Harold Greenwood and the Kidwelly Poisoning

Dr. Jonathan Oates

All correspondence for
Harold Greenwood and the Kidwelly Poisoning
should be addressed to:

Irregular Special Press
Endeavour House
170 Woodland Road
Sawston
Cambridge
CB22 3DX

*****

Overall Copyright © 2024 Baker Street Studios Limited
Text Copyright © 2024 Jonathan Oates
The right of Jonathan Oates to be identified as the author of this work has been asserted by him in accordance with the Copyright, Designs and Patents Act 1988.
All rights reserved

Typesetting is in Times New Roman font

ISBN: 978-1-901091-95-3

A CIP catalogue record for this book is available from the British Library.

Front cover picture: Harold Greenwood, Rumsey House and Mabel Greenwood.

*****

All rights reserved. No part of this publication may be reproduced, stored in a retrieval system, or transmitted, in any form or by any means, electronic, mechanical, photocopying, recording or otherwise, without the prior permission of the Irregular Special Press in writing.

*****

Every effort has been made to ensure accuracy, but the publishers do not hold themselves responsible for any consequences that may arise from errors or omissions. Whilst the contents are believed to be correct at the time of going to press, changes may have occurred since that time or will occur during the currency of this publication.

Contents

Introduction 7
1. A Family in Wales 11
2. The Death of Mrs. Greenwood 47
3. Suspicions 75
4. Investigations 89
5. Adjourned Inquest 119
6. At the Magistrates' Court and After 133
7. The Case for the Prosecution 157
8. The Case for the Defence and the Summing Up 183
9. Aftermath 211
10. Conspectus 239
Notes 257
Further Reading 275
Index 277

Acknowledgements

Researching and writing this book was a collaborative effort. I would like to thank the following for their help in its production. Firstly, there is Lindsay Siviter who has lent me many valuable texts from her unique true crime library, as well as talking through the case and commenting on the final chapter, which as always has been invaluable. Then there is Dr. Anna-Lena Berg for reading through the text, commenting upon it and especially assisting with the medical intricacies of the case. Jennifer Mercer was kind enough to use her professional knowledge of the law to improve the work. Fr. Jim Flanagan of Kidwelly provided local photographs and information and read the text. He also acted as my guide on my visit to Kidwelly as well as being a most hospitable host. Mark John Maguire gave encouragement and contacts. John Coulter, foremost historian of Victorian Forest Hill and Sydenham, assisted with information about this south London suburb. Nicholas Gibbs kindly shared his knowledge of the Bowater family with me. Jonathan Hewlett assisted with pictures and family knowledge. John Gauss gave mostly accurate genealogical information and advice, as well as reading through the draft for errors in English. Paul Lang lent postcards from his collection for use in the book and also read through the text. Sophie Leyshon of Llanelli Library provided a copy of the local newspaper. Gareth Long permitted use of the picture of Forest Hill. Thanks to Bob Hinton for the use of some of his photographs and sharing his solution with me. Anonymously, staff at the National Archives, the British Library, the Guildhall Library and Leeds Local and Family History Library all helped with the provision of crucial documents and books. My thanks to Kelsea Toulouse for her company on my return trip from Kidwelly. Pictures on pages 95, 152,

153, 157, 206 (top) and 252 are all taken from the book by Winifred Duke, *The Trial of Harold Greenwood* (1930) while all other non captioned pictures were ones bought by myself. Finally, my family for having to listen to me discourse on the case for several months, in visiting Greenwood's birthplace and one of Greenwood's descendants.

This book is dedicated to Lindsay.

Introduction

In 1920 Harold Greenwood was charged with the murder by arsenic poisoning of his wife, Mabel, in the previous year. He was found not guilty at his trial, but was this the correct verdict? This was once a well known case, but has been overshadowed by that of Major Herbert Rowse Armstrong, which in many ways is very similar, occurring as it did two years later. Both cases were graced by a volume of the *Notable British Trials* series shortly afterwards. However, since then, the Armstrong case has been dealt with by three major books and by a television drama; there has only been a stage play and an American television play loosely inspired by the Greenwood case.

This is the first book to solely cover the Greenwood case since the trial volume of 1930. Unlike previously published short accounts and summaries, it has been far more extensively researched. It will use the files of the Metropolitan Police, the department of the public prosecutor, the Assizes and the Home Office held at the National Archives, which provide new insights and statements not hitherto made known. It will also utilise the contemporary press and the transcript of the trial. Material well known to the genealogist such as census returns, wills, parish registers and other evidence will be used to build up pictures of the major characters in this intensely human drama. In particular there will be more weight given to the early life of the Greenwoods, the police investigation, the aftermath and an examination of the previous works on this topic.

This is a story that could have been written by an author of detective stories in their golden age. The trial was held in the same year, coincidentally, as the first ever Hercule Poirot novel, *The Mysterious Affair at Styles*, by Agatha Christie, was published. Indeed, in four later stories the same author implicitly draws from or cites the Greenwood case. Another famous author, George Orwell, also referenced the case in his essay *The Decline of the English Murder*.

This is a classic domestic story of the middle classes. The victim was from a very wealthy family of manufacturers and her husband was from a family of gentry in Yorkshire. They lived with their children (those not at boarding school) and servants in a detached house in a small country town in Wales. Their friends included the doctor and the vicar. Both Greenwoods were busy in the social, religious and sporting life of the place. He was a solicitor. There is no violence and there are no professional or habitual criminals.

Yet underneath the veneer of middle class respectability, trouble was brewing. Chiefly this arose from the fact that Greenwood had an all too common Achilles heel – he was too fond of the company of younger women, though to what extent has been debated. His wife, older and richer than he, was full of charitable and good works, and was, perhaps, an incumbrance on his activities.

There are two diametrically opposed views as to whether or not he killed his wife. The first, as espoused by Winifred Duke, writing about the case in 1930, was that the evidence and motivation for Greenwood to kill was very slight indeed and so he should be given the benefit of the doubt, as, after all, if found guilty he might have been hanged. This is the general consensus in the many chapters in books and websites that deal with the matter. It is apparently a story without a solution. A few give Greenwood an unqualified 'not guilty' verdict. More recently Mark John Maguire has put forward the hitherto novel hypothesis, that Greenwood had the motive, means and opportunity to kill his wife and indeed got away with murder. Only one of these positions can be the correct one.

It is up to the reader to sift through the evidence that will be put forward before them, evidence taken from a number of sources, and to determine their own retrospective conclusion. The reader is now the jury, but with more information to hand than those twelve men had in 1920.

I was drawn to this case by two people already mentioned in this introduction. Firstly, by the 2019 YouTube episode, *The Case of the Gooseberry Tart* in Mark John Maguire's *They Got Away With Murder* channel (subsequently published in book form). Secondly as part of a perusal of the Agatha Christie canon for references to true crime and criminals, which are numerous. This made me realise that there had been no full length study of a case which is surely deserving of one. Previous authors had not used all the sources which are now available and so a new study was needed to bring all the hitherto unknown information to light in one place.

Chapter One

A Family in Wales

[1] Baptism font at St. Mary's church, Ingleton, 2024. (Author's photograph)

By 1919, the Greenwood family had lived in Kidwelly for just over two decades but were relative newcomers, having neither been born there nor being Welsh. Harold Greenwood had been born in Ingleton, a small village in the west riding of Yorkshire, bordering Lancashire, with a population of 1,625 in 1881, on 1st January 1874.

He was baptised on 1st February of that year in the Norman font of the parish church of St. Mary's **[1]**. There had been Greenwoods at Ingleton since Isaac Greenwood of Heptonstall settled there in the early 18th century. David Greenwood had died in 1799 and his son was James, who lived at Bank Hall in Ingleton village. His brother, William (1777-1857), succeeded him and married one Elizabeth (1819-1888) and had three children. The eldest, of which, and only son, was William Norman. The Greenwood family was the most important family in the parish in terms of influence and wealth.[1]

[2] Ingleton village and church.

Ingleton was 219 miles from London and 9 from Settle. It had an Anglican parish church **[2]**, whose vicar from 1874-1879 was the Reverend Thomas Sherlock, and also a Wesleyan Methodist chapel. There was a National school, a police station and three railway stations, each for a different railway company. In 1886 it was described thus, as 'a long, uneven, curiously old fashioned looking village … exceedingly plain, primitive and unpretentious in appearance'. Houses were mainly two storeyed and made of stone. As to its inhabitants, 'There are a few well to do people in and about Ingleton, but the bulk of the inhabitants are of the ordinary working class kind'. Most worked in nearby mines, quarries and in lime burning.[2]

A Family in Wales 13

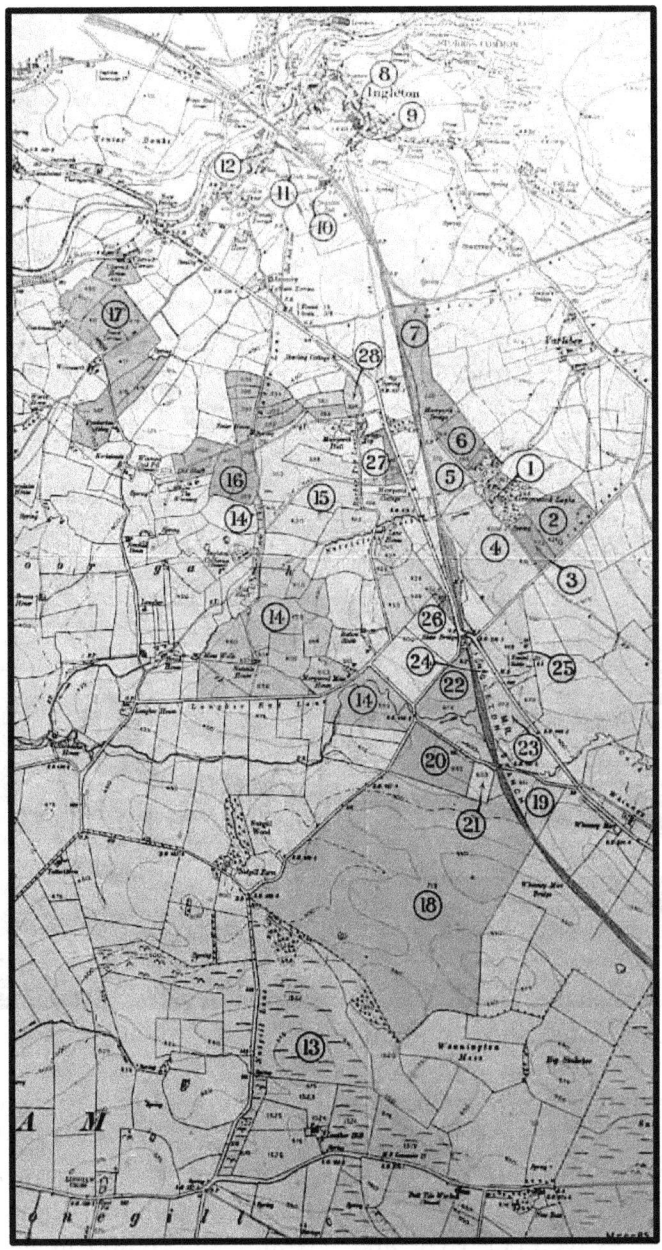

[3] Numbered/shaded areas showing the extent of the Greenwood Leghe estates when put up for auction in 1924. (Jonathan Hewlett's collection)

Harold Greenwood was the son of this William Norman Greenwood, the latter being baptised on 19th October 1849 at the same church. As an adult William described himself as a gentleman, which indeed he was. His landed estate [3] consisted of 536 acres at an annual rental value of £653 4s. He married at the parish church on 7th October 1871. His wife was Isabella Anne, nee Balderston, a vicar's daughter, and she had been born in Port Natal, near Durban in South Africa on 1st May 1851, though was also from an old established family in Ingleton (the Balderstons had lived there since at least 1607 and many had been churchwardens, but none were listed there in 1861). Harold Greenwood had an elder brother, William Norman, (1873-1944) and two younger ones; Percy Stobart, (1875-1936) and Oscar (1877-1960).

[4] Three Horse Shoes pub, Ingleton 2024. (Author's photograph)

Their father seems to have been benevolent and is recorded as treating the bell ringers, work people and others at the village's Three Horse Shoes Inn [4] (which was owned by the Greenwoods) in January 1873 to celebrate the birth of his first son. He died aged only 27, on 7th November 1876 and left almost £18,000 in his will; a wealthy man indeed.[3]

[5] Gravestone of William Norman Greenwood, 2024. (Author's photograph)

At the funeral were a hearse, a mourning coach, seven carriages and a local newspaper noted, 'During the service the church and churchyard were crowded with spectators [5]. Deceased was a man who was held in the highest regard in this locality'.[4]

[6] Isabella Kirk (left), then her seated son Gerald Kirk. The woman on the right is probably Fanny Balderston; the identity of the other two is unknown. (Jonathan Hewlett's collection)

A will had been made in 1872 and after sums for his wife and mother, the residue of the estate, was valued at under £18,000 in 1877, so presumably between £17,000 and £18,000. After several bequests, this was to be equally divided between the children of the marriage. Before reaching the age of 21 years the income from these portions was to be administered by the executors; their mother, Mrs. Isabella Greenwood [6] and James Henry Vant (1848-1919), a solicitor of Whitefriars, Settle, for the maintenance and education of the boys. On attaining the age of 21 years the capital sums were to be given to the young men. It would seem that Harold was allowed a sum of £400 prior to attaining the age of 21 years; presumably to pay for his education.[5]

[7] Greenwood Legh, Ingleton. (Jonathan Hewlett's collection)

In 1881, now a widow, Isabella was living with her four sons as an annuitant. The family was then residing at Greenwood Legh [7] in Ingleton. This large house had been built on Riggs Hill, on the site of an older house, in 1874. Apparently, 'It was a fine stone mansion, gabled and towered, approached by a half mile drive, and about three quarters of a mile from the village of Ingleton'. It had a dining room, a drawing room, a breakfast room, a butler's pantry, a lavatory, a kitchen, a scullery, bathroom with hot and cold running water, a laundry, five bedrooms, four servants' bedrooms and two dressing rooms. There were 6 acres of grounds, some laid out as a garden, with stables and coach houses. The house had views of woods to the west and of Ingleborough mountain to the east. There was a carriage drive both from the front and back of the property.[6] The family lived in comfortable circumstances, with a cook, housemaid and coachman. Isabella was equally gracious to those less well off, giving tea to the deserving poor, 'all of which was no doubt thankfully accepted' in 1879.[7] On 20th December 1882 she married Alfred Samuel Kirk, a wine and spirits merchant, a year her senior. He was later director of the Leeds Forage Company, chairman of the Ingleton Conservative Association, a freemason, a liberal benefactor (he and his wife paid for a new pulpit for the church) and was an active local speaker. There was a son born to this marriage, one Gerald (on 14th July 1883), who, despite the age gap, Greenwood may have been close to or held in some affection, as shall be later noted. Isabella was widowed again, as Kirk died on 1st April 1893, aged 43 years. The chief mourners were the widow and the four sons from her first marriage.[8]

Virtually nothing is known about Harold Greenwood's childhood and upbringing. In later life he referred to having lived an outdoor life, 'I had been fond and a constant user of the gun from boyhood' and 'as a son of the open'. So he probably took part in shooting grouse and pheasants as part of shooting parties with family and neighbouring gentry when he was at home during the school holidays. Whether he was close to his brothers, having lost their father when very young, is another question. They do not seem to have featured much in his later life, so presumably they grew apart from each other, perhaps in part due to geographical distance.[9] However, it will be noted that Percy, his younger brother, did maintain some contact with his older brother, possibly because Percy was a keen huntsman, fisherman and shootist, as Harold was.

As for the four Greenwood boys, they all seem to have been mostly educated outside Ingleton. William and Percy were boarders at the ancient Royal Giggleswick Grammar School, about 7 miles to the south of Ingleton. William was later a boarder with the vicar at Sawrey Vicarage, probably being tutored. It is likely that Greenwood was taught by a governess or a tutor at home before being sent off to school, perhaps at the age of 10 years (this is the age his brother William was sent to school and the age that Greenwood was to send his youngest son to boarding school). The school he attended was far removed from his home and why he was treated differently to William and Percy who attended a good school not too far from home is a mystery. He was educated at Fir Lodge College, No. 57-59 Kirkdale, in Upper Sydenham, south east London. Founded in 1847, it was in a large house near to Sydenham railway station. It had a lower school and an upper school. In the 1880s the principal was a Miss Higgins. Mr. Joseph Hirste Haywood (1857-1940) M.A. of Hertford College, Oxford, was the headmaster of the upper school and in 1890 was the principal. It was described as being for 'the sons of gentlemen' who would be 'carefully prepared for the public school, the various examinations and professions'. In the last decade a dozen boys at the school had won open scholarships; some attending Dulwich College. The school took boarders (17 in 1891) as well as day pupils such as Greenwood.[10]

[8] Sunderland Road, Forest Hill. (Gareth Long)

In what must have been a major culture shock, Harold was living at Parkhurst, a detached house, now No. 57 Sunderland Road [8],

Forest Hill (adjacent to Sydenham), south east London, in 1891. He was then a boarder with his mother's sister, Fanny Balderston (1850-1906), and his cousin Robert, aged 18 years, another boarder and a servant. Mrs. Balderston had been resident in Sunderland Road, Forest Hill from at least 1887 (possibly as early as 1884) and that might well be when he first arrived there to be educated at Fir College. If he was there in 1885 he would have known a fellow student, the Anglo-Irish Ernest Shackleton (1874-1920) who became a famous Antarctic explorer in the next century. On 1st July 1891 he took exams at Fir Lodge College, in French and Latin. His residence was to have important results that no one could have foreseen at the time. Meanwhile, the four Greenwood sons were all brought together again in January 1894 when there was a large local celebration for William's 21st birthday. There was a concert in Ingleborough for the tenants, the elderly and the poor, who were feasted. Speeches were made honouring William's late father and praising him with hopes for the future. Meanwhile, there was a tea for the children at the local National (i.e. Church of England) School, over 200 of them. Harold, Percy and Oscar served them. Oscar and Percy remained bachelors at home until at least 1901, though William served in the Imperial Yeomanry during the 2nd Boer war in 1900 and on his return was given a hearty local welcome, with a ball and dinner being held in his honour. Their mother died on 10th April 1903 and the church was full for the funeral service.[11] In the following years Percy moved to Bank House, Oscar to Moorgath Hall and Greenwood Legh was rented or sold to one Mr. A. T. Whittle. William was married, working as an actor and living in Devon in 1911.[12]

Greenwood was proud of his family roots as he wrote in 1920:

> I am still a Greenwood, the Greenwoods who were squires in Yorkshire, proud of the name of Greenwood and of those who bear it.
> They have occasion to be proud rather than ashamed of one who has been humiliated through the clumsiness and, I cannot help but say, the injustice of British law.[13]

The Greenwood family motto was, in Latin, *'Dum Spiro Spero'*, or in English, 'While I breathe, I hope'. Their coat of arms was a shield, divided by a chevron. Above the chevron were two saltire crosses and one was below it, and the chevron had seven upwardly pointing arrows. The crest on top of the helm was a lion (denoting courage) holding yet another saltire. At St. Mary's church is a plaque in the chancel to William Norman Greenwood, Harold's father, and his parents, as well as plaques to his step-father and half-brother. The family graves are just outside the church porch; slabs in memory of his grandfather and predecessors; his father having a horizontal tomb.[14]

Harold Greenwood presumably continued living in Forest Hill in the mid 1890s; however, in 1895 he is listed at No. 7 Argyll Place in Notting Hill, presumably temporarily, as he was described as being of Forest Hill in 1896. He was articled to Mr. Arnold William Whittel Holt (1862-1914), a solicitor of No. 7 Argyll Place. Holt was a gentleman's son from Leeds who was married in Keighley in 1885. Given the social status and geographical proximity to Greenwood's birthplace, he may well have been previously acquainted with him or his family or was recommended or introduced by those who knew both. Furthermore, Greenwood's aunt, Mrs. Balderston, was resident in Keighley in 1881, where Holt's wife once lived. On 24th January 1895 the young man took three of his law exams; Heads I, II and III, scoring a total of 179 marks, which was a middling achievement.[15]

By this time (January 1895), Greenwood had attained the age of 21 years and so his inheritance from his father's estate would have accrued to him, being hitherto held in trust for him by his mother and the family solicitor. It is unknown exactly what this sum would have been; almost a quarter of somewhat under £18,000 might have meant that he gained a sum of perhaps £4,000 and thus was a rather eligible bachelor.[16]

Life was not all spent working for his legal career, however. He also met one Mabel Bowater, probably in Forest Hill as she also resided there, with her family. As a soon to be solicitor and with some family money in his possession he would seem like a good marital prospect. The two were married at All Saint's church, Edmonton in Middlesex on 2nd June 1896. He was 22 years to her 24 years. A newspaper noted, 'GREENWOOD-BOWATER, June 2nd, at All Saints, Edmonton, by the Reverend L. Hughes, M.A. Harold, second son of the late William Greenwood, Esq. of Greenwood Legh,

Ingleton, Yorks. Mabel, younger daughter of William Vansittart Bowater, of Bury Hall, Edmonton, London N.'[17] On 15th June 1897 he took his final law exams, scoring 82 in conveyancing, 79 in equity, 88 in common law and bankruptcy and 28 and 36 in probate and divorce A and B, a total mark of 313; higher than some and lower than others. A Yorkshire newspaper noted that he passed his final law exams in 1897.[18]

Greenwood's bride was from a rather different social background and it has been supposed that they looked down on him. Mabel Bowater had been born on 3rd September 1871 in Cheetham, a suburb of Manchester. She was baptised at Manchester Cathedral on 28th September 1871. Her father, William Vansittart Bowater (1838-1907), born in Edgbaston, Birmingham, was then an ambitious manager of a paper manufacturing firm owned by Robert Wrigley. He had married Eliza Jane Devey of Bristol in 1861 in Islington. In 1871 they were living at No. 12 Polygon, Salford with their six children and two servants. Mabel was the sixth of their offspring and the second daughter.[19]

The others were Thomas (1862-1938), Edith Jane (1864-1930), Frank Henry (1866-1947), Frederick (1867-1962) and Herbert J. (1869-1872). They were soon joined by others; Arthur (1873-1874) and Sydney (1874-1939). All had been born in Manchester. However, their father was a bad tempered man and fond of the bottle. Arguments with his employer led to him seeking employment elsewhere. The family moved southwards and from at least 1881-1884 they were living in Derby House, a detached house in Sunderland Road (now No. 38) **[9]**, Forest Hill. There Norman (1882-1934) was born. Frank and Sydney were then presumably at boarding school as neither are listed there in 1881. Thomas was employed in his father's new paper manufacturing company, which was established in the City of London in 1881. The company sold paper for the expanding newspaper industry and became very profitable, as the press was expanding substantially in the new era of mass literacy. Mabel, Frederick and Sydney were then all described as scholars so presumably all attended private day schools in the locality. Perhaps the latter went to the same school as Greenwood. Shortly afterwards the family moved. By 1886 the family lived at a house called Broughton on Church Road (destroyed by a flying bomb in 1944), which runs parallel to Sunderland Road. By 1891 Frank was then described as an agent and Sydney a clerk in the family firm; Norman was attending a nearby day school. Mabel and her elder sister Edith still lived at home and were unmarried; there was no need for them to have paid employment, so we do not know what they filled their time with, but perhaps church or charitable volunteer work took up some of their lives and, as Christ Church on Church Rise was the nearest, perhaps this was the one they were associated with. A cook and a housemaid served the family.[20]

[9] No. 38 Sunderland Road, Forest Hill, 2024.
(Author's photograph)

According to a descendant, the eldest Bowater was a hard man to his family as well as in the workplace. He posited that this may have led Mabel to draw in on herself and become emotionally distant.[21]

Their impact locally was limited. Bowater senior, in 1887, complained to the local council about street cries in Forest Hill on

Sundays and women loitering on Westbourne Road and Park Road at night time; they told him that this was the responsibility of the police. Frederick played in the Sydenham cricket team and seems to have been quite good at both batting and fielding. He and his two sisters attended a *Twelfth Night* festivity at Forest Hill Baths in 1891.[22]

The family paper making business (W. V. Bowater and Sons) had its offices on No. 28 Queen Street in the City of London. In about 1894, to set the seal on their worldly triumphs, the senior Bowaters bought Bury Hall, an 18th century mansion in the north Middlesex parish of Edmonton, moving there in about 1895. The elder Bowater and his three elder sons (Thomas, Frank and Frederick) formed a partnership, but this was dissolved in 1903, quite possibly by boardroom coup on the part of the sons against their overbearing father.[23] The Greenwoods were comfortably off, but the Bowaters were even more so; when William Bowater died on 28th April 1907 his will left his family £53,865 5s. 8d. They were the last family to live in Bury Hall; in 1920 it was demolished. His widow moved, by 1911, to live in a 12 roomed house, No. 51 Plaistow Lane, Bromley, Kent, with her unmarried daughter Edith, now 46, a cousin and three servants.[24]

Those writing about this case have noted that Mabel was wealthy, an heiress and there have been various estimations of the money she brought to the annual family income. This has been used to indicate either that Greenwood would not have killed his wife because he would have been the financial loser in that eventuality, or to suggest that he inherited some money from his late wife's estate, which was derived from her family and so this was a motive to kill. Mark John Maguire notes that Miss Bowater was 'an heiress and a daughter of Sir William Vansittart Bowater' and so 'they lived comfortably due to Mabel's generous income from her family'.[25] Winifred Duke wrote 'I am informed from a private source that it was between £600 and £900'. Greenwood himself said at the trial as to his wife's income, 'I don't exactly know how much, but about £900 a year'.[26] We shall now examine what the financial settlement really was.

It did not take effect until 1907. On her father's death in 1907 (Greenwood attended the funeral at Edmonton Cemetery alongside his brothers in law and he and his wife sent a wreath for the funeral), Mabel received the income from the sum of £3,000 to be held in trust for her during her lifetime. This money was invested for her and she was paid the interest on this sum as an annual income (her single sister, not having a husband to provide for her, received £6,000). She could not touch the capital. She could dispose of it in her will after her death but if there was no will, the income would be divided equally between her children on reaching the age of 21 years for boys or on marriage for the girls. There was nothing for Greenwood personally.[27] With a bank base rate of 5% in 1919, this trust fund provided an annual income of £150, which wasn't peanuts but nor, by itself, was it the income of the upper middle class. A little more accrued to Mabel, when her mother died on 23rd June 1912 at her house in Bromley. Various items of clothing, two rings and a gold watch were given to her. A third of the residue of the estate, which amounted to a total of £1,310 9s. net before about £120 had been taken away, was given to her in trust.[28] At some point in the next few years Edith, as the unmarried daughter, joined the Greenwoods in Kidwelly. Her income of about £300 per year would certainly have helped to allow the family to live a comfortable lifestyle, and with a detached house, servants and children at boarding school they would certainly need it, though at the trial it was said that she only contributed 25s. per week.[29]

As to Greenwood's finances, it is impossible to know what use he made of the inheritance he gained in 1895, but given his later financial concerns, it is probable that it was mostly spent by the 1900s and so he was chiefly dependant on what his profession would bring in.

Money values are pre decimal, so 12 old pence (abbreviated to d.) made up a shilling (abbreviated to s.) and 20 shillings was a pound. Given that money values do not increase at a uniform rate, to multiply those of 1919-1920 to those of 2024 is a misleading exercise. The fact that in 1920 a detached house in Kidwelly could cost £1,500 and a car could be bought for under £100 should give the reader a notion of what money would buy at that time.

Two of Mabel's brothers became very wealthy and important indeed. The eldest, Thomas, became a sheriff of the City of London in 1905, and was knighted in 1906. He had become a common councillor and later an alderman in the City of London and was a member of the Girdlers' livery company.[30] He became Lord Mayor of the City of London in 1913. On his death he left £74,195. Frank fought in the First World War as a major and was also Lord Lieutenant of the City of London. Mabel's existence was one of the comfortable middle classes; her brothers that of the new business plutocracy.

[10] Harold Greenwood on his first wedding day, 1896.
(Bob Hinton's collection)

As said, Mabel and Harold Greenwood were married in 1896 [10]. It is not known how and when they met but given that both lived in close proximity to each other in Forest Hill they may have met at church or at a social or charitable group. His aunt, whom he boarded with, is noted as having been involved in church work at Christ

Church from at least 1887, so it would seem probable that both Greenwood and Mabel attended the same church and so met there. Mrs. Balderston is recorded as assisting with the church decorations for the harvest festival, helping organise a treat for the poor and helping man a stall at a church bazaar. Miss Bowater, probably Mabel's sister, assisted at a harvest festival for the same church and it was at that church that her elder brother Frank was married in 1891. Greenwood may have been attracted to her to an extent by her family's wealth.[31] Greenwood may also have known something of the family's importance, with Lady Louisa Knightley being prominent at court and politically; earlier Bowaters had been prominent in the East India Company, in the armed forces and at court.

[11] All Saints' church, Edmonton.

They then lived at a house he called after his birthplace, Ingleton, at Wellington Road, Enfield (north London), close to the church they had married in and near to her parents' new home in Edmonton. In 1897 he passed his final Law exams and could now practice as a solicitor; qualifying in January 1898; it had taken him at least six years when the usual period was three to five years as an articled clerk. This suggests that he was not blessed with a particularly high aptitude as a solicitor. On 3rd April 1898 the first of their four children was born, Edith Irene Isabella (1898-1980), known as Irene, and was baptised at the church her parents had been married in, All Saints' church, Edmonton **[11]**, on 28th May. Greenwood put an announcement in the London press, '3rd April 1898 – Greenwood, birth, at Ingleton, Bush Hill, Enfield, a daughter'.[32]

[12] The Priory, Lady Street, Kidwelly, 2024. (Fr. Jim Flanagan)

They then moved to south west Wales and in 1898 resided at Broomhill, a detached 11 room house (demolished in the later twentieth century; now rebuilt with the same name) just north outside the main settlement of Kidwelly, Carmarthenshire. It was the home of Holmes Stead in 1898, a fellow solicitor and then from 1899 Alfred Stephens. By 1901, but probably from 1899, they lived in a house called Castle Terrace, Kidwelly, employing Margaret Davies, a 20 year old, as a cook and Margaret Jones, a 23 year old, as a nurse to look after Irene. By 1902 they were also living at The Priory [12], between Nos. 39 and 47 Lady Street, in the centre of the same small town, a 10 roomed detached house. There were soon three more children; Mabel Eileen (born on 15th November 1902 and baptised on 20th December), Norman Ivor Vansittart (born on 1st November 1904) and finally John Kenneth Vansittart (born on 13th February 1910). It will be noted that the two sons took their maternal grandfather's middle name, the eldest daughter took one of her aunt's names and the younger daughter took one of her mother's Christian names. There were then (1911) three servants; Lilian Price, a 25 year old from Kent employed as a governess to teach the three youngest children (Irene was then a boarder at Northumberland House Girls' School in Bristol, quite possibly recommended by her grandmother who was born there), Elizabeth Harries, aged 25 years and the cook and Mabel Powell, aged 29 years, the housemaid, both of whom were Welsh. The three servants slept in the same room. By 1918 the two youngest children were attending a local day school, whilst Norman attended the prestigious Malvern College in Worcestershire from 1918-1920.[33]

The move to Wales may well have been influenced by the fact that Elizabeth Mary Balderston, a younger sister of Greenwood's mother, had married one Dr. David Traherne (1860-1927). He was the brother of Sage Traherne, later Jones, of Llanelli, a large industrial town 8 miles to the south east of Kidwelly. In this way Greenwood was to be introduced to the Jones family, who owned *The Llanelli Mercury*. This was to be of immense significance in 1919 as shall be seen.

In 1920 Greenwood was described thus, 'A well groomed middle aged man, rather short of stature, with a grey moustache, thick bushy eyebrows, and a keen, alert appearance'.[34]

The Greenwoods bought Rumsey House [13], Bridge Street, from George Bowen, in November 1916. It had been designed by Thomas Williams Angell Evans, architect and later mayor of Kidwelly, in 1862 and he and his family lived there until his death in 1897. It was a detached house in its own grounds and stood on Bridge Street, part of the road from Carmarthen to Llanelli, described in 1904 as an 'exceedingly desirable and commodious residence' when it was home to John Beavan. On the ground floor were, leading off from the hall, a sitting room, drawing room, a dining room, a school room, kitchen, china pantry and a store room, and a scullery. Stairs went down to the cellar and up to the bedrooms and bathrooms. There were bedrooms on the second floor. In the grounds were a kennel, a firewood shed, a potting shed, a fruit store, stables/garage, a coal store and a dustbin. They also kept hens; no other birds or animals seem to have been there.[35] It was described in 1920 as 'a large three storeyed house, situated on the bank of the River Gwendraeth **[14]** and commands a splendid view of the beautifully hilly country which encircles the village'.[36] It certainly stands out from its neighbours, perhaps purposefully so.

[13] Rumsey House, c.1920.

[14] The Bridge over the Gwendraeth and Rumsey House, 2024. (Author's photograph)

Chief Inspector Ernest Edward Haigh (1871-1938) described it in 1920 as:

> ... probably the largest house in the town. It fronts upon Bridge Street, into which it has two separate exits. Behind and at the side of the house are fairly extensive grounds, over an acre, and there are exits there from two other thoroughfares. In the grounds there are stables, a cottage and a garage.[37]

Mrs. Greenwood ran the household as a middle class wife would. She frequently had to advertise for female servants in the local press in the 1910s. In March 1914 (twice), July 1915, January 1916 and January 1917 (four times) she advertised for a cook. A governess was advertised for twice in August 1916 and a parlour maid in November 1918 (twice). The governess was to look after her youngest son and also to care of the two others when they were back at home for the holidays, as well as undertake other light duties.[38] It is possible that this turnover of young female servants was due to her husband's attentions to them, but this cannot be verified. Or it could perhaps have been because they saw their mistress as being strict. Many young women chose to work in factories and took other jobs, especially in World War One, as the less well paid and more exacting domestic service was increasingly unattractive as a career option. However, a neighbour and family friend, Miss Mary Adeline

Griffiths, later remarked that 'At one time there was talk that Mr. Greenwood was carrying on with one of the Governesses they had at the Priory'. This may have been Lilian Price, who was employed as such there in 1911.[39]

Kidwelly is a small town near to the Carmarthen coastline. In 1921 the population was 3,350 persons living in 686 houses. It is on both banks of the Gwendraeth Fach (river). It is a town of fairly narrow streets with terraced housing. There was the Anglican parish church of St. Mary's and six nonconformist chapels, two banks and numerous pubs. Some residents were employed in the mines and some in the local tinworks to the north of the town. A nearby brickworks was another major local employer. There were a number of small farms in the locality. It was governed by a corporation since 1885. It had a railway station and the substantial ruins of a Medieval castle. There were four elementary schools and in 1924 there had been 46 deaths due to natural causes.[40]

In 1930 the following was written about the place:

> The stranger to Kidwelly alights at its picturesque little station, and, in order to visit the village, follows a country road for about a quarter of a mile. Kidwelly's crooked main street, a double row of low-browed houses and small, dark shops, climbs at one end towards the open landscape, and at the other one over a bridge across a sluggish river. Just before the bridge is reached a substantial three-storeyed stone mansion [Rumsey House] used to stand back from the road in its own grounds.[41]

It is worth introducing some of the town's other characters who will play an important part in the ensuing drama. Dr. Thomas Robert Griffiths (1871-1934) was educated in 1886-1889 at Llandovery School, described as the Welsh Eton, founded in 1849 and which was then a public boarding school for boys with an emphasis on teaching the Welsh language, history and literature. He then attended University College London to study medicine and took his M.R.C.S. and L.R.C.P. in 1900 and took additional medical qualifications at Edinburgh and Glasgow and then returned to Kidwelly as its principal doctor. He was also medical officer of health to the borough and certifying factory surgeon. In 1916-1918 he had been a member of the seven man Kidwelly tribunal to assess cases for military exemption to conscription. In 1908 the then vicar, the Reverend David Daven Jones, published a history of the town and included the doctor in his chapter entitled *Local Celebrities*; clearly he entertained a high opinion of the man.[42] He had been born in Kidwelly and only left it for his schooling and university life.

[15] Henblas, 2024. (Author's photograph)

Dr. Griffiths was from a wealthy background, his father being termed a 'landed proprietor' and given that the doctor left over £22,000 in his will, he was a rich man. In 1911 he was living in Henblas [15], an 11 room house, on Bridge Street and opposite Rumsey House, with his unmarried three sisters and one servant. His sisters, the second of whom plays an important role in this narrative, were Anne Clementine (1872-1913), Mary Adeline (1873-1933) and Katherine, (1876-1916). None of them needed to go out to work. Given that there was only one servant, some of the household duties were doubtless undertaken by these three women, though Mary was very active in voluntary and church activities locally; she was also a good whist player. It is possible that he was close with money; employing one servant in 1911 and none in 1921, whereas the Greenwoods had two or three. He was also a keen sportsman, being a member of the London Welsh Rugby Club and the Ashburnham Golf Club. As with Greenwood, he played in the Kidwelly cricket club and once sat on the same town council.[43] The Greenwoods became his patients in January 1903 and he helped deliver their two later children. Between January 1915 and September 1919 he made 125 visits to the family and undertook 16 consultations.[44]

However, a police report in 1920 gave a less than flattering account of him:

> Dr. Griffiths is a bachelor living with his sister and has a private income. His practice depended principally upon a levy from the industrial workers. The principal private patients in the district are attended by doctors in neighbouring towns. He is not regarded by many who are quite friendly with him as particularly competent rather the contrary, especially at diagnosis. He has been the sole practitioner in Kidwelly for many years.[45]

He was definitely not a specialist in poisons; few doctors are. When asked he admitted such and claimed that he had not heard of the 19th century Reinsch or the Marsh tests for arsenic.[46] It is quite possible that he and Greenwood were friends, at least in part, because both had a modest level of competency in their chosen professions.

Another important member of the local middle class community was the Reverend David Ambrose Jones (1866-1940). This Oxford educated Welsh clergyman had held a number of clerical posts in Wales before becoming vicar of the Anglican parish church of St. Mary's at Kidwelly in 1914. He was also a published author and in 1919 his *Philosophic Thoughts and Religion* appeared in print. Given that Mrs. Greenwood assisted in church activities the two knew each other quite well. In fact, all the family were regular churchgoers.[47] The vicar was married with two daughters, one of whom, in 1921, was employed in a bank.[48]

Miss Florence Lorraine Phillips **[16]**, born in Grantham, Lincolnshire in 1878, was probably Mrs. Greenwood's best friend.

She was unmarried and an artist, living in The Cottage, just two minutes' walk from Rumsey House and had lived there since at least 1911. Once her parents died later in that decade she lived there alone. She said 'I was intimate with Mrs. Greenwood for 10 or 11 years'. The police described her as being intelligent and well educated and the vicar said that he was to be trusted; she also helped out at St. Mary's.[49] As with Mrs. Greenwood and Miss Griffiths, she was active on local committees and in church work.

[16] The Reverend David Ambrose Jones,
Miss Florence Phillips and an unknown man.

We should also mention another Jones family, albeit one that lived in the industrial and dockland town of Llanelli, but known to Greenwood by the family connection already mentioned and proximity of their living in the same street in that town as his workplace, Frederick Street, where several other solicitors had their offices. They were headed by William Benjamin Jones (1853-1917) and his wife Sage (1850-1942). In 1901 they lived at No. 42

(Greenwood's office comprised of three rooms was at No. 1). Jones was a journalist and editor of *The Llanelli Mercury*, one of two local newspapers, as well as serving as a local councillor, he served on the Board of Guardians and was general secretary to several friendly societies. The couple had ten children and most of important for this book was one of their daughters, as we shall learn in the next chapter. The family had one servant and can hardly be called wealthy, however.[50] It does not seem that Greenwood's family had much contact with them; he kept his business and family life at arm's length, geographically and socially.

The Greenwoods were outsiders in Kidwelly. They were English in a small Welsh town. Yet they threw themselves into local organisations and events. This was especially the case with Mrs. Greenwood; less so her husband. It led to social acceptance.

[17] Mabel Greenwood, nee Bowater.

Mrs. Greenwood, 'a rather tall, handsome woman, with a fair complexion' [17] was well thought of locally, being involved in a great many charitable and voluntary activities. These included the local Red Cross and church work for St. Mary's.[51] Irene said that 'She visited the sick people and did whatever she could for the poor'.[52] She was regarded as a local 'Lady Bountiful', being benevolent to the poor and generous to deserving cases. She was a member of numerous local committees.[53] There are many references in the local press to her being involved in local activities, especially church work.

These included, in 1906 addressing a Band of Hope meeting alongside Sir Thomas Bowater, and the curate, the Reverend Llewellyn Davies, in the parish hall. Bowater declared that he had charge of a branch of the Band of Hope in London.[54] Soon afterwards, Mrs. Greenwood, Mrs. Annie Priscilla Smart (1871-1933) of Mountain View, Kidwelly, chairwoman of the Nursing Association, and the mayor oversaw a variety entertainment in aid of reducing the debt of St. Mary's church.[55] Mrs. Greenwood manned a Christmas tree stall with the Davieses at Kidwelly jumble sale.[56] She was also in a needlework group.[57] Other church work included helping decorate the chancel for Easter and the windows there.[58] Here she mixed with other ladies form the local elite, such as the three Misses Griffiths and Mrs. Smart.[59] Greenwood and Dr. Griffiths were sidesmen at the church for a time, at least from 1905, but clearly Greenwood did not share his wife's devotion to the church.

Estimates as to her public character were universally positive. The vicar later said 'I had always found her quite cheerful, genial, kind-hearted and thoroughly upright with an excellent character. She was most highly respected'.[60] Miss Griffiths said that 'Mrs. Greenwood was very reticent and very particular as to her personal appearance' but did not use artificial beauty aids.[61] Another local woman said 'Mrs. Greenwood was the soul of kindness and probably nobody in the village was better liked'.[62]

Her family were very socially, financially and politically prominent in London. One of her brothers was Sir Thomas, who had taken over from their father as head of the paper making company. He had been Lord Mayor of London in 1913.[63] The Greenwoods were anxious to remind the world of their existence to their rich relations and so put news of the birth of their first son in a London newspaper.

Their younger daughter, Eileen, was a maid of honour to her aunt when she had been Lady Mayoress on Lord Mayor's day in 1913. It was noted that Mrs. Greenwood had many friends in London.[64]

[18] Sample letter from Greenwood, 1914.
(Bob Hinton's collection)

Greenwood was a solicitor in practice in Llanelli. In 1898 he bought into the partnership of Thomas Johnson and Holmes Stead, presumably using the money from his inheritance to do so. However, by the following year he concluded that this was not a profitable association for him and so he left it, dissolving the partnership in July 1899. He consulted Samuel Watkinson and Mr. T. J. Williams about this and paid £99 in fees for them to act for him in the matter of the dissolution. However, in August 1901 at the Llanelli County Court he was sued by Watkinson and Oliver Williams for not having fully paid all the fees they claimed he owed them. The court found for the plaintiffs, so Greenwood as defendant had to find £82 plus legal costs.[65]

His work **[18]** does not seem to have been of a very high powered nature. In 1898 he defended a number of men at the magistrates' court for salmon fishing without a licence.[66] In 1901 he acted for a client in a debt case for £42.[67] On 18th April 1906 he represented one Morgan Walters, a 25 year old boot dealer of Llettynewydd at the Carmarthen Bankruptcy Court.[68] Most of his work seems to have been in conveyancing, i.e. the drawing up of transfers of property as it was sold or leased. There are a number of reports of him acting for clients, such as in October 1904 when he worked for the vendors of property auctioned at the Castle Hotel.[69] In 1902 a Mr. W. D. Davies lent £35 to Evans Lewis and Smith on Greenwood's recommendation, the transaction occurring in Greenwood's office, but on not repaying him with interest, the case went to the courts.[70]

He also instructed barristers on behalf of clients who were going to court in civil cases. In August 1898 he instructed a barrister in the defence of his friend, Benjamin Jones, secretary of *The Llanelli Mercury*, which claimed £500 damages in a libel action against Jenkin Howell, a printer. The case went in Jones' favour.[71] In 1904 he was employed by the trustees of the Order of True Ivories (a Welsh friendly society) against the Widows and Orphans Fund at Brecon Assizes.[72] Two years later he instructed the barrister for Mr. H. Ellis, a Llanelli auctioneer at the Glamorgan Assizes.[73] In 1907 he instructed a barrister in a case where a farm worker was owed money from his former employer.[74]

However, a police report of Greenwood in 1920 was less than flattering:

> Harold Greenwood may be described as a man of little ability, a certain amount of simple cunning, and a large measure of conceit, is a solicitor and has an office in Llanelli. His small practice has mostly to do with Jews, moneylenders and dealings in house property.
>
> He has a poor reputation, both as a lawyer and generally, no one seems to have good word for him.[75]

Greenwood had occasional reason for recourse to the law himself. Having been involved in conveyancing work for one John Williams regarding a property sale, Greenwood had not been retained to complete the transaction so felt that he had lost the income due to him. Thomas Richard Ludford (1866-1950) represented Greenwood in the Llanelli County Court and was successful in winning the case with costs.[76] As we shall see, Ludford was to be an important man in Greenwood's subsequent life. Apart from having been a solicitor since 1891, Ludford was also the proprietor of the other of the two Llanelli newspapers and had been the editor of the *Llanelli Argus* since 1905.[77]

[19] Two plaques illustrating that Alfred Stephens was a valued and respected citizen of Kidwelly. (Fr. Jim Flanagan)

Greenwood also had modest political ambitions, as befitted a man of his local social standing. In November 1899 he was elected for a year as a member for Kidwelly council, with 215 votes, the lowest of the four successful candidates.[78] He was designated as a Stephenite, allied to the cause of Alfred Stephens [19] of Broom Hill, proprietor of a nearby brickworks and a man of political ambitions; he stood as Unionist (i.e. Conservative) candidate and so presumably Greenwood was politically a Conservative.[79] His wife was certainly one, attending meetings of the Kidwelly branch of the West Wales Unionist Women's Federation.[80] The council met on the evening of the third Friday of every month, so membership was not onerous. Yet a year later he did not stand again because he and another councillor were disgusted by the bickering and unprofessional nature they witnessed at council meetings.[81] He attended a ratepayers' meeting at the town hall (which is at the end of Bridge Street) about the council's leasing property they owned to Messrs. Smart and Stephens, and spoke up to object to a non-ratepayer speaking to them and was told they 'did not think Mr. Greenwood would have the courage to speak up among so many people'. Greenwood was the only dissenting voice against the meeting which opposed the council's offer.[82] A few years later his taste for public office recurred, though he was less successful. In 1908 he stood for the council but withdrew his candidature prior to the election.[83] In September 1911 he applied, as did another six men, for the position of town clerk for the borough of Kidwelly. This was a post which was usually held by a solicitor as the principal executive officer of a council and would have been part time, given the small size of the borough, so enabling a man to maintain his private practice. Alas, he was not chosen. He also stood for election as one of the four Kidwelly councillors for the county council. He gained 200 votes but this was not enough to secure a seat; the winning candidates took between 220-342 votes, but he did gain the most votes of the four candidates who were not elected.[84] At a Unionist meeting held to oppose Irish Home Rule by the then Liberal government, in which Stephens gave the main address, it was Greenwood who seconded the vote of thanks to him.[85]

Greenwood briefly attempted to form a company to produce aerated water locally. To do so he sought to rent Colman Well from the council for £12 10s. per week. It does not seem that this proceeded for at the next council meeting it was said that they were awaiting a letter from Greenwood but had yet to receive one.[86]

Greenwood was a big fish in a small pond. He clearly lacked the drive, ambition or ability to flourish in a larger setting. The professional scope in Llanelli was limited. Some solicitors would have sought to further their careers in London where there was opportunity for advancement but Greenwood did not avail himself of such but lived and worked in what workwise was a backwater.

[20] Kidwelly Cricket Team (Harold Greenwood bottom row, 2nd from the left, Dr. Thomas Griffith, bottom row, far right).

Some books about the case refer to Greenwood as being unpopular locally; at least where men were concerned, citing an anonymous male acquaintance 'describing him as not having a single man friend'.[87] Yet the contemporary evidence of his life in Kidwelly shows that he was involved in many local activities. He seems to have been fairly sociable and prominent locally. Although he never learnt Welsh, he threw himself into local activities; political, sporting and social. He played for the local cricket team [20] from at least 1906-1909 and may have captained it. He does not seem to have been particularly good at cricket, though. In a match against a Llanelli team in 1906 he made a single run and was then caught out. However, two years later he scored 13 runs before being run out. In another match that year he caught one of the opposition out.[88] There must have been a hiatus in his playing for in 1908, 'The reappearance of Mr. H. Greenwood in the team is heartily welcomed by all local lovers of the summer game and we trust his score of 20 is a foretaste of greater things' and later in the season he and the captain 'made a long stand against the fine bowling' of the opposition.[89] In 1909 it was noted 'H. Greenwood played his usual steady game'.[90] In 1913 he was one of the founders of the Kidwelly Tennis Club, being its captain with Dr. Griffiths as treasurer.[91]

More sedentary, he was also a card player, and in a tournament in 1910 was presented with the winner's silver vase by the doctor, it being stated that Greenwood was 'the champion whist player in the district, so many prizes he secured'.[92] On another occasion, he made a humorous public speech, citing Daniel in the lions' den.[93] He was also on committees organising other sports, as with a Kidwelly cycling meeting in 1903.[94]

A local newspaper described him as being 'a typical sporting countryman, fond of all outdoor sports, with a great pride in the beautiful gardens of Rumsey House'.[95] Another newspaper described him as 'a well known South Wales sportsman and athlete'.[96] He was noted as taking part as one of the seven guns on a grouse shoot in Ingleborough, Yorkshire, on the Glorious 12th of August, 1912. His brother Percy was also there.[97] Greenwood described himself in 1920 as 'A son of the open' and loved 'the wondrous vernal beauty of Carmarthenshire's wooded slopes'.[98]

Greenwood was also fond of entering livestock and produce in a variety of local agricultural shows. He often won prizes. In 1898 at the Llanelli flower show he won third prize for his roses, first for dahlias, broad beans and intermediate carrots.[99] Later that month he entered a horse and rider, John Griffiths, on a hackney gilded mare of over 15 hands high and it came second place.[100] The next year he entered a pullet into another such show.[101] He was later one of the judges of the Kidwelly Agricultural show in 1905, judging butter and cheese.[102]

On one occasion there was almost a serious accident. Greenwood was being driven on a horse and trap from home to the railway station, when the horse bolted and the trap capsized and smashed. Fortunately both Greenwood and the driver were unscathed.[103] There was another accident 9 years later when there was a fire at his office, caused by burning papers, but the fire brigade and police arrived there before much damage was caused.[104]

The Greenwoods were both involved in a concert at Kidwelly town hall to raise funds for the St. Teilo's Mission church, Mynydd y Garreg. Mrs. Greenwood was one of the women organising it and Greenwood was one of the men 'rendering valuable help'. In particular, he helped organise an advertisement competition among the guests and this was one of the most successful parts of the concert.[105]

Greenwood performed a little service in the First World War, in which 48 Kidwelly men gave their lives for King and Country. Given his age and lack of previous military service, taking an active role was unlikely. His younger half-brother, Gerald Kirk, served as a second lieutenant with the first battalion of the Royal Lancaster (Territorial) Regiment. When he died of wounds received at Ypres in April 1915, the local newspaper reported him as being Greenwood's brother and for which great sympathy was extended towards him for his loss.[106] Along with the mayor and other local notables he saw local men march off to war in 1914 and at a meeting about Belgian refugees suggested that the town hall be used to house them. He was later a member of the mayor's committee for welcoming the soldiers home.[107]

However, his wife was very active, unsurprisingly given her charitable and church work in Kidwelly. She presided over the committee for the relief of Belgian refugees. She was honorary treasurer for the flag days to help Welsh soldiers. She provided stationery for the troops and along with other needlewomen made clothing for the soldiers. At a fete for the Red Cross held at Kidwelly castle in 1916, organised by Miss Griffiths and Miss Phillips, presided over by Mrs. Smart, Mrs. Greenwood, Eileen and Ivor helped out to man some of the stalls. At the war's end she and others who had been so involved in such work, such as Miss Griffiths and Mrs. Meredith, gave a presentation to the former mayoress who had also done a great deal in such work.[108]

In 1918 or 1919 a Mrs. Little of Yorkshire offered Greenwood a post in India on a cotton plantation. He turned it down because he said he was a married man and did not want to leave his family.[109] Had he done so his life would have changed out of all recognition, though whether his stated reason was entirely truthful may be later questioned.

In 1919 the household at Rumsey House was composed of Harold and Mabel Greenwood, Irene and John Kenneth Greenwood (the other two children being at boarding schools). Greenwood was usually at work from 10.00am to 3.00pm. He was often home at 5.30pm and the family ate at 7.30pm. This suggests a rather leisurely lifestyle on his part, dependant to an extent on his wife's income and presumably he had few clients. Overwork was not one of his failings. Irene then worked in a bank in Carmarthen, travelling there and back each day. The Greenwoods held a dance in April 1919 at their house to celebrate her coming of age. John Kenneth had private lessons from a Miss Gough who came to Rumsey House each day. Edith Jane Bowater, Mabel's unmarried sister, lived with them, paying 25s. per week, but was not there in May and early June; it is not known when her residence with them began (in 1911 she lived with her mother in Bromley). Their servants were Hannah Maggie Williams, aged 18 years, house parlour maid, employed there since about October 1918, Margaret Ann Morris, aged 38 years, the cook, who had been there since about 1917, and another maid, Lily Gwyneira Powell, aged 20 years and who also had looked after the little boy since about 1917. There were also a couple of men who did casual work in the gardens and Mary Morris, a woman who came in to do daily work but lived elsewhere in Kidwelly.[110]

> Gravell, Mr. W., Gordon Terrace, Kidwelly.
> Gravell, Rev. W. J., B.A., St. Michael's College, Llandaff, Cardiff.
> Gray, Mr. Thomas, J.P., Underhill, Port Talbot.
> Green, Rev. Prof. E. Tyrrell, St. David's College, Lampeter.
> Greenwood, Mr. H., Solicitor, Kidwelly.
> Greville, Mr. David, 12 Doughty Street, London, W.C.
> Greville, Mr. T., Maesderwen, Pontyberem, Llanelly.
> Griffith, Rev. John, Llangynwyd, Glamorgan.
> Griffith, Rev. Wm., Villa Master, 67a Hampton Road, Southport.
> Griffiths, Dr., Kidwelly (two copies).
> Griffiths, Rev. D., Llangranog Rectory, Henllan, Cards.
> Griffiths, Mr. John, Ferry Road, Kidwelly.
> Griffiths, Mr. Joseph, 1 St. Peter's Terrace, Cambridge.

[21] List of subscribers to Reverend Jones' *A History of Kidwelly*, 1908 (note Harold Greenwood and Dr. Thomas Griffiths' names).

It seemed a conventional and comfortably off middle class household. The entry for Kidwelly in the 1920 South Wales and Monmouthshire directory lists 14 individuals in the *Residents* section; of these six were clergymen and of the eight others one was Greenwood and another was Dr. Griffiths.[111] He was, therefore, one of the social elite of the town, at the top of the little local tree. Local newspapers in the 1900s and 1910s which covered Kidwelly activities frequently list the Greenwoods, the Smarts, the Merediths, the Griffiths and others being involved in the same social and charitable activities **[21]**. Yet events were to impinge on this apparently comfortable existence.

Chapter Two

The Death of Mrs. Greenwood

There were cracks in the comfortable edifice of life for the Greenwood family. We now come to Greenwood's private life, unrecorded in public until 1920. Apart from the possible monetary motive for murder, the other one touted is whether Greenwood had an amatory reason to kill his wife. Those opposing this argue that none existed. Duke wrote 'he was accused of 'carrying on' – a convenient term conveying anything from affability to adultery – with sundry ladies in the neighbourhood'. She later added 'Servants, friends, acquaintances, the family doctor, all described the Greenwoods as a happy couple, and apparently attached to each other'.[1] A later author has echoed this, writing, after quoting the previous statement with approval, 'Greenwood was a pompous man, dapper and moustached, and his facetious little efforts were more probably attempts at the former than the latter, but even so had been noted with disapproval'.[2] Another author thought that this 'probably meant no more than he took pleasure in the company of a pretty woman'.[3] Dr. Thompson was more agnostic, writing that Greenwood 'had the reputation of being very much of a ladies man ... flirting, if nothing more, with a number of women, single and married, in and around his home ... Just how far he indulged himself with these various ladies, is difficult to know'.[4] Anything but agnostic, Mark John Maguire makes a number of damning comments, that Greenwood was 'something of a philanderer', 'known as a ladies' man', 'a man of relentless amorous ambitions' and so spent his time 'pursuing local girls'.[5] Which assessment is more accurate is up to the reader to determine by examining the known evidence, some of which is to be found below. It should be said that there is no surviving contemporary paper evidence in the form of letters or diaries.

Certainly some evidence can be cited to support the view that the Greenwoods were a contented couple. On the surface, the marriage seemed a happy one and the two appeared compatible, the Greenwoods 'appear to have led the placid life of country people and found diversions in local pursuits', as a newspaper reported.[6] Dr. Griffiths, when asked if he always found them on the 'most affectionate terms', agreed. Martha Morris, a servant, said 'So far as I know, Mr. and Mrs. Greenwood lived in good terms'. Nurse Elizabeth Jones said almost the same. Margaret Morris, another servant, thought that the couple 'seemed all right' and 'quite happy'. Finally, yet another servant, Lily Powell, who had been there for two years said 'Mr. and Mrs. Greenwood were living on very happy terms'.[7] Evidence from those in Greenwood's employ is not necessarily accurate; if they wished to continue in said employment they would hardly speak against their employers (when the servant of Mrs. Light gave a statement against her son, Ronald, accused of murder in 1920, the servant was dismissed). Greenwood himself said 'we were very happy together. We were married for twenty-three years, and I can honestly say we never had a quarrel. It was always give and take with us'.[8]

Then there were other views. One was by Miss Phillips, a great friend of his wife and so perhaps best placed to know the concerns of the normally reticent Mrs. Greenwood. She was at first equivocal and hesitant when asked about the state of the Greenwood marriage. Eventually she said that, when asked if they were on good terms or not, she said 'Sometimes' but 'I have seen so many differences between them' she finally volunteered. To be more precise, 'Mr. and Mrs. Greenwood used to have tiffs and brawls about women'. Such occurred in early 1919.[9] Miss Phillips also said, eventually, 'If you must have the truth, when Mr. and Mrs. Greenwood had tiffs it was always about women, the last time perhaps was about a few months or a few weeks before she died … they were so frequent … I can recall a good many more going back, three, four, five years …'[10]

Additionally, Miss Phillips, added, 'Mr. Greenwood was very fond of making his wife jealous and irritating her, and that caused unpleasantness … A few weeks before Mrs. Greenwood's death I was present on the occasion of such unpleasantness'. Miss Griffiths later said 'Things were not very comfortable at times with Mr. and Mrs.

Greenwood because he was a flirt and Mrs. Greenwood knew it. She had often said to me 'That is Harold's weakness, he is fond of women".[11]

A police report on Greenwood in 1920 was also less than flattering:

> He was too friendly with other women, during his deceased's wife's life, which caused a certain amount of domestic infelicity, so that their married life could not be described as a particularly happy one.[12]

The key woman in the case was Miss Gwladys Amelia Jones who was born on 4th February 1888 in Llanelli, where she lived until 1919. In 1911, when the family were living at Sunnyside, Tyr Fan, in Llanelli, she is not listed as being in gainful employment and was unmarried, but seems to have assisted in the family business later in the decade. Greenwood had done business with her father and so had been known to the family for some years. Gwladys Jones' character and history are enigmatic. Very little is known about her and yet she is a crucial character in this case. She was never interviewed by the press nor questioned by the police. We can deduce a little of her character by her actions, which are mostly commented on by others.

In May 1915 Gwladys Jones was engaged to one Frank Astley Russell (1890-1960). He had been born in Burma and in 1911 was an apprentice motor mechanic living in Swansea. He joined the army in 1914 and rose from private to 2nd lieutenant in the 5th battalion of the Wiltshire regiment, fighting at Gallipoli in 1915 and then serving in Mesopotamia and India, where his health suffered. Having been introduced to her in 1912 by one of her brothers, Hubert Jones, when visiting his home, the two wrote to each other, becoming engaged in May 1915 (and exchanged rings), but by the summer of 1919 he thought that she was becoming cooler in her replies. In her letters she mentioned Irene Greenwood as a friend and also Greenwood as the solicitor her family employed.[13]

The police report went on to state that when Mrs. Greenwood was absent from home in 1918, he invited Gwladys Jones, whom he had known for 20 years, to stay with him. Elaborating on this, Irene Greenwood stated that 'Father wanted Gwladys to stay for a weekend. She came and brought her sister with her'. It was Irene who invited

Gwladys and by letter, at her father's urging. Gertrude Jones, Gwladys' soon to be married sister, was also present at the time as well. As was the children's governess, one Miss Davies. Mrs. Greenwood had no prior knowledge of this and the subsequent weekend visit. The police noted that 'Greenwood had for a long time lunched with her' and 'had become on extremely friendly terms' with her. At the same time, 'There has been a longstanding flirtation between Greenwood and the Doctor's sister'.[14] Apparently Irene and Gertrude left on the Monday by the 9.00am train and Gwladys Jones an hour and a half later. Miss Griffiths reported 'I heard that when Mrs. Greenwood came home she found a number of chocolate boxes in the house and there was a dreadful row about the young ladies ... The impression he gave me was that he was not a devoted husband. He never took Mrs. Greenwood anywhere for the day'.[15]

Agnes Mary Davies had been a servant at Rumsey House in 1917-1918 and had additional comments to make about these times. She said:

> During this stage Mr. Greenwood spent a good deal of his time with his present wife in the sitting room, and Miss Irene and Mrs. Greenwood's sister would sit in the [nearby] drawing room. Before Mrs. Greenwood returned from her holiday, Mr. Greenwood said to me, 'don't tell Mrs. Greenwood that I have had the two Miss Jones' here two week ends, but say that two Miss Evans' had been here for one week and only'. I said 'Suppose Mrs. Greenwood asks me as I cannot say an untruth to her'. He then said 'Well, it will mean a divorce'.[16]

She was not the only one asked to lie on Greenwood's behalf, as we shall see, and when this is the case the relationship in question is unlikely to be innocent. Irene later said that her mother did learn of the weekend from her.[17]

Mrs. Annie Elizabeth Groves [1] (1868-1949), caretaker (and resident) at Greenwood's office at No. 1 Frederick Street, in Llanelli, had some pertinent remarks on this subject. She told how in 1918 and 1919 Greenwood took his lunches in the offices of the Mercury newspaper, where Gwladys worked (before 1918 he had eaten his lunch at his office). She later said 'He was on very friendly terms with Miss [Gwladys] Jones and she frequently came to the office at Frederick Street and was alone with Mr. Greenwood … I have frequently seen him kiss her … Miss Jones did not resent this', though later denied that she had seen them doing so until after they were married. She said that from a Saturday in late October 1918 Gwladys Jones often visited Greenwood at his office.[18]

[1] Mrs Annie Groves.

The two often spoke on the telephone regularly as Miss Griffiths reported; lacking a telephone of his own (ironically fellow English solicitor in Wales, Major Armstrong, had a telephone at his house but not a car) Greenwood relied on that of the Griffiths in the house just across the road. As with two employees just cited, Greenwood would lie to cover up what may have been an illicit relationship. She stated:

> Miss Jones used to telephone to Henblas and ask me to get Mr. Greenwood to the telephone. I asked him one day 'Who is this person that rings you up on the phone?' He said 'Oh it is the woman that cleans the office'. I said 'No, it is Miss Jones, she gave me her name'. He said nothing in reply.[19]

The need and desire to talk to each other when apart suggests at the least a close friendship and providing the conversation is private, it is far safer than written communication which can be seen by others.

Of course, it could be argued that a married man and an unmarried woman can be just good friends, who enjoy each other's company and conversation without any romantic intention or action on either side. That he did not mention such to his wife could be because his wife had a jealous nature (she certainly resented his friendship with Miss Griffiths which she did know about) and so it made his home life easier if he did not mention to his wife this friendship. However, such is human nature that alas any such friendship will be assumed by others to be of a non-platonic nature, regardless of reality. Whether this was the case in this instance is for the reader to judge.

Greenwood was also on good terms with the doctor's sister and she admitted that this was so, though no more than that. She agreed that he was 'Always very pleasant' and said this extended to all the fair sex. She added that his wife once teased him about it, 'That is Harold's weakness. Too fond of the ladies'. Greenwood frequently visited the doctor's house, though this was in part to receive telephone calls from Gwladys and he was also on good terms with her brother, Dr. Griffiths.[20] It was said at the trial that 'No human being could say what the relationship was between Greenwood and Miss Griffiths'.[21]

As with Gwladys Jones, relatively little is known about Mary Adeline Griffiths, the sister of one of the town's most prominent citizens, Dr. Griffiths. She was born in Kidwelly in 1873 and had lived in Henblas, Kidwelly all her life (and from 1916 just across the road from the Greenwoods' house). Her father was an affluent landowner and once mayor of Kidwelly. She was presumably educated locally but given her parents' wealth never needed to work. The local press noted that she, as with Mrs. Greenwood, did much voluntary work for the church and various charities, especially during World War One. In recent years (1913 and 1916), she had lost her two sisters and so now lived alone with her brother. She was unmarried and by 1919 was 46 years old and so unlikely to be otherwise.[22]

Miss Griffiths denied any romance with Greenwood and stated to the police 'I have been friendly with Mr. Greenwood for many years, it is quite untrue that I have been other than on friendly terms with him, the suggestion that I sat on his knee in a railway carriage is perfectly untrue'.[23] Yet Greenwood, when asked, stated that his wife was jealous of his friendship with Miss Griffiths; given their physical proximity, she could hardly fail to observe this.[24] This could, of course, be also why he concealed from his wife his friendship with Gwladys Jones.

He later tried to exonerate himself from any wrong doing on his part with Miss Griffiths by focussing on one act which apparently gave cause to gossip. He claimed 'Our names have been linked together, though there was not a scintilla of truth'. It was all 'through a concatenation of perfectly innocent, ordinary and unavoidable circumstances, I frequently travelled with Miss Griffiths between Kidwelly and Llanelli'. This was on the train, when travelling home each evening from work, taking one that left about 5.00pm and it was an infrequent service but he took that one so he could be home early for the family dinner. It was often the case that Miss Griffiths was on that train and so they travelled home together. 'There was no earthly reason why I should have gone out of my way to avoid Miss Griffiths'. He even said that she often called on his wife and there was friendship between the neighbours; to avoid her would be suspicious.[25]

There was also a suspicion that Greenwood was rather friendly, whatever that means, with nurse Elizabeth Jones. The grounds for this are slender. In early 1919, she and a Mrs. Chambers were walking near Rumsey House. Greenwood called them over and he asked to have his fortune told. Nurse Elizabeth Jones said that she was not very good at it but that Mrs. Chambers was and so she consulted her playing cards and divined what she thought was Greenwood's future (unrecorded).[26] It is also possible that Harold Greenwood cultivated a friendship with Miss Griffiths for the purpose of suggesting that there might be more to it than this in order to create an alibi for his real romantic interest in Gwladys Jones.

There is also some evidence on how the Greenwood family interacted with one another. Greenwood himself related in 1920 how he was a liberal father, with reference to 'the fun and frolic I fostered in my home among my children, to whom I have been a pal as well as a father'.[27] Relations between Irene and her mother were also commented upon by Miss Phillips. She said that Irene 'did not show [her mother] much affection'. She added 'I do not think there was quite as much affection as between some mothers and daughters. I do not think she was especially fond of her mother'. On the other hand, Irene herself spoke of her mother's kindness to others and added 'She was very devoted to her children'. A servant thought that the daughter was on good terms with both her parents. Quite possibly, though, Irene had a better rapport with her father, calling him daddy, whereas her mother was termed simply mother.[28]

We shall now turn to the subject of Mrs. Greenwood's health which later became a matter of more than purely personal and family importance. Miss Phillips said that she was 'a wiry type of woman' who took care of herself and would always seek medical aid if needed. It is generally believed, though, that her health was poor and especially in the months and weeks prior to her demise. Agnes Davies recalled that in 1917 and 1918 'Mrs. Greenwood was frequently complaining and suffered from biliousness and headache ... She used to go to the doctor's herself and was continuously taking the doctor's medicines'.[29] Greenwood later wrote that she had been especially ill since about the end of 1918, when she had a breakdown. Apparently, she had taken a great interest in the case of Billie Carleton (1896-1918). She was a young actress who had enjoyed great success during the First World War. Unfortunately after attending the Victory Ball at the Royal Albert Hall she took an overdose of cocaine and died. Greenwood took to hiding all the newspapers about this story. He once said to her 'Look here, Mabel. Tell me the honest truth. Have you taken any drugs?' She replied she had not and he was relieved, though she did take sal volatile. He remained concerned about possible drug possession, however. He was worried but kept it a secret from their children and relatives; praising his wife's 'heroic fortitude and her suffering, and her modesty'.[30]

In 1919 she was a woman of 47 years who had borne four children, one as recently as 1910. Dr. Griffiths, who had attended her from about 1903, later told the inquest that 'she was in fairly good health' but also remarked that she was 'delicate and frail, and not by any means robust'. Since late 1918 her health had been failing. Recently, he stated, 'She complained of weakness and haemorrhage'. He put this down to 'change of life or some organic trouble. There was uterine trouble also. I prescribed for her and made up a preparation'. It caused him some concern, he said, attributing it to the change in condition or something growing. Menopause or cancer in other words. There was also a growth on one of her organs but it was not cancerous or dangerous to her life, though it was painful.[31] The doctor had treated her in 1917-1919 for gastric trouble, sickness and biliousness, attacks which lasted a day or two and led to fainting fits.[32] However, he also remarked 'Her health was fairly good up to a few months prior to her death' and 'I did not expect her to die so soon as she did'.[33]

Dr. Griffiths reported that Greenwood had been calling in various specialists to see his wife. One such was apparently Sir Milsom Rees (1866-1952), a prominent Welsh doctor who had treated members of the royal family and notable opera singers. However, his speciality was the health of the voice box and this does not seem to have been one of Mrs. Greenwood's ailments so quite why Greenwood would have paid him for a diagnosis is hard to see. Possibly it was so because he was such a well known Welsh physician and Greenwood was a snob.[34] Greenwood himself said that he was considering asking one of his brothers-in-law for advice about a specialist to treat his wife for cancer but never made the enquiry because he claimed that his wife would not have wanted him to do so.[35]

Greenwood later said that his wife had been taking medicines before her death but that he did not know 'what was in it'. He said 'They were treating her for catarrh, supposed cancer, her heart and her nerves'. He thought they could not have been poisonous because 'If there had been she would have been writhing in pain would she not?' However, on another occasion he suggested 'I should not have been the least surprised to know that they found poison of some kind'. Her daughter later recalled that she had been taking iron jelloids.[36]

She had also been losing weight. Greenwood reported that 'she had become painfully thin', being reduced to a mere six stones and one pound in weight, from being eight stones seven pounds, which is an extreme and dangerous loss of weight (and a symptom of arsenic poisoning). She put stuffing in her corsets to ease their pressure on her body. She seemed emaciated. Miss Phillips, however, said that she had not noticed this and presumably it had been hidden from her. There were also, apparently mental health concerns, with hallucinations that she claimed she could hear her son Kenneth 'our dear little boy' who she thought was calling out to her at night.[37]

Others thought that she was in bad health. Martha Morris, a former servant, claimed that she had seen her faint several times, once in May 1919, and that she had been in low spirits in the week prior to her death. She had always been unwell, she recalled.[38] On 19th May Greenwood was with Gwladys Jones and a brother of hers and Greenwood rang Edward Roberts to ask him to drive them back to Kidwelly because his wife was very ill.[39] The vicar said 'She had not been looking well for several months'.[40]

In May 1919 Gwladys Jones told her neighbour Gwyneth David in Llanelli that Mrs. Greenwood was very ill and had been unconscious for a week. That puzzled Gwyneth because she had had a letter from Irene that morning and there had been nothing there about her mother being so ill. Gwyneth, who was also a friend of Irene Greenwood's, then made enquiries and on 5th June received a letter[41] from Greenwood, which read as follows:

> Dear Miss David,
>
> I am indeed very much surprised to hear that you told Miss Alice Jones yesterday that Mrs. Greenwood was not ill and that her brother had not been to see her. Why and what was is your object in telling her these deliberate lies? Your only object that I can see is that you, for some unknown desire, wish to break my friendship with the Jones family, which I feel happy to say is more than your flippant tongue can achieve. I must ask you in future to let me and mine alone, unless you can speak the truth concerning them, but I must call for an explanation

> concerning the innuendo you suggest by making the false statement you have.
>
> Yours truly,
>
> H. Greenwood.

Martha Morris also noted that Mrs. Greenwood had been suffering from diarrhoea in early 1919. It is perhaps worth noting that this is one symptom of, amongst other ailments, arsenic poisoning (weight loss as noted above, is another). Since there are no other comments on her exact symptoms, it is impossible to be sure if this was the case, even in retrospect. It may be a coincidence that her health worsened after her sister left in April 1919 for a short holiday of a few weeks. 'She was wasting away and she knew it', Greenwood later said.[42] Possibly Irene was also absent, in London with friends, at this time and she recalled seeing a play in London, *Our Mr. Hepplewhite* at The Criterion.[43] It may also be a coincidence at this time that Mrs. Greenwood began to become noticeably ill and Dr. Griffiths began to see her more regularly in the four of five weeks from mid-May onwards, though believing she was suffering from cancer or heart disease.[44]

Greenwood said that his wife thought that after her sister-in-law's departure, a servant had been tampering with the wine. According to Miss Phillips, both Greenwoods thought a servant (probably Hannah Williams) had been watering it down and so he decided not to drink it. She said 'They were both laughing about it'.[45]

As far as the outside world knew, the death of Mrs. Greenwood was swift and unextraordinary. But months later its exact circumstances became the focus of much importance. Those witnesses intimately involved with her death gave their testimonies; her husband, her eldest daughter, a friend, two medical professionals and the servants. All these recounted their recollections almost a year later and this account is based on what they said to the police, at the inquest and on subsequent occasions. We shall first survey the days leading up to her death, mostly narrated by her husband a year later.

On the Monday of 9th June, a Bank Holiday, Miss Griffiths and Mrs. Greenwood were having tea together at the ruined castle [2] during the Eisteddfod, 'and then Mrs. Greenwood was quite well'.

She had never heard Mrs. Greenwood say that she was very unwell.[46] Meanwhile Greenwood recalled that 'the greater part of the day I spent in the garden'. Next day both the Greenwoods were in their garden for much of the day. Greenwood claimed his wife was unwell, complaining of weakness and depression.[47]

[2] Kidwelly Castle. (Paul Lang's postcard collection)

On Wednesday 11th June 1919, and not mentioned (perhaps significantly) by her husband, Mrs. Greenwood visited his office in Llanelli, where her husband and Gwladys were together in the back office. Knowing they were there, when Mrs. Greenwood called, Annie told her that her boss was out and she did not know when he would be back. Mrs. Greenwood left, but not before seeing her husband's coat hung up. Later that afternoon, Annie saw Greenwood alone and she apologised to him for having told an untruth to his wife. He said 'It is alright'. Gwladys visited him on the next day as well.[48] Needless to say this went unrecorded in Greenwood's later accounts of his wife's last week. That Wednesday evening, he drove his wife for a trip in his Calthorpe car, that he said he had bought for her and had cleared out the stables behind the house for use as a garage. There must have been very few cars in Kidwelly for the place neither had a petrol station nor a garage; clearly Greenwood prioritised having a car over a telephone, though both would have been of use to his lifestyle. Possibly cost was the issue. However, this, her first and last journey in a car, made her very nervous. On her return she was in a fit of restlessness.[49]

On the Thursday Mrs. Greenwood went to the first meeting since the war of the Carmarthen Antiquarian Society and Field Club, which was at Kidwelly town hall, to view some of the relics and documents held there. Apparently she was so ill that she had to be helped up the steps of the town hall. Greenwood wrote 'One of her friends said they had never seen her look so ghastly as she did that day. She had reached the stage when her feeble condition was becoming obvious to others'.[50]

[3] Phoenix Stores, Bridge Street, Kidwelly, 2024.
(Author's photograph)

Greenwood later recalled that on Friday 13th June a friend visited his wife and she later told Greenwood how she thought his wife looked and perhaps she had not much longer to live. That day Mrs. Greenwood also went to Bertha Isaac's milliner's and dressmaker's shop at Winsham House on Bridge Street. She went for a dress fitting for a summer frock and 'she seemed quite pleased with it'. She also ordered a cream skirt and talked about her forthcoming holiday.[51] She intended to go on holiday with her sister to Portishead on 22nd June.[52] On Saturday 14th June 1919 Mrs. Greenwood seemed healthy and well, however Greenwood later wrote that her heart was bad and that she needed to change the medicine she took. He did not go to Llanelli that day.[53] She also went to the Phoenix wine stores on Bridge Street [3], next door to Rumsey House, and bought a bottle of Reo red wine from the proprietor, Sarah Edwards. She often drank a half glass or three quarters of a glass of burgundy at lunch; occasionally port. Greenwood often bought a bottle of whisky from the shop and his wife bought burgundy there. Most of the household's wine, though, was bought from Frederick Brigstocke's shop at No. 54 King Street, in Carmarthen.[54]

That afternoon she went to Ferryside, a village 4 miles to the north west of Kidwelly on the way to Carmarthen, by train, to a meeting of the tennis club with which she was involved. Greenwood later said he took her to Kidwelly station by car. The vicar went with her, travelling in the same train compartment after meeting her on the railway platform, then walking the three quarters of a mile trip to the club from Ferryside railway station. He recalled, 'She took a lively part in the discussions'. Miss Phillips, recalling her presence there, later said that she had been 'in good spirits and very bright'. The vicar thought, 'She was not looking well, but she made no remark about her health then ... she was quite cheerful and active'. However, Greenwood later claimed that she declined a game of croquet there and that was a game she enjoyed playing. She returned that evening, travelling with the vicar by train, quite well and they parted at the railway station at 7.00pm.[55]

However, that Saturday evening, Mrs. Greenwood called to see Martha Morris, an occasional servant of theirs (and who had once been nurse to Irene), who lived further down Bridge Street. She regularly gave Martha a pound of butter. On this occasion she paid her for some sewing and needlework she had done for her. Martha recalled 'She seemed very weak and sat down on the sofa'. Martha went to Rumsey House later that evening between 9.00 and 10.00pm and found Mrs. Greenwood and Miss Phillips together. The former said that she could not give her the butter now but that she should call for it later in the week and that Irene would pass it on to her.[56] Miss Phillips later said that that evening her friend 'seemed bright, but her voice was low, and she had some difficulty in speaking'.[57] She also recalled 'Mrs. Greenwood seemed quite bright and unusually well. We laughed and talked for some time. What particularly struck me was her complexion. It was a lovely sort of pink which was quite unusual'.[58] Greenwood's recollection of that evening was that his wife was in an exhausted state and was feeling depressed due to her weight loss. Apparently, she cried that night in the garden and only fell asleep at midnight.[59]

[4] St. Mary's church, Kidwelly, 2024.
(Fr. Jim Flanagan)

On Sunday 15th June she was at home with her husband, eldest daughter and youngest son. Hannah noted that Mrs. Greenwood came downstairs at 9.30am and went to the dining room.[60] Irene later remarked that she, her brother and 'Daddy' had breakfast at 10.00am. They had eggs, tea (coffee according to Hannah) and bread and butter. Greenwood claimed his wife was depressed and complained of being ill at breakfast. It sees that she had had hallucinations that night and believed she has had a conversation with her late mother. Greenwood asked his wife to excuse him from church [4] that morning because he wanted to overhaul the car. She said that she was not feeling well enough to attend; the 11.30am service (in English) was presumably the one that they missed. Greenwood commented, 'It was no triviality which could interfere with her custom, extending over her life, of attending service on Sunday morning'.[61]

Irene then went to her room to tidy it up and then went downstairs to the kitchen to help Hannah with the preparation of the pastry.[62] Hannah recalled, 'Mrs. Greenwood appeared to be quite well after breakfast and spent the whole morning on the lawn writing letters'.[63] Greenwood said that he had put out a deck chair for his wife and that she was reading 'a library book of the light kind'. She seemed very restless, he thought. Later that morning he saw her nervously pacing up and down and once went over to the garage.[64]

There is also a suggestion of yet more marital discord that morning. Hannah Williams recalled hearing raised voices behind a closed door, 'In the morning that Mrs. Greenwood was taken ill. Mr. and Mrs. Greenwood were in the sitting room. They were quarrelling. I don't know what they were quarrelling about'. In conjunction with Miss Phillips' earlier comments the reader can be fairly certain about the subject in hand.[65] It is possible that she recalled going to husband's place of work on the 11th when he was apparently not there but his coat was (and he was with Gwladys Jones in another room).

Late that morning, about 11.00am, Thomas Foy (1887-1947), of Alpine House, Kidwelly, the local cinema proprietor/manager who also worked on cars, came to the garage to work on the family motor car. He also sold cars; in 1919 he advertised one for £55. Greenwood was already at work there, dismantling the car's engine and taking out and cleaning the parts 'a dirty job' which meant that he became smeared with oil and grease up to the elbows.[66] Foy and Greenwood worked together, until the gong went for lunch at about 12.55pm, it being rung by Hannah. Irene had been out into the garden at about noon as well and sat on the lawn, just outside the dining room window. She did not notice her father enter the house from the garage at that time.[67]

When the dinner gong was sounded, Irene got up and went to the dining room. She was followed by her mother, then Kenneth and then her father, last of all. The family had lunch, a meat joint (either roast lamb or beef as the servants differed in their memories of what was eaten) and vegetables, then gooseberry tart and custard. Greenwood later claimed, 'I told my wife not to have any [gooseberry tart]. As she had had diarrhoea on the Saturday previous, and she had it on that Sunday afternoon also'.[68]

[5] Sideboard in the dining room which contained the bottle of wine. (Bob Hinton's collection)

The lunch may be a pivotal episode in the drama. There are several accounts of what happened. Hannah recalled that she took a bottle of red wine (a black bottle with a red label, she thought) and a bottle of whisky from the sideboard cupboard [5] of the dining room and placed them on the dining table. The bottle of wine was three quarters full; probably someone had had a glass on the evening before. It is uncertain whether the sideboard cupboard was normally kept unlocked so anyone could have accessed it or whether only Mrs. Greenwood had the key, as Greenwood later alleged, to stop the servants drinking the family's wine.[69]

Hannah recalled, in contradiction to what Irene later said:

> In the morning of the Sunday Mr. Greenwood was in the garden, and from there he went to the china pantry, where he remained a quarter of an hour and from there he went into the dining room, where he remained about five minutes. I have never known him to do that before and I had to wait for him to come out.[70]

The crucial question later was who drank what. Least controversial was that Greenwood claimed that he 'probably' had a whisky and soda and his daughter agreed on this point, as did Hannah, that Greenwood drank whisky. What was less certain was what his wife and daughter had to drink. Greenwood claimed that his wife 'may have had' whisky and soda and also said that she often drank it.[71] Yet Hannah and Irene thought otherwise. Irene said that her mother drank wine. Hannah said that she placed the wine bottle next to Mrs. Greenwood and that she helped herself, but on another occasion she claimed that she actually poured out the wine for her mistress, which was the only time she had ever been asked to do so. Mrs. Greenwood clearly did drink wine with her meal. Most controversial of all is what Irene drank. Hannah claimed that she drank soda water (as did Kenneth) and said that no one else drank the wine on that occasion. Hannah said that Irene never drank wine (unless she was unwell) and 'I did not see any other members of the family taking port wine'. Irene said that she did drink wine and had wine on that lunchtime. Lily Powell claimed that both Irene and her mother drank burgundy generally but she was not present at the lunch to know what they drank on that occasion.[72] To confuse matters, Hannah, another time claimed that she put two wine glasses on the table, one for Greenwood and one for his wife.[73]

If Hannah was correct in recalling that she put two wine glasses onto the table, this can surely only be taken that two people drank the wine at the meal. Or perhaps only Mrs. Greenwood did and Mr. Greenwood, drinking whisky (and soda), drank from a wine glass.

The question is, whether or not Mr. Greenwood would have drunk whisky from a wine glass or from a (smaller) whisky tumbler (he certainly denied that he drank whisky from a wine glass and convention suggests that he would not have done so). The latter seems more probable. Maybe Hannah erred in her recollection and Irene was right in that she did partake of wine that lunchtime. The question of who drank what is very important as we shall see. Much would depend on how fastidious the Greenwoods were.

After having served the gooseberry tart, Hannah left the room.[74] She continued, 'After the dinner was over I replaced the wine bottle and the whisky bottle in the cupboard'.[75] Clearly not all the wine was drunk at this lunch, but whether one or two glasses had been drunk is unknown.

The midday meal had been cooked by Margaret Ann Morris and the remnant was eaten by the servants. Miss Phillips visited, though she did not go into the dining room but saw her Mrs. Greenwood, perhaps in the hall. It was about 1.00pm and the change in her friend was noticeable and she later said 'she looked very, very ill and her voice was low and uneven' and 'she appeared pinched and pale and spoke very quietly'. She invited Miss Phillips to supper that day. Irene said that she and her mother went out into the garden after lunch. Kenneth and his father also went into the garden. Towards 3.00pm her mother went inside whilst Irene left with Foy for her driving lesson, and they saw Mrs. Greenwood as they were driving away and she spoke but he could not hear what she said. They returned at about 3.30 or 4.00pm.[76]

Mrs. Greenwood then went inside and Hannah later recalled, 'I can't say whether she was eating chocolate in the sitting room but she often did eat chocolate'.[77] Greenwood recalled, a year later, 'we were taking our usual stroll together in the garden [6], when she suddenly exclaimed, "Oh my heart" and put her hand to her side. I thought it was another of her fainting attacks'.[78] He elaborated, 'Barely had we started when she stopped suddenly and said she had a frightful pain at her heart and could not go a step further. I helped her to a chair and asked her what it felt like. She replied that it was just like a red hot skewer going right through her heart and she felt very faint'.[79]

[6] Grounds of Rumsey House, 2024. (Author's photograph)

This was witnessed by no one else for Foy had taken Irene out in a car for a driving lesson as pre-arranged. It was about 3.00 to 4.00pm when this occurred. Mrs. Greenwood had waved the two off. He thought that Mrs. Greenwood seemed in good health.[80]

Afternoon tea was served between 4.00 and 4.40pm. The same four members of the family partook of the light repast. They had tea and bread and butter. Mrs. Greenwood told her daughter that she felt sick, that she had pains in her heart and flatulence. Greenwood asked his wife if she had taken anything that might make her unwell and she said no. She then drank some brandy, which was given to her by her husband. They took her upstairs to her room; it was now about 6.00pm.[81]

Hannah put the wine and whisky bottles on the table in readiness for the family's evening meal, before leaving the house at 5.15pm, as it was her evening off. When she returned later that evening, everything had been cleared away.[82]

The crucial events of the evening were witnessed in part or whole by six people; Greenwood, his daughter, Dr. Griffiths, his sister, Miss Phillips and nurse Elizabeth Jones. They did not all agree. Therefore, the following narrative is discordant.

Once the unwell Mrs. Greenwood had been taken upstairs by her husband and daughter, they decided that they should call the doctor, who lived just across the road from Rumsey House. Greenwood did so and the two came back almost immediately. It was 'sometime between six and seven' that Dr. Griffiths claimed that Greenwood came to see him at Henblas and told him that his wife was unwell. He found Mrs. Greenwood sitting on a couch in her room. She had been sick around this time. Mrs. Greenwood told Dr. Griffiths that she had eaten gooseberry pie and that as always it made her sick, as she said 'I do feel frightfully faint and have awful pains in my head as I always get'. She complained of gastric pains and was suffering from bile. He said he thought that her heart was bad, but that she was just suffering from bile. He gave her sips of brandy and iced water, also suggesting that milk and soda water or barley water could be given as well. He asked Irene to put her mother to bed, which she did.[83]

The doctor then left the house. He went into the garden with Greenwood, leaving Irene with her mother in her bedroom. Greenwood claimed he said 'I think you had better stay a bit' to which the doctor replied, 'Oh! She will be alright now that she has had more bile up'. The two men played two or three games of clock golf in the garden. This is a game played with a single hole in which to putt the golf ball, and twelve numbers which are put into the ground in a circle at distance from the hole and from which the golf ball is putted. It is ideal for garden play. Greenwood persuaded him to have another look at his wife and the two went up to her room again.[84]

Meanwhile, Miss Phillips, who had been asked at lunch by Mrs. Greenwood to come to supper, arrived at 7.15pm. The front door of the house went unanswered (the servants had this evening off) so she tried the side door. There she saw Greenwood on entry and he said 'The wife is very ill: run upstairs', so she went upstairs and found that Irene was just coming out of her mother's bedroom. She told Miss Phillips 'Mother is very ill: I am undressing her'. Meanwhile, Miss Phillips made up some hot water bottles for her friend.[85]

Although Greenwood and his daughter claimed they asked her to ask the district nurse to come over, Miss Phillips said that she did this on her own initiative; the nurse's home, Whinstone House, was only three minutes walk away. On arrival there she said 'Oh! Nurse, come at once, Mrs. Greenwood has a very bad attack with the heart'.[86]

[7] Nurse Elizabeth Jones.

Nurse Elizabeth Lewis Jones [7], aged 35 years, who had known Mrs. Greenwood for several months and had attended her youngest son, took 10 minutes to make the journey, and arrived at 8.00pm. Earlier that year it was said that she was 'well known and highly thought of in the town and district'.[87] The Kidwelly Nursing Association that employed her had been established in April 1919, with Mrs. Smart as secretary and Mrs. Meredith as treasurer. It was financed by voluntary subscriptions. The nurse was paid £110 per annum.[88] She later said, 'I found Mrs. Greenwood in a state of collapse. She had been vomiting slightly. Her pulse was very weak. She had diarrhoea, which was practically continuous up until midnight'. She complained of pains in the abdomen, but 'she was not one to complain much'.[89] Admittedly she had not seen a poisoning case since 1906 and that was a suicide by carbolic acid.[90]

Dr. Griffiths then returned to Mrs. Greenwood's bedside at Greenwood's behest. It was about 7.30pm. The doctor later recalled 'The vomiting had ceased and she seemed a little better. Her pulse was weak from the commencement. I thought she was getting better. I left Rumsey House and sent over a bottle of medicine containing a bismuth mixture to act as a gastric sedative'. It was given in a two ounce bottle of red fluid which had 16 doses. This would be a sedative for the stomach and would allay the sickness there. It was to be taken every four hours.[91] Mrs. Greenwood said it 'caught her at the back of the throat'. She gave her the medicine that the doctor had prescribed, but not before trying it herself.[92] Mrs. Greenwood's symptoms were sickness and diarrhoea and white vomit and diarrhoea.[93]

In the lull, Miss Phillips, together with Greenwood and his daughter went downstairs to have supper. Irene later recalled drinking burgundy and offering the same to Miss Phillips, that is from the same bottle as had been drunk from at lunchtime. Conversely, Miss Phillips thought that Irene and Kenneth drank lime juice or water, however. According to her only a decanter of whisky and a tantalus of brandy were evident on the table. Which is right? This is a not insignificant point because of the possible importance of the contents of the bottle of wine; this was the same as that being served at lunch; if Irene is right then it was not poisoned; if Miss Phillips is right then perhaps it was and that is why it was not there. The former may be true because Hannah stated that she had taken the wine bottle that was partially drunk at lunch and put it out on the table for the family to drink that evening. This suggests that it was not poisoned. There was probably not much left given that it was three quarters full prior to the lunch, and after more had been drunk at lunchtime, and so it may well have been finished at this supper. Nurse Jones remained with Mrs. Greenwood. At about 9.00pm, but possibly earlier, she briefly went home to put her son to bed and to see to her aged father, a retired Methodist minister in his 70s. The other three sat with Mrs. Greenwood.[94]

At some stage in the evening they decided that Dr. Griffiths should be recalled. Miss Phillips thought that this was at 8.00pm, Miss Griffiths thought it was 9.00pm but nurse Jones thought that this was at 10.00pm.[95] No one doubted it but it was Greenwood himself, as before, who went across the road to the doctor's house. Earlier in the evening he had been there and back in a matter of a few minutes. This time the errand took considerably longer.

[8] Bridge Street, Kidwelly, 2024. (Author's photograph)

One Mary Williams recalled, at about 8.00pm, walking up Bridge Street [8] and seeing Greenwood rushing across the road to Henblas. She said 'He appeared to be very agitated'.[96] This suggests that Miss Phillips was probably right as to time.

The doctor was then in the surgery, so Greenwood was met at the door by Miss Griffiths and then the two went into the drawing room. She recalled that he told her that his wife was unwell and he needed her brother. She asked 'was it one of the usual fainting attacks?' and Greenwood replied that it was 'worse than the usual ones'. After that, he apparently forgot his main errand and seemed his usual self, in ordinary spirits and jocular. However, despite his manner, he said to Miss Griffiths, 'I don't think she will get over it this time. She is worse than usual' or words to that effect. However, his other words did not quite agree with this, as 'He seemed to be quite alright' and after she referred to a possible imminent holiday, he even talked about going to Ramsgate on honeymoon. She said 'He said that as a joke to me'. Apparently, this was in connection with what a fortune teller had recently told him about his future. She thought they had been chatting for ten minutes, in total, though when talking to a friend time can fly, but the others, more objectively perhaps, thought it was nearer an hour.[97]

Meanwhile, nurse Jones gave Mrs. Greenwood brandy which led to a slight revival, but she was still very weak. Miss Phillips sat with young Kenneth in one of the front bedrooms. After 45 minutes of Greenwood's absence, she remarked on the fact to Miss Phillips.[98] Miss Phillips, however, thought that Greenwood had been gone for an hour and so asked Irene to fetch her father and the doctor.[99] Irene went to Henblas and waited for her father and the doctor to come back with her, which they eventually did.[100]

The doctor later recalled, 'she was still sick and in a very, very weak state. She was weaker than when I had last seen her. There was a nurse then in attendance [nurse Jones said she was not present at the same times as the doctor]. I saw Miss Phillips downstairs. I examined Mrs. Greenwood again and I found the pulse and the heart were very, very weak, I prescribed two morphia pills [he also later said that these were opium pills but the matter was never cleared up] with the instruction that one was to be given immediately and the other in half an hour's time', though nurse Jones claimed that these were prescribed at a visit the doctor made at 1.00am. Greenwood went to the doctor's house to collect them.[101] At about 9.30 Hannah Williams returned to Rumsey House after her evening off and was told by Irene and the nurse that Mrs. Greenwood was unwell.[102]

It was now, perhaps, about 10.00pm, the doctor thought. He recalled 'I did not anticipate anything serious', although I was afraid of the heart's condition'. An hour later he was leaving Rumsey and saw Greenwood standing at the gate. 'He told me he thought Mrs. Greenwood was much easier and in view of that I did not think it was necessary to go into the house'.[103] Greenwood went back indoors and came in and out of his wife's room. The nurse said that Mrs. Greenwood felt a little better and did not think Miss Phillips needed to remain there and that Mrs. Greenwood said that her friend and daughter could leave her then. Miss Phillips said that she was reluctant to leave but that her friend was always considerate in that regard and she left. The nurse said that she would speak to the doctor about the sickness and diarrhoea. 'She said it was of a very peculiar nature and that she said she had never seen anything like it before. She was very worried by it'. Irene went to bed as well at this time.[104]

Miss Phillips was leaving Rumsey House at this time too and she had a conversation with Greenwood at this point, who was standing by the gate. He noticed that she was looking worried and told her, in contrast to what he had told the doctor's sister, 'Oh, she will be quite alright by the morning'. He told her that she had seen his wife in much worse conditions and that she had pulled through. Miss Phillips was told not to worry. She thought Greenwood was in high spirits.[105]

There is a difference of opinion whether Dr. Griffiths made a fourth visit that evening. He said not but nurse Jones said that he was called over. Neither Irene nor Miss Phillips were there so neither could corroborate this. Nurse Jones claimed that Dr. Griffiths was sent for at 12.30am and came within 10 minutes, leaving again at 1.00am. However, this may be to conflate the earlier visit and the last one, as the nurse refers to the doctor giving pills on this occasion and also Greenwood failing to rouse the doctor and then the nurse going over to rouse him, which sound like the final visit.[106]

In October 1920, Picton Phillips, the chief constable of Carmarthen, wrote that he once had thought that the nurse gave the incorrect statement 'to cover her almost criminal neglect in not sending for the doctor', but now he thought differently. That is to say, 'I am now strongly of opinion that it is the nurse who is telling the truth about the Doctor's visits, and that the Doctor has suppressed them for the reason I suggest, that it might appear he hadn't much opportunity for proper diagnosis'.[107]

Meanwhile nurse Jones remained with Mrs. Greenwood. She later recalled, 'She was conscious up till 1.00am. About that time she asked me to tell Miss Bowater if she did not get well again to mother her children and bring them up in the way she would have wished. Mr. Greenwood kept asking me how she was and she kept replying that she was very, very ill'.[108] At 2.00am the nurse was convinced that her patient was dying. She gave her the two brownish pills that Dr. Griffiths had given her, putting them on a spoon and then onto the patient's tongue one after the other. Later she said that it was

Greenwood who gave her the pills, 'I did not read the directions on the box. I did not see the box. They were brown pills'. She did not wake again. She moaned but not very loudly.[109] Irene recalled being woken by her father at 1.00am, and then she was able to speak to her mother.[110]

Greenwood went over to find the doctor at about 3.00am, but claimed, on his return, to the nurse he was unable to rouse him. So she went instead. It was at about 3.00am on the morning of Monday 16th June that he was awoken by the nurse knocking on his front door. He opened the window and spoke to her; Mrs. Greenwood was in a bad state and he was asked to come over. He said, 'When I saw her between 3 o'clock and 3.30, she was in a moribund state, and she died a few minutes after I got there. I did not take her temperature as she had gone past that. She died ten minutes after her arrival'. Greenwood and his daughter were also present at her death.[111]

The nurse told the doctor that Mrs. Greenwood had been suffering from diarrhoea. There had also been vomiting. He did not see the excreta or ask to see it. He made out a death certificate to state that she had died of valvular disease of the heart.[112] Later he claimed that he had not been told by the nurse or the others all of Mrs. Greenwood's symptoms; as said in a previous chapter his medical standing was low and if this is an example of his slackness that would seem to fit in with the general views held of his professional repute.

Yet he was not the first or last doctor to misdiagnose a death as being natural. In 1914 in Montgomeryshire, a Thomas Roberts died and the doctor stated that the death was due to valvular disease of the heart; it later transpired to be a case of strychnine poisoning. In 1921 Dr. Hincks thought that the death of Mrs. Armstrong in Cusop was down to natural causes; a post mortem a year later showed that she died of arsenic poisoning.

It might also be noted that not one of the three servants made any reference to the comings and goings that evening. They were all out in the early evening but would have been home long before midnight and so were certainly at the house during the time of crisis. No one made any call on them either.

Irene asked Hannah to run to tell Miss Phillips and she did so, but did not arrive before her friend's death. She later said, 'When I got into the room I found the nurse was very upset, too agitated to talk, and crying. Mr. Greenwood was also walking about the room, crying'. Irene agreed with this reference to her father's actions.[113] A grief stricken husband or a great actor?

Yet the death was unexpected. Dr. Griffiths, though he knew she was in poor health and had been for some months, said 'I did not expect her to die so soon as she did'. However, no further inquiry was felt to be needed prior to burial.[114]

Chapter Three

Suspicions

The story could well have ended with the death and subsequent burial of Mrs. Greenwood on 19th June 1919, she having died an apparently natural death. There was a brief news story in the local press about the death and burial of this well known local woman, the wife of a prominent local man; her family connections were noted. Life would have proceeded as normal, except for that of family and close friends. This was not the case for two reasons. One was because of what had already happened and this became common knowledge. Secondly, and this fed into the first, Greenwood's subsequent actions.

Nurse Jones talked about the death to several people shortly after the event. Possibly the first person she addressed was at 7 o'clock on the morning of the day of Mrs. Greenwood's death and that was the vicar. She told him, naturally enough, that Mrs. Greenwood was dead. But there was more to come. She also said 'I think there ought to be a consultation. I think another doctor ought to be called in'.[1] The vicar asked nurse Jones about Mrs. Greenwood's symptoms prior to death.[2]

Greenwood visited his office that same morning. He asked Annie Groves whether there were any letters for him; there were and so she gave them to him. He then told her that if anyone called, he would not be there again until Friday. He also told her about his wife's death to which she replied, 'Oh God, don't tell me that'.[3] Meanwhile, nurse Jones also asked Mrs. Sarah Ann Meredith (1863-1952), wife of Daniel, a colliery manager, if she had heard of the death. She also spoke to Greenwood about the pills that the doctor had given her to give to his wife.[4]

That morning the vicar called at Rumsey House but Greenwood was not there, as he was in Llanelli. According to one source, he was also conferring with Llewellyn Jones, who agreed to arrange the funeral with a Llanelli undertaker and he then went with Gwladys Jones, whom he borrowed £20 from, to buy a mourning suit. On his return to Kidwelly, he went with the vicar to the churchyard to ascertain where his wife should be buried. He was sympathetic with the widower, who remarked that his wife had died of heart failure, having been told so by the doctor.[5]

At some stage, probably on this day, Greenwood asked Martha Morris to throw all the medicine bottles found in his wife's room into the river at the bottom of the garden.[6] Whether any of the contents of these would have provided clues as to her death is another question.

Finally, nurse Jones spoke to Mrs. Smart, chairman of the Nursing Association whom she worked for, 'The case has worried me a lot. I do not understand it. I had never seen anything like it before. I wish I had my time over again'. She then allegedly, though she later denied it, added 'I would insist upon a post mortem, but I don't like them'.[7] Back at Rumsey House, Hannah Williams found that the bottle of wine which had been drunk from on the previous day, had been taken from the cupboard. The empty bottles were heaped up in the cellar.[8] She later said 'I thought it strange that the bottle had disappeared' but she did not tell anyone about this thought until much later.[9] Perhaps she assumed that the contents had all been drunk at lunch and supper and so it was empty.

Bad news spread fast and later that evening, Mrs. Greenwood's sister, who had not seen her for the last six weeks, arrived in Kidwelly by train. She soon learnt that the doctor had been with her sister for most of the previous night.[10] She subsequently discussed her sister's death with Irene and the latter was able to recall most of the events of the past two days in her attempt to ascertain what had happened to her mother.[11] It is not known what conclusions, if any, they reached.

On the next day, a telephone call was made from Gwladys Jones to the doctor's house and Miss Griffiths answered it. Gwladys asked for Greenwood and Miss Griffiths found him for her.[12] On the same day, the following announcement was made in the Deaths notices in *The Times* newspaper:

> GREENWOOD – On the 16th of June, suddenly, Mabel Greenwood, the dearly beloved wife of Harold Greenwood, Esq., of Rumsey House, Kidwelly, and the youngest sister of Colonel and Alderman Sir Vansittart-Bowater, Bart.

The local paper was very brief and another newspaper just stated 'Mrs. Greenwood, sister of Sir William Vansittart Bowater, ex Lord Mayor of London, has died near Llanelly'.[13] Another gave a more extensive account of her life, applauding her extensive charitable works and Christian character. It stated, 'The deepest gloom was cast over Kidwelly' and that 'The hearts of the community go out in respectful sympathy' towards Greenwood and his children.[14]

[1] Site of Mabel Greenwood's grave marker, 2024.
(Author's photograph)

Two days later the deceased was buried in the churchyard of St. Mary's church. It took place at 11.30am on Thursday 19th June. It was termed 'private', which was fitting for her character, and so presumably only her husband, children, sister and one brother and Miss Phillips were there with the clergy.[15] Mrs. Greenwood had died intestate and her estate amounted to a mere £378, which went to her husband once the formalities had been completed in August. Not having made a will is suggestive that Mabel did not envisage death in the near future. The burial was carried out by William Thomas Morgan, undertakers, of Station Road, Llanelli.[16] The corpse was placed in a double coffin; the inner one of elm and the outer one of oak. It was lowered into a brick cavity and was covered by a stone slab.[17] Greenwood laid a wreath on the place where his wife was buried, by the side of the path leading to the church. It read 'In loving memory to a perfect wife'.[18] No gravestone was ever erected for her, though, despite him later attesting in public to his great love for her. There is, however, a small stone marker by the side of the path leading to the church, to mark the position of her mortal remains [1].

At the funeral, conducted by the vicar and his curate, the Reverend Rhys Curzon Jones, Greenwood told Irene, Miss Bowater and Sir Thomas Vansittart Bowater, that it was nurse Jones' opinion that his wife had died of the pills that had been given to her inadvertently by Dr. Griffiths. He had earlier spoken of this concern to the doctor but the latter replied that the pills were not injurious to health. Greenwood did not report this officially, so as to protect the doctor, or so he said.[19] Miss Phillips was also present, of course, and she later recalled that, in contrast to this, that Greenwood was being most complimentary about the doctor, telling Miss Bowater that 'The doctor was so good he came every half hour' which was a patent mistruth.[20]

On 20th June, Irene registered the death of her mother with William Trevor Evans of Leeswood, Burry Port, the Llanelli registrar, and obtained two copies of the death certificate; one she gave to the vicar and the other to her father.[21]

Meanwhile, on 24th June, Hannah Williams, who had been housemaid at Rumsey House since the autumn of 1918, left her job there and took up another position in the town; at Gordon House, Alstred Road. She had been given her notice to quit by the late Mrs.

Greenwood, for staying out too late on an evening off.[22] She said that her aunt had needed her to help in the haymaking and so had written to Mrs. Greenwood some time ago to release her niece from her employment.[23] Whether this has any relevance to the narrative is another question, but it did mean that when she later gave statements to the police and in the various courts she was freer to state what she was to do which would not have been the case if she was still in the employ of Greenwood and wished to remain so.

Some days after the death, nurse Jones met the vicar in the street and they talked about the recent demise. The nurse remarked that it did not look good for the vicar because he had spent a lot of the previous day in Mrs. Greenwood's company. She added that the death was very sudden. These are strange words; was she suggesting that some might think that the vicar was in some way involved in the death of Mrs. Greenwood? No more came of this and it is a curious insight into the woman's character.[24]

Taking possession of his late wife's property, Greenwood decided to distribute her rings to his daughter. He gave the engagement ring to Irene, but later took it back and gave her a half hoop ring.[25]

The sudden death of his wife and the comments made about it by nurse Jones may not have been enough to keep the rumour mill active. More was needed and more was forthcoming. Greenwood's own actions after the funeral fed the existing flames of the wagging tongues. Some commentators have blamed what he then did as the cause of his own later downfall. Duke, for instance, wrote of 'Possibly in time the gossip and rumours touching Mrs. Greenwood's end, might, unlike the unfortunate subject of them, have died a natural death had it not been for her husband's insane folly of marrying again within four months'.[26] Another author noted that this was 'a foolish slip 'and 'the crowning folly'.[27]

The context to this should also be recalled. Mrs. Greenwood had been very popular locally. Her work with the church and local charities had made her so. Her husband was less well thought of. Local bias was therefore all too prevalent to rear its head for her against him.

On 4th July, Greenwood, writing from his office in Llanelli, sent a letter to a Mr. W. E. Hurscomb Esq., of No. 170 Piccadilly, London. It read:

> Dear Sirs,
>
> I require a Diamond Lady's Marquise Ring somewhere between £30 and £40. The size of the finger is enclosed herewith; you will see it is rather small. I want one worth the money. You have my banker's reference some 18 months ago when I bought a Diamond Horseshoe pin from you which gave every satisfaction. Do you wish me to send on cheque, or will you send on approval.

They replied on 8th July and clearly asked for more specific guidance on the type of ring he wanted for he replied on 10th July, again from his workplace:

> A good Cluster ring would suit quite as well – if the stones are nice and large; I don't want a lot of small stones. I have a Diamond ring which I would like made into a Horseshoe Pin. If I sent the same to you would you convert the same. It is a ring that belonged to my late wife.

On the same day he wrote to another branch of the same firm:

> Herewith I return the rings and have kept the £55 one for which I enclose cheque. Also a cheap ring I bought today giving the exact size of the ring required, so please have same altered and let me have it back as soon as possible and oblige'.

They prepared what he wanted, viz., a diamond cluster ring for £55 on 15th July.[28]

There is no doubt therefore that from at least 4th July 1919, 18 days after his wife died, Greenwood was set on matrimony again and wanted there to be no delay. That he was writing from his office also suggests that he wanted to keep this secret from his sister-in-law and his eldest daughter, both of whom resided with him at Rumsey House, for as long as possible. When his thoughts, as opposed to positive action on his part, first turned to remarriage is unknown (he later claimed it was not until 12th July, but these letters suggest a rather earlier date).

It was at this time that Frank Russell, who was engaged in a four year long distance romance with Gwladys Jones, began to detect a cooling off in her ardour for him. Then it was definite; she returned her engagement ring to him and spoke of her intention to marry Greenwood. This as a surprise to Russell, who thought that her only relationship to Greenwood was that of him being their family solicitor.[29]

According to him, Greenwood proposed marriage to Gwladys Jones on 12th July; about four weeks after his first wife's death. She asked him for a fortnight to consider it. Two weeks later, she wrote a letter to Russell, breaking off their engagement. On the next day she accepted Greenwood's proposal. It was then that Greenwood gave her the diamond ring that he had recently bought. He later said that 'She accepted me the day after she wrote to India breaking off the engagement. I had no intention of marrying for a year, but because my wife broke off the engagement with the man in India, she wanted me to marry her at once'.

At least that was his version of events and we have no other. This suggests that she had waited a time for him and wanted no further delay once minds were made up.[30]

The next known event is that on 11th September when Greenwood and Gwladys Jones met, having travelled together from the railway station to his home. He asked her if she wanted to see his car, and so opened the garage and she entered the vehicle, saying 'This is just the thing I would like to go for a honeymoon in'. He told her he would like to do so himself. He added that he thought he would be going for a honeymoon in the said car, allegedly saying that as a joke. He did not tell her who he thought he would be going with. Then he claimed that Gwladys Jones said that his name had been romantically coupled with that of Miss Phillips, nurse Jones and two other women who he did not know.[31]

On 24th September he informed Thomas George Anfield, the registrar of Llanelli, that he desired a marriage licence in order to wed Gwladys Amelia Jones. The paperwork was completed and the die was cast.[32]

However, Greenwood had dealings with more than one local woman, as has already been suggested and his actions with her are uncertain because there are two opposing views as to what exactly happened between them, and in what sequence. One, given by Greenwood, is that at some point, either in the morning or late evening, of Friday 26th September, Greenwood wrote a letter[33] to Miss Griffiths. It read as follows:

> My dearest May,
>
> I have been trying to get to you this last fortnight, but no luck, always someone going in or you were going out. Now I want you to read this letter very carefully and to think very carefully, and to send me over a reply tonight. There are very many rumours about, but between you and I this letter reveals the true position. Well, it is only right that you should know that Miss Bowater and Miss Phillips between them have turned my children against you very bitterly, why I don't know. It is only right you should know this, because you are the one I love most in this world, and I would be the last one to make you unhappy. Under these circumstances, are you prepared to face the music? I am going to do something quickly, as I must get rid of Miss Bowater at once, as I am simply fed up. Let me have something from you tonight.
>
> Yours as ever,
>
> Harold

He also paid a visit to Henblas that evening to talk to her. He later said that he told her that he was to marry Gwladys Jones that Wednesday, and he later recounted the conversation between the two. According to him, once he had broken this news 'she began to cry, and told me I had let her down very badly', saying 'You led me to believe that you were going to marry me'.

He told her that he had suggested nothing of the sort, to which she retorted 'You paid a tremendous lot of attention to me'.

Apparently, Miss Phillips, Mrs. Smart and Miss Meredith had teased her on the subject and she was in tears, then turned on Greenwood, saying 'Will you say you have proposed to me?'

'If it will help you'.

Crying again, Miss Griffiths said 'But they won't believe me unless I have something to show. Will you write me a letter, proposing to me?'

'If it will help you, certainly. If you think I have compromised you in any way, I am ready to help you'.[34]

With that she calmed down and Greenwood went home. He claimed he wrote four letters before he was satisfied with what he had written and then sent it to her.

Apparently, she read it on the next day, a Saturday. According to her, but not him, she asked him what he meant by it. On the Sunday, Greenwood said that she then laughed at what he had written.[35]

This is one version of events, but there is another. Miss Griffiths said that far from suggesting the letter was her idea, that it was his and that it was hand delivered at about 11.00am on the 26th September. She read it and that evening, about 9.30pm, Greenwood visited. She asked him if it was true that he planned to marry Gwladys Jones, having been told of the marriage licence by nurse Jones, 'Are you going to be married next Wednesday? Miss Griffiths asked, and then what had he meant by the letter. 'There is nothing in it', Greenwood allegedly replied. He also told her not to listen to gossip. Miss Griffiths later claimed that she had meant to burn the letter but did not do so.[36]

Three days later, Greenwood told Irene of his intended marriage and it came as quite a shock to her. It is noteworthy that despite being a regular churchgoer, until his first wife's death, Greenwood chose not to be married at St. Mary's church. Possibly this was to avoid his impending marriage being widely known about before it happened, as banns would have had to have been read out in church on three Sundays prior to the wedding.[37]

Nurse Jones spent part of the evening of 30th September with Greenwood at his home; on the eve of his second marriage. She went to him on business (he helped fund the nursing post that she held and he also undertook some legal work for her family) and was with him until at least 10.00pm; it was suggested it was 11.30pm but she denied this.[38] The nurse was clearly on good terms with Greenwood; on one occasion she had visited him and the two went to a separate room where they could be together so she could tell him his fortune and this showed 'the degree of intimacy between them'.[39]

The marriage of Harold Greenwood, widower and solicitor, aged 45 years, to Gwladys Amelia Jones, spinster, aged 31 years of no stated occupation, took place on 1st October at the Welsh Congregationalist Bryn chapel to the east of Llanelli. The Reverend John Evans was the minister presiding. The witnesses were several of her siblings; Llewellyn Thomas Jones, Arthur Thomas Jones and Alice A. Jones. They then went off on a motoring honeymoon and returned about three weeks later to live at Rumsey House.[40]

A local newspaper reported the event thus:

> A very quiet wedding was solemnised at Bryn chapel, near Llanelli, on Wednesday, the contracting parties being Mr. Harold Greenwood, solicitor of Kidwelly, and Miss Gwladys Jones, daughter of the late Mr. W. B. Jones, J.P., and Mrs. Jones, Sunnyside, Tyrfan.[41]

The timing of this marriage has been universally condensed by subsequent writers. Duke wrote, as to a possible reason for remarriage in haste, 'The only way in which the wretched widower could assume the mastery of his own house was by a second marriage'. She goes on to providing a context as to why this should not have been seen as being scandalous:

> ... it should be remembered that these events took place less than a year after the conclusion of the Great War. Death had lost its dignity and importance. Mourning was regarded as obsolete, and the outward observances of bereavement were curtailed or disregarded. Speedy remarrying and giving in marriage, war wedding, followed by a similar ceremony in a few months' time had become commonplace.

She reminded readers that this was not a crime *passionnel*, that Gwladys was over 30 years of age (aged 31 years) whom Greenwood had known for a long time and that 'it cannot be stressed too strongly that the usual sordid reason [pregnancy] for a hurried marriage was entirely lacking'.[42] Quite why two people, one just over 30 years and one in his mid-forties cannot be passionate about each other is unclear; all that can be said is that Winifred Duke thought so.

Greenwood later wrote in a newspaper as to his motivation:

> I will now tell you why I married again.
>
> Counsel has described it as a sudden resolve. Are the sudden resolves of love so uncommon?
>
> As Sir E. Marshall Hall has put it – I had done an unpardonable thing in the eyes of Kidwelly in marrying before the expiry of a purely artificial conventional period of twelve months.
>
> It is more than probable that, had my second marriage fulfilled that necessary stipulation of narrow minded gossips, there would have been no Greenwood case, no whispered rumours, no gathering cloud of suspicion, no inquiry and no trial.
>
> But what was my position? I had a young family, used to the extravagant cares of a deceased mother. I had two children at school. I had one daughter becoming a woman, at an age when the older woman's care and counsel, such as a father cannot give, are in the highest degree necessary.
>
> What more natural course could I take than to remarry.
>
> What sin is there in having the woman I did marry, the woman who has made me so happy, and has suffered a burden many of her sex would give way under? I thought that marriage was provided by the law of God and man for those free to embrace it.
>
> Was I not free? Free, not by my own hand, but the visitation of the Higher Form'.[43]

How much of this was self justification for the wider public? It is not unknown for a middle aged man to be in love with a younger woman; in fact it is commonplace, even though he may be married to someone else, and the object of his affections is inevitably someone younger and perhaps more physically attractive than his spouse. Greenwood later said that sexual relations between himself and his first wife had ceased two years ago; again not uncommon for middle aged couples who have been married to each other for a long time. Sexual attraction may have well played a part in his feelings for Gwladys Jones (and they were later to have a son together). However, in public he could hardly admit this. Most importantly, she reciprocated his feelings.

No comment was made at the time or later from Gwladys Jones as to her motivation for marriage or her relationship with Greenwood at any time. None of her family, who seem to have been supportive of the marriage, commented either. She seems to have been a loyal wife to her husband (whilst he was in prison and even after his death) and so would have been unlikely to have spoken out of turn. Yet it is worth indulging in some speculation. She was already engaged, albeit to a man that she can have seen little of in recent years (he being on active service abroad and distance did not make the heart beat fonder on this occasion). She did not have to fear being single 'on the shelf', as it were, as many women were in a post war world with far fewer young men. She also presumably had a secure home with her family and nor was she pregnant, as far as we know (she may have had a miscarriage early in pregnancy).

Would the aging Greenwood have been attractive to her and more so that her younger and war veteran fiancé? Clearly he was to her, despite outward appearances. Greenwood was middle aged but looked far older, with his greying hair and at five feet seven inches was short in height for a man. He was not particularly good looking, nor rich, but had a well established home. Yet he clearly seemed to her to be a better match than her existing fiancé, whom she dumped by letter. Perhaps she saw Greenwood as a father figure and perhaps he was kind towards her.

The marriage resulted in the departure from Rumsey House of both Irene and Miss Bowater; the latter went to live temporarily with one of her brothers at No. 8 Prince of Wales' Terrace in Kensington, London. It is likely that the latter's departure was a relief to Greenwood. Miss Bowater's exit in the second or third week of the month was noted in a local newspaper, with the comment that she had been very kind towards the poor.[44]

The Chief Constable of Carmarthen, William Picton Phillips (1866-1955), made a statement about local feeling on the matter:

> There is a very prevalent belief, freely voiced, in Kidwelly and Llanelli that Mrs. Greenwood met her death through foul play. Miss Phillips who does not hesitate to say it thought so when she was at the bedside during the evening of the 15th and still thinks so but of course she has only psychological grounds for it. As an indication of the local feeling I may instance the opinion of Mr. Smart (Mrs. Smart's husband) who informed me that he was perfectly satisfied in his own mind that Greenwood had poisoned his wife. He knows Greenwood very well and they have always been on good terms.

And the vicar who has been heard to say that he had very grave suspicion (this was before the police had moved) and told Police Sergeant Herbert Lodge Lewis (1877-1949), Kidwelly's policeman, 'When that body is got up people will stiffen their backs and you will get to know a good deal more'.[45]

Miss Griffiths gave it as her opinion that 'The village has been full of rumour and I heard that it originated outside Kidwelly'.[46] The rumours were that Greenwood had poisoned his wife in order to marry Gwladys Jones. Quite how he had done so was another question, however, and there would be only one way to find out.

How widespread was the gossip is unclear. Both Greenwood and his eldest daughter claimed that they knew very little about it. But then, perhaps, as he was the prime suspect and was of a high social class, no one would have mentioned it to his face or in his presence. He, after all, was one of the town's most prominent members, not that this would do him much good in subsequent months, though perhaps he thought it might.

Chapter Four

Investigations

It seems that it was on 28th September 1919 that the county police began to investigate the case; three days before Greenwood remarried, but possibly after they had heard that Greenwood was to remarry or maybe for another unconnected reason. Unfortunately there are no known surviving archives for much of the local investigation which began in the autumn of 1919 and so there is much that is unknown about this; principally why it took so long before a conclusion was reached to take it to the next level.

The Carmarthenshire County Constabulary then numbered 131 men. At their head since 1908, as Chief Constable, was William Picton Phillips (1866-1955), based at the Shire Hall, Carmarthen Street, Llandeilo. He had been a policeman since 1883 and his father had served as chief constable for 33 years.[1] Under him were his two superintendents, the one in charge of this investigation was Superintendent Samuel Jones (1861-1949) of the Llanelli division, based at the police station in Market Street in Llanelli. He had worked down the mines from the age of 10 and then served in the police since 1883, rising from sergeant to superintendent in 1913. He was a devout Baptist, helping found one chapel and then being treasurer of another; noted as being an impartial witness and upholder of fair play.[2] His division included Kidwelly and Llanelli. As with many small county police forces there was no detective force; presumably on cost grounds and the fact that cases needing investigation were very few indeed. In murder cases, county forces often contacted Scotland Yard to send down an experienced detective chief inspector; as was to occur in the event of the murder of Irene Munro in Eastbourne in August 1920. It was not mandatory; in 1930 the Cornish Constabulary did not apply to London when there was the suspected fatal arsenic poisoning of Mrs. Alice Thomas. Whether the

Carmarthenshire force should be criticised for failing to do so is a moot point, but at this stage there was only suspicion of murder.

Making investigations on the ground was Police Sergeant Herbert Lodge Lewis (1877-1949), who had been in the dock police and the county constabulary for two decades; in 1912 he was employed in Llanelli as a sergeant. He was Kidwelly's policeman. He interviewed a number of people in the small town. He and Superintendent Jones interviewed nurse Jones and she told them that the vomit spewed up by Mrs. Greenwood was 'of a yellowish-green colour'. She also said to Lewis, backtracking, 'You can look through me sergeant; I am telling the truth. I have had many cases like this. There is nothing unusual about the death'. She went onto say 'I will not tell you anymore unless compelled. I have never had a case like this before'. She was further evasive when she told the sergeant, 'There is one thing I'll never tell – it is a private matter'. This was about the vicar asking her if she thought that there might have been foul play as regards the death. She was interviewed many times; the first being 28th September and was later said to be 'Just to obtain information whether there was anything in what they had heard'; clearly rumours had led to the beginnings of an investigation.[3]

On one occasion both Superintendent Jones and Mrs. Phillips, Mrs Greenwood's best friend, spoke to the nurse. She said that the diarrhoea looked as if Mrs. Greenwood had been drinking a lot of milk because it was white.[4] Lewis also took a statement from Miss Phillips.[5] He also took several statements from Hannah Williams, one a month, she later recalled. In detail, she was first spoken to in November, then a week later, then several weeks later (December) and then two months later (February). On the third interview, Lewis asked if she had seen Greenwood in the pantry.[6] She said that she had not given the matter any thought until Lewis asked her about it.[7] He also interviewed Dr. Griffiths and his sister, Foy, the vicar and Mrs. Phillips. He took statements from Mrs. Smart and Miss David.[8]

One witness they did not take a statement from was Irene; nor were any of the servants at Rumsey House questioned. John Greenwood, aged nine years, was not questioned either (in the 1928 Pace poisoning case the victim's nine year old son did make a statement). In the case of Irene, she was not living at home from October to December 1919 but she did return at the end of the latter month. Perhaps it was thought too difficult, time consuming and expensive to pursue her in London and possibly once she was back in Kidwelly the initial impetus for the investigation had gone. Or maybe Superintendent Jones or Lewis had assumed the other had done it and neither they nor Picton Phillips noticed the omission. It was, though, a missed opportunity to have additional eye witness testimony as to the events of the lunch and the evening of 15th June. Possibly the servants went uninterviewed because of their dependant position with regards to Greenwood meant that they could not be relied upon. Nor was the new Mrs. Greenwood interviewed; probably because a wife could then not be obliged to testify in court against her husband.

On the return from the honeymoon, Superintendent Jones visited Greenwood for a few minutes because he had not sent his wife's death certificate to the vicar. Apparently, Greenwood had given it to a servant to take over, but they had failed to do so. The policeman made a note of this and seemed satisfied, so left.[9]

On 24th October, Greenwood provided Superintendent Jones with a statement when Jones and Inspector Daniel Nicholas visited him at his office and it read as follows:

> There was a no more united family at Kidwelly, than the wife and I. On 15th June 1919, myself, wife, boy, daughter and one maid were present at lunch. We had gooseberry tart. I told my wife not to have any as she had had diarrhoea on the Saturday previous, and she had it on that Sunday afternoon also. I would probably have had a whisky and soda, and she may have had the same, as far as I can remember.
>
> I afterwards went to my car, as it was not in good order at the time. I do not think the car was out that day with Foy. I feel quite sure it was not out. My daughter and Foy were out on the 8th and the only other day she went out with Foy was some weeks previously.
>
> On the morning of 15th June my wife was sitting on the lawn reading while I was in the car. She did not sit there in the afternoon after lunch. She went to lie down, and came to me about 3.00 to 3.30pm, while I was still in the car, and she said that she had had another attack of diarrhoea. I told her she had

no business to eat that gooseberry tart, and I took a chair from another part of the lawn and placed it in the sun for her to sit there.

Soon afterwards I had finished the car, and I went to have a shave and a change. The gong for tea went when I was changing. I came down. The tea was laid in the drawing room, and they were half through it. She hardly had any tea. She said that she was going to lie down, and I went to feed the fowls.

About 5.30pm my wife and daughter came walking slowly up the garden, just past the stables, and she sat down, and I sat down with her. The little boy was there. We sat there for half an hour. It was then getting cold. She went into the house for a cloak. I met her on the steps. She took my arm and we walked up the garden as far as the stable. She told me she had a suffocating pain in her heart and that she could not go on any further, so I brought her back to the same chair on the lawn as she had sat on before. She sat there for four or five minutes and said she felt much better, and would try again, so we started again the same way, as she said she felt alright.

I don't think we had gone thirty yards when she fell against me and said 'I can't go another yard', so I took her back again to the chair. She complained of a frightful pain in her heart and said she was fainting. I put her on the chair, and Irene, my daughter, came down. I told her to look after her until I brought some brandy. She did so, and I brought a bottle and a glass and I gave her a wineglass neat. That made her a little sick, and she said she felt a bit better and I said 'Come to the sofa and lie down'. She wanted to stay, and said she would be alright in a minute. She said she felt bad again and very faint, so Irene and I took her by the arm. I felt her pulse and could not find it, so I said to Irene, 'We shall take her to the sitting room' and that I would fetch the doctor.

We got her to the room and she said she felt very faint indeed, so I said to Irene 'We shall take her to the bedroom' and when we took her to her room she said 'I do feel frightfully faint and I have awful pains in my head as I always get'. Irene helped to put her to bed and I went for the doctor. He was there in the sitting room and he came at once. There was no one present and I can't say who opened the door for me. That would be about 6.45 to 7.00pm.

The doctor came immediately. He examined her and said the heart was very bad. She had some more brandy – I can't say whether it was at the doctor's orders or not – and after taking the brandy she became very sick. The brandy was given to her neat and was not diluted. I think it was Irene who gave her the brandy. The doctor told me we should not have given it to her neat. He examined her and said it was bile. I asked her if she liked nurse Jones and she said 'Yes' so I went for her. The doctor said that if she kept quiet she should soon come alright.

I said to the doctor 'I think you should stay a bit' and he said 'Oh. She should be all right now that she has had more bile up'. I did not feel so sure in my own mind so I asked the doctor to come round the garden. We went round, and when we came to the clock golf at the other end of the garden, I suggested to the doctor to come and have a game. We had two or three games. I did not want to keep him, and in the meantime, nurse Jones had come in. I had asked Miss Phillips to go for her. She had come in for supper. I met her coming in when I was going to the doctor's. The doctor stayed for about an hour and before he went I asked him to come up again and see my wife, and he did, and said 'I will send a bottle of medicine'. He said she was much better then, and had absolutely no pain, but was very weak. I was with the doctor and saw him out. I then stayed in her bedroom all the time with nurse Jones, Irene and Miss Phillips.

'About twenty minutes after, nurse Jones said that she [Mrs. Greenwood] was so much better that she would run home and put her little boy to bed, but that she would not be away more than an hour. nurse Jones went and I said to Miss Phillips would she mind sitting alone with her while Irene and I had supper. After supper, Irene and I went back again and she said that her hands were very, very cold and that she had no feeling. Nurse Jones came back just then. This would be in about an hour and a quarter. Mrs. Greenwood's arms looked quite white and the fingers of both hands quite blue. I pointed this out to nurse Jones. Of course I rubbed them to see if she had any feeling in them. She was quite rational, and told us all what she felt. We were giving her brandy in sips all the time and nurse Jones told me it was her heart – she had a diseased heart.

At about three o'clock we lost her pulse absolutely. She was quite conscious, and nurse Jones asked me to go for the doctor. I ran for the doctor and knocked for him, but failed to hear an answer. I went back to the house and told the nurse that I failed to wake him. My wife then got a little better again and I got Irene to her. She sent Irene to bed. Soon after that we lost her pulse absolutely. Nurse Jones said she would go to the doctor. She did, and the doctor came in after her. I went down to meet him, and he said she was much better in herself, but her heart was very, very weak, and to keep on with the brandy and if I went with him he would give me two pills to give to her. She was quite rational all the time and complained of no pains, but once – that she had some pains in the stomach.

That was about 3.30am and only a slight pain. We put mustard leaves over her heart and mustard plasters all the time. Her chest was perfectly raw and the skin red. When taking the two pills, she said 'Put them on my tongue. I will swallow them'. She talked for about five minutes and then went to sleep. About four o'clock she began to breathe quite heavily, so I felt her pulse, and said to the nurse, 'I cannot feel it a bit'. The nurse felt it and she said 'No, it has stopped. Run for the doctor at once!' I went for the doctor and told him that since she had those pills her pulse had stopped and said 'Come over at once!' He did come and tested her, and said 'There is not much hope now'. I called Irene and she came in. Her mother died about a quarter of an hour after Irene came in.

I think if she had not had the two pills she would be alright today. They were too strong for her. She was so rational all the time, and after taking the pills she went off to sleep, and never woke up from the sleep. Her life was not insured at all, either by herself, or by me, and all her property was hers for life, and afterwards for her children. The death was registered. The certificate I gave to Irene with a guinea to take to the vicar. It was Irene who registered the death and had two certificates from Mr. Evans. The yellow one she was to give to the vicar, and the white one was for us. I had the two certificates from Irene when she came back. Miss Bowater saw me give it to her.

I told him that the vicar had not received the certificate, and he said, 'I gave it to Irene but I will look in the safe now'. He made a search in the safe. Failing to find it he said 'I will have a search at home again'. He further stated 'The doctor had been attending her for the last few months for her heart. She had been unwell all the week for her heart. She felt better on 14th June and she went to Ferryside'.[10]

[1] Harold Greenwood in his office.

Greenwood was later to repudiate the final part of his statement as we shall see **[1]**.

Greenwood later said he told the police, 'If you can show me why I should have my wife's body exhumed, I will do it at once, and you need not bother any further'.[11]

On 31st October, Jones and Nicholas returned to Greenwood's office. He was able to show them the copies of his first wife's death certificate that Irene had collected. They were in his eldest daughter's room. This seems to have been the last time the police officially saw Greenwood until the next year.[12]

Meanwhile, there were changes afoot at Rumsey House. Irene left to stay with her mother's family in London (though returning to her father's house at Christmas). Yet if Greenwood and his new wife thought that they could carry on life with each other without any hindrance, they were to be living in a fool's paradise and they had only months to enjoy such.

After this the investigation appeared to lapse; for what reason is unknown, but it was some months later that it resumed its course. There seem to be no archives existing made by the force, so their inactivity, if such it was, cannot be discussed. The next that is heard is just over four months later. On 9th March 1920, Picton Phillips wrote to Edward Short (1862-1935), Home Secretary, K.C., M.P., beginning, 'I beg to bring to your notice the following particulars which concern the death of Mabel Greenwood with a view to the exhumation and examination of her body, should you consider there to be sufficient justification for making the order'.[13]

Meanwhile, Dr. Griffiths' medical career was coming to an end. He had already tendered his resignation to the council as its medical officer in March 1919 and was replaced in the December of this year. He ceased practising as a doctor at the end of 1919. He was independently wealthy; he did not need the money and perhaps he decided that he had had enough of doctoring and wanted to spend his time pursuing other activities.[14]

Despite comments about the doctor's incompetence, he had some local testimonies to his medical ability. Firstly, his teaching of the local ladies' ambulance classes during the war was deemed 'very efficient'. The council gave him a testimonial to his 'admirable service' to the town as their medical officer. Whether this was at least in part due the doctor's wealth and local status is another question.[15]

Picton Phillips recounted the story to Short, erring in thinking the Greenwoods had but three children, outlining the fact that Greenwood was 'too friendly with other women'. He deemed Miss Phillips 'a truthful and reliable person'. He wrote that 'I am informed on good authority' that Dr. Griffiths told a Dr. Owen Williams of Burry Port (and a magistrate) that death was due to food poisoning. The latter, though, usually affects more than one person, so presumably Dr. Griffiths was displaying his ignorance of matters medical by making such an assumption. Phillips attached importance to Gwladys Jones (the second Mrs. Greenwood) spreading a story about Mrs. Greenwood being in very poor health in May 1919, 'There must have been some object in spreading this report. It might not unreasonably be attributed to an attempt to create an impression that Mrs. Greenwood was in such a case of health that she might die suddenly, so that when she did it would not be unexpected'.[16]

He also laid store by nurse Jones' suspicions, 'These remarks justify the view that there was something mysterious … about the death, and she had the best opportunity of forming an opinion generally and professionally'. Yet her conduct was seen as 'most unsatisfactory' as she gave information reluctantly and in a confused manner, perhaps she wished to conceal something and her friendship with the Greenwoods was thought to be inhibiting her and Phillips thought that she had been told to act in such a manner by Greenwood, to whom she was close.[17]

Greenwood's behaviour was being viewed as appearing distinctly odd:

> Greenwood before being cautioned by Superintendent Jones did not act in the manner one would regard as that of an innocent man. It must have been obvious to him that foul play was suspected in connection with his wife's death. He showed no indignation and did not resent in any way the implication (contained in the caution) that he was being suspected of being involved, and acted as if he knew there was something to explain.

> He dwelt very much on the pills given by the doctor as being too strong and causing her death as if he wanted to shift the responsibility onto someone else.
>
> When the rumours were mentioned to him he did not enquire what the rumours were nor did he make any attempt to ascertain who was responsible for them. ... His whole account is full of misstatements.

It was thought odd that he appeared indifferent to his wife's sudden death yet was cheerful enough in conversation with Miss Griffiths at this time when he realised what was happening at home. His statement about his wife possibly drinking whisky at the lunch contradicted that of housemaid Hannah Williams who had declared 'She always took port wine and was never known to take whisky'. There was also a difference of opinion with her sister-in-law about who benefitted financially after his wife's death; she said he did but he said it was all to the children. In this, though, Greenwood seems to have been largely in the right. However, in telling her 'Doctor was so good he was over every half hour' he was, as usual, in error.

It was no surprise that Phillips should then write, 'It is impossible to estimate what importance should be attached to anything he says. He is ordinarily one of the irresponsible and unreliable type'. After Superintendent Jones had spoken to Greenwood, he said 'having regard to the rumours which were about and the matter being so very much talked of by the people I am afraid we shall have to apply for an order to exhume the body'. Greenwood replied, 'Just the very thing I am quite agreeable'. Phillips commented 'He might have thought that any objection would increase suspicion'.

Phillips concluded, 'These are the suspicious circumstances connected with a death surrounded by mystery, falsehood, and, it seems to me, culpable negligence and callousness, which I have respectably to submit as reasons why the body should be exhumed, either in the interests of justice, if that should happily not be so, then to relieve the husband of a terrible suspicion which will otherwise probably cling to him for life'.[18]

Sir Charles Edward Troup (1857-1941), Permanent Under Secretary of State for the Home Office from 1908-1922, wrote six days later to give a green light to the investigation:

> I think that the suspicion is sufficiently well founded in this case for the coroner to order an exhumation of Mrs. Greenwood's body for the purposes of a post mortem, and it certainly seems to me that this is the only way in which the suspicion, which the chief constable reports to be intense in the immediate vicinity will either be verified or dissolved. The nurse has behaved very strangely but in my opinion there is no case against her.[19]

Philips was also told to monitor Greenwood and nurse Jones lest either attempt to escape the district; both were seen as the prime suspects.[20]

There were concerns as to the effectiveness of the police investigation. Archibald Bodkin (1862-1957), director of the public prosecutions from 1920-1930, was not impressed, writing on 19th March, 'The chief constable's procedure is incomprehensible. There is not a single date to show when suspicion arose, or when any of the numerous statements were taken. Possibly the chief constable has been guilty of delay. It is nine months since the death'. He also noted that Dr. Griffiths, Greenwood and the coroner all knew each other and so, 'I feel that there may be difficulty in getting any real investigation'.

In similar vein, the Home Secretary wrote 'It would have been better if this step had been taken sooner … he is unable to gather the reason for the delay'.[21]

The district coroner, John William Nicholas (1863-1931), who was a solicitor and also Clerk of the Peace for Carmarthen, had been informed on 25th March about suspicions about the death. Apparently 'he had a wide experience of criminal law before becoming clerk to the Carmarthenshire county council and he carried on an extensive practice in the courts and society'. There was then correspondence with the Home Office and eventually an exhumation order was given.[22]

Yet Nicholas was far from enthusiastic about such a proceeding. In a letter of 27th March he outlined his concerns:

> After considering the circumstances, I am inclined to order exhumation, though I doubt whether it will afford any very definite result in view of the fact that the death occurred more than 9 months ago.

He also drew attention to the Coroners' Act which stated 'If there be danger of infection by digging it [the body] up, the Inquest ought not to be taken by the Coroner unless we have a special commission for that purpose'.[23]

Greenwood was apparently informed about the exhumation on Tuesday 13th April; he informed the Bowaters immediately. Nurse Jones visited him at Rumsey House at about this time. She was surprised at the impending exhumation and apparently stated 'I thought that had fallen through', though she later denied saying so. Greenwood told her that he thought the pills given by the doctor had killed his wife and the nurse replied, 'Don't you say anything about those pills to anyone' as nurses are not supposed to repeat anything about doctors' prescriptions. She added 'I have to work for doctors, and it will never do for me to say anything about doctors' prescriptions'.[24]

Greenwood also visited Dr. Griffiths as well to discuss the letter he had received about the impending exhumation. Greenwood asked him, 'Don't you think those morphia pills were too strong?' 'Certainly not' replied the doctor. The latter said that nurse Jones' gossip was to blame for the current situation. Greenwood told him that he thought the police were on 'a wild goose chase' and would not find anything pointing to his first wife having died an untoward death.[25]

The body was exhumed by the light of four lanterns in the early hours of Friday 16th April, at about 1.30am and took an hour. The local newspaper reported, 'There were strange proceedings in the ancient churchyard in the early hours of Friday. It was a wild and boisterous morning'.[26] Present then was Superintendent Jones and Lewis. The coffin was taken to the town hall.[27] Kidwelly Town Hall had been built in 1877 in the Gothic style. It had a spacious hall. The upper floor hall was for the magistrates' business. In the basement were police cells, a public reading room, institute and market place.

Dr. Alexander Dick (1878-1925) of Llanelli was the police surgeon and he undertook the post mortem that afternoon. Dr. Griffiths and two other local doctors (Dr John Davies and Dr Alexander Dixon Smith (1890-1960) were present. The brain of the deceased was largely decomposed but the rest of the body was intact. He removed some of the organs, placed them in sterile sealed jars and wrapped them in paper.[28]

Lewis received three jars from Dr. Dick and he took them to London by train. On 17th April he gave these to John Webster (1877-1927), who was Deputy Senior Analyst to the Home Office and was employed at St. Mary's Hospital and was given a receipt for them.[29]

These jars contained the following:[30]

Jar One
Stomach (4½ ounces), small intestine, pancreas with omentum and presentary (23 ounces), large intestine (5¾ ounces), liver (15 ounces), spleen (11/2 ounces), 2 kidneys (2 and 2¼ ounces), uterus (5¼ ounces), and rectum (3½ ounces).

Jar Two
Heart (4 ounces), lungs (11¼ ounces) and oesophagus (3¼ ounces).

Jar Three
Brain (20 ounces).

What was not done was to take samples from the hair and nails of the victim. This had been done in the case of the Seddon poisoning investigation of 1912. The exhumation had not been carried out with any input from the experts in question. It is a great pity that this was not performed because it would have provided far more evidence for the investigation, for arsenic can be detected in hair and nails. This can be used to show how long arsenic has been introduced into the victim, with what frequency and the amount. Perhaps Dr. Dick did not know of this and it is unlikely that he would have come across similar cases before in this part of Wales. This was one of the investigation's faults, but by no means the only one. When Mrs. Armstrong's body was exhumed at Cusop churchyard in 1922, the far more experienced pathologist Dr. Bernard Henry Spilsbury (1877-1947) carried out the post mortem and he certainly did not neglect to take samples of the deceased's hair and nails. There was later talk of his being involved in this case but he never was.

[2] Kidwelly Town Hall, 2024. (Author's photograph)

Apparently, the exhumation was 'the sole topic of conversation in Carmarthenshire'. Speculation and gossip was rife locally. Hundreds visited the churchyard but the gates were locked.[31] Another newspaper stated, 'Speculation is rife as to the causes that have led to this step being taken and there is no lack of rumour and gossip for it to feed upon'.[32] However, an alternative view was given by another newspaper on this occasion, 'much sympathy has been expressed with Mr. Greenwood and the members of his family. Most local people have already made up their mind that the whole affair is much ado about nothing'.[33]

The inquest opened that afternoon in the town hall **[2]** at 3.00pm by Nicholas, the district coroner. It was a very short affair. Beforehand the jury had had to view the corpse as was then common.[34] Dr. Griffiths gave evidence to the extent that he had known the deceased prior to her death and had attended her in her final illness. He had not been present at the disinterment but had been at the post mortem. Dr. Dick stated that he had undertaken the post mortem, taken out several organs and had them put into jars and sent them to London. Mr. Morgan, the undertaker, gave brief details of the original interment and the disinterment, as did Lewis. The coroner noted that he had received a report on 25th March about the suspicious circumstances of the death from the Home Office and so ordered an exhumation. It was then adjourned in order to allow for the analysis of the organs removed from the corpse.[35] Greenwood told his daughter again that it was the pills the doctor gave that were fatal.[36] He did not attend the inquest but was legally represented by Ludford. Superintendent Jones and Lewis were there, as well as many local people. The jury was headed by George Jones and of the other Kidwelly men whose identity can be ascertained, one was a draper, another a butcher and another a publican. None of them put any questions to the witnesses. The coroner thought that he would have the results of the analysis in two or three weeks and said 'We have gone about as far as we can carry today under the circumstances'.[37]

According to the local press, 'The news was received with consternation in the ancient borough where the family was so well known'.[38]

Meanwhile, on the evening of the exhumation, Greenwood sent Irene to the vicarage to ask the vicar to see him at Rumsey House at

6.00pm that evening. The vicar did so, 'where I found he and his wife very perturbed and distressed'. He later said, 'Of course he was very upset and he asked me if I knew how the whole thing had arisen. Then he remarked that Mrs. Greenwood was often depressed, and that she had taken to staring at water, and that he wondered whether she had taken something herself'.[39]

This is in contrast to the statement he had made earlier in the day that it was the doctor's pills that killed her. If his suggestion was that of suicide, then this is strange, too. Suicide was a criminal offence until 1961, but not only that, his wife was by all accounts a God fearing woman and would have known, as did Mrs. Armstrong in 1921, that suicide or its attempting was not only an offence against Man but more importantly, against God, too.

On the Tuesday after the exhumation, Henry Edward Smart (1862-1938), a brick manufacturer and twice mayor of Kidwelly (husband of Annie Smart) was on the same train from Kidwelly to Llanelli and talked to Greenwood. The latter said, 'They say that I was seen on the Town Bridge, the night my wife's body was exhumed. That was not true, I was in bed fast asleep'. On another shared train journey, Greenwood told Smart, 'They are a long time over my case. I don't suppose they can find anything'.[40]

An examination of the organs taken from Mrs. Greenwood's body was undertaken in London four days after the exhumation. Webster found that the organs showed that:

> ... arsenic was present in all the organs, the total amount being found was 18 milligrams or about a quarter of a grain. The distribution showed that it was taken by the mouth. It must have been taken several hours before death and that there was little arsenic in the stomach suggested that none was taken after three hours prior to death.[41]

In detail, Webster used the tested and tried Marsh test, which had been devised in the previous century, for arsenic, adapted for the current purpose. First he destroyed the organic matter found in the stomach, then put portions of the stomach in the hydrogen apparatus as stipulated by the test. If there was arsenic it gave off a gas. There was also arsenic found in the heart and spleen. There was also arsenic in the stomach.[42]

Furthermore, in finding arsenic present in the all the organs he wrote that in the stomach were 0.58mg, in the small intestine, omentum and mesentery 4.33mg, in the large intestine 0.55mg, in the liver 8.5mg, in the spleen 0.4mg, in the two kidneys 1.21mg, in the uterus 0.75mg, in the rectum 0.39mg, in the heart 0.27mg, in the lungs 0.79mg, in the oesophagus 0.21mg, and in the brain 0.09mg. In total he found 18.07mg.[43]

This is a relatively small amount. Customarily two grains of arsenic are required to kill. However, the amount of arsenic ingested is always far more than what will be found in a corpse upon investigation. This is because after ingestion the body's defence mechanism will reject most of the poison in vomit and diarrhoea and we know that Mrs. Greenwood reacted thus. The absorption (uptake from the gut to the blood) after oral ingestion is high (80-90%) although it can be lower if an insoluble form is used. Assuming a person ingests 1 grain soluble arsenic, there is immediately a reduction of 10-20% of the dose, meaning the absorbed dose is 0.8-0.9 grain. After absorption into the blood, the arsenic is metabolised mainly in the liver and after that excreted in the urine (a very small amount is also excreted in the faeces). About 45–85% is excreted in urine within 1-3 days after ingestion. It is also possible that if arsenic poisoning had been taking place over weeks or months then a small dose could have proved fatal.[44]

Yet there was to be a poisoning case in Cornwall in 1922 when a mere 3.73 mg of arsenic was found in the body of the victim, a Mrs. Black. To be fair, usually a great deal more is found in the deceased; 131.37mg in the case of Miss Barrow in 1912; 208.2mg in that of Mrs. Armstrong in 1922 and 602.7mg in that of Mr. Pace in 1928.[45]

In some ways, arsenic was an ideal poison and was often used in the 19th and early 20th centuries. It was cheap and easy to buy in the form of weedkiller, that anyone with a garden can legitimately buy without comment. Weedkiller was chiefly made up of it and that could be bought over the counter in a shop after the poisons book has been signed. It is tasteless and so can easily be introduced into food, drink or medicine without arousing the victim's suspicions. Its symptoms are similar to other medical complaints, especially gastritis and food poisoning. This is not the case now; such lethal products have long since been taken off the market or reformulated.

[3] Sir Thomas Bowater in Kidwelly for inquest.

Sir Thomas Bowater [3] made the suggestion to the police that the arsenic might have found its way into the bottle of wine by accident. He passed on correspondence about a like case in 1914. Then, a City of London merchant who sold wholesale spirits and wine had a complaint from a customer Messrs. Box and Co. of Brentford that a customer complained that a bottle of port wine that the company had supplied, had caused the buyer to be ill with vomiting. On investigation it was found that arsenic was there, but this was a very rare instance in 30 years of business.[46]

In the midst of these suspicions, Greenwood decided to give interviews to the press. The first was on the day of the exhumation itself. He told:

> I am the victim of village gossip, of village scandal, and if you know Welsh village life you will know what that means.

> It all started from the fact that four months after my first wife's death I married again. That started the gossip. It is only fair to say that my first wife suffered from ill health for at least two years before her death. Not only was her heart bad, but she also suffered from an internal disease, which caused her intense depression. It was, however, from the heart attack that she died on 16th June. No one, not even the doctor, thought that that attack would be fatal.[47]

He was interviewed again only a few days later. He attacked the lying slanders that had brought down the attention of the Home Office and the police. He was angry that relations between him and his first wife were stated as being allegedly unhappy:

> My neighbours know better than that. They know how happy we were. They also know that for two years my wife was under the care of Dr. Griffiths, the family medical attendant, on account of an affliction of the heart. During the last six months of her life, I noticed that my wife seemed to be wasting away daily and I put this down to the fact that she was suffering from an internal malady.

There was a rumour that he had insured his late wife's life for £10,000 and to this Greenwood responded:

> That is another malicious falsehood. She was not insured for a brass farthing, and, painful as the enquiry is to me and to the family of my late wife, I welcome it, as an opportunity to bring to an end, once and for all, the tissue of lies that has been circulated in Llanelli and Kidwelly for the last ten months. I want the whole thing cleared up and I have no doubt at all what the result will be.
>
> If I had known there was going to be this suspicion I would have insisted myself upon an enquiry being held. Who the people are who have instituted this investigation, I cannot conceive. I would very much like to know. I have never been

> asked for a statement, nor have any member of my household, as far as I know.
>
> She had been in very bad health for at least two years before she died, and had been the subject of fainting fits ever since we arrived. She has also expressed fears that she had an internal compliant'.[48]

On a later occasion he talked to a journalist in his house and told him 'there is nothing at all I can tell you – absolutely nothing at all'. He claimed to welcome the enquiry as he had said previously 'for I have nothing to hide'. Acknowledging that there would be an inquest he remarked, 'I shall certainly volunteer to give evidence'. As to the forthcoming investigations by the Home Office analyst, 'I know there can be nothing wrong – or at least I shall be very much surprised if there is'.[49]

As said, the Carmarthen Constabulary, as with most county police forces in England and Wales at that time, did not have a separate detective force. Instead when such were needed, a chief inspector would be sent from Scotland Yard to undertake the investigative work that was required in conjunction with the local force. It was now clear that this was not merely a suspicious death, as was thought previously, but one of murder and so more help was needed. Blackwell wrote to Phillips on 1st June to tell him that 'having regard to the very serious nature of this report' (that of Webster about the poisoning, received on 31st May), he would be sending down an experienced officer 'to render you all assistance in his power'. This probably rankled.[50] This is in contrast to a violent murder in June 1920, near Abergavenny, when the chief constable had wired to the Yard on the day of the discovery of the body. Though to be fair, the Greenwood case was initially only a suspicious death not an obvious murder.[51]

In this case the lot fell to Detective Chief Inspector Ernest Edward Haigh (1871-1938) [4]. He had been born in Fulham on 4th April 1871, the son of Police Sergeant Henry Haigh. He had joined the police at Peckham on 13th June 1892, became a sergeant third class in 1899 and a detective inspector in 1909 and a detective divisional inspector in 1910, rising to his present rank in 1919, earning £10 13s. 4d. per week. He had brown hair which was greying, blue eyes and stood 5 feet 9¼ inches tall. He was married to Mary and they had four children, and lived in Bighton in Hampshire. By 1920 he had served 28 years with the Metropolitan Police and so was about to retire in July. This was his last case.[52] With him was Detective Sergeant Henry Edgar Helby (1881-1962), who had joined the Metropolitan Police in 1902 and had been a detective sergeant since at least 1912.

[4] Chief Inspector Ernest Haigh.

Haigh later recalled that it was at noon on 1st June that he was called from his office at Scotland Yard and told to report to the public prosecutor. He was given a file of papers and instructions. He had a bag at the Yard already packed for such expeditions into the country.

Haigh was then taken by official car to Paddington station and took a train westwards. He read through the dossier and so 'became acquainted to a certain extent to the general outline of the case I was called upon to handle'. It was clear that his provincial colleagues had already undertaken a lot of work into what was a confused situation.[53]

The instructions given were almost certainly those contained in an undated and unsigned memorandum found in the relevant police file, and as shall be seen, one clause was to hamper the investigation. They were as follows:[54]

1. Funeral – Undertaker – Grave number.
2. Exhumation – Order for – Date – To whom sent – By whom grave opened – By whom body and coffin identified.
3. P.M. Examination – by whom made – when – Obtain copy of Report – Cause of death.
4. Organs of body – by whom removed – Sealed by and handed to Sergeant Lewis – when and by whom.
5. Certificate of cause of death – By whom given and when.
6. Certificate for Burial – By whom given and when.
7. Greenwood's second marriage – Date of – When notice given.
8. Copies of all Prescriptions written or given by Dr. Griffiths.
9. Copies of all entries in Dr. Griffiths' books.
10. Take no statements at present from the Greenwood family.
11. Take statements from all the servants.
12. Collect information as to the commencement of Mrs. Greenwood's indisposition – symptoms – dates.
13. Inquire if the Doctors have read up Arsenic in the Text Books.
14. Obtain if possible specimens of the soil from Mrs. Greenwood's grave.
15. Were any other persons in the house sick when Mrs. Greenwood was ill.
16. Enquire about the bottle of port.
17. Who paid the nurse – when – how.

The 10th clause ordered that neither the present Mrs. Greenwood nor Irene were to be questioned and there is no evidence that they were. Of course, then a wife could not be obliged to give evidence in court against her husband and so it might have been seen as pointless to have done so. As to Irene, her whereabouts was not always in Kidwelly. She seems to have spent some of her time this summer elsewhere; in Bristol and Cardiff. And the phrase 'at present' may have meant that questioning could take place at some point, but never was.[55]

Another problem may have been that Haigh was a London policeman and he was investigating a crime in the Welsh countryside where many spoke Welsh as their first language. That and the common nature of surnames may also have been a problem, as he wrote to his superiors, 'I have found it extremely difficult to keep a grasp of the various statements owing to the names of so many of those interviewed being called Jones'.[56]

Possibly Haigh assumed that the county force had already done so, but presumably he had seen the statements that had already been taken and so should have known that there was none from Irene and given that she had been present at the time of both lunch and thereafter, she was a material witness. The failure to take a statement was, as with the failure to take nail and hair clippings from the corpse, another problem with the investigation.

He later wrote:

> My training and my success in the detective calling had, if I may say so, been by preserving a perfectly open mind in the details of any case placed in my hands. And I should like to add here that my secret instructions included one to the effect that this case must be approached with perfectly unbiased mind.[57]

Because of the blaze of publicity that had surrounded the case so far, Haigh, wanting to work 'in my own quiet unobtrusive way' decided to make Carmarthen rather than Kidwelly, his base of operations, arriving there at 11.15pm on 1st June, notifying the local police once he had done so. Here he was able to meet and interview a number of the people who later gave evidence at the trial. It was six days before any journalist was aware of his presence in the locality.

He decided to go to Llandeilo on 2nd June to see the Chief Constable there. After doing so he arranged to meet Superintendent Jones and Sergeant Lewis. The three met at Carmarthen that afternoon; the other two could not get to Llandeilo and if he went to see them at Llanelli or Kidwelly it would be known to the press. In fact, a reporter from *The Daily Mail* had been at Llanelli for three weeks already and Haigh wanted to avoid him. Haigh asked the officers if a discreet observation could be kept on Greenwood, but they were unimpressed by this idea.[58]

Haigh's first visit to Kidwelly was at midnight (this secrecy was similar to that used by the investigating Yard officer in the following year in the Armstrong case; albeit prior to the exhumation). He went there by car in order to get a sense of the geography of the place and especially that of Rumsey House and its grounds. He wrote 'I am sure my movements, very quietly made, disturbed the slumbers of no one'. It was on a later visit to the town that he met a journalist from *The Weekly Despatch*. Haigh had just left the grounds of Rumsey House. He realised, after his visit, noting the local geography and the fact that Greenwood had a car which he constantly uses, surveillance on him would be impossible.[59]

He continued, 'this was the day of which I first saw Mr. Greenwood'. He visited him with the full knowledge of his solicitor, Ludford 'a most estimable gentleman for whose capacity I entertain a very high regard'. Haigh and Greenwood strolled 'like two old friends in the beautiful old world garden'. Neither alluded to the business in hand though Greenwood knew who Haigh was and since he had already been interviewed twice by the local police, Haigh saw no need to do so again. Haigh recalled that 'He spoke to me without restraint or nervousness. With pride he showed me the lawns, and pointed out trees which he claimed to be remarkably fine specimens of their kind. In parting he told me cordially that I was free to make any use of the place and the staff'.

However, in private Haigh painted a rather different picture, 'The enquiry is an extremely difficult one because of the fact that the suspected murderer is keeping in close touch with particularly all the persons concerned, most of whom are his friends or members of his family and business staff'.[60]

In fact, there were only two of the witnesses that Haigh could question without Greenwood's knowledge. Even then, 'I am sure he has such a degree of influence upon them that until he is under detention it will be hopeless to attempt to interview them, especially those in his home and office'. He also interviewed the coroner, who had fixed the adjourned inquest to 8th June but who had now postponed it for another week. Such was the need for discretion that he advised that any communications be sent to him in plain envelopes addressed to 'Mr. Haigh', adding 'The place is so small that every precaution against publicity is absolutely imperative'.[61]

The initial results of Haigh's enquiries were far from decisive. Guy Stephenson, of the Home Office, was not optimistic, writing:

> ... it does not appear that Greenwood derived any financial benefit from the death of his wife; and I may say that unless the evidence at present available is supplemented by further developments I feel grave doubts as to its being sufficient to justify the finding by a coroner's jury of a verdict of murder against the husband of the deceased woman or any other person.[62]

The police also crucially found evidence of some of Greenwood's recent purchases. One was a note of 14th April 1919 from Greenwood to Messrs. Dobbie & Co., seedsmen of Edinburgh, 'I should be obliged if you will let me have the 20s. worth of weed killer I ordered some months ago'. There was also a note from the said company sending a tin of Eureka weed killer.[63]

Meanwhile, the police investigation continued locally. It was found that on 8th June 1917 Greenwood had signed the poisons book at Lewis Jones' chemist's shop at No. 19 Bridge Street, Kidwelly. He had just bought two quart tins of Cooper's weedicide, 'which I understand is practically all arsenic'. The contents of such tins contained 36% arsenious oxide combined with soda, with a variation of 2% more or less. This is highly poisonous, though a fatal dose will depend on the constitution of the person, the method of administration and the state of the stomach, to name three factors. The weedicide was essentially colourless, though up to 1915 there had been a dye in it. Two single drops would produce half a grain of arsenic.[64] Apparently 'He [Greenwood] stated he wanted it for the destruction of weeds and signed the Poisons Book, which is still in the possession of Mr. [Superintendent] Jones'.[65]

The police also looked into the wine that the household bought. This was the responsibility, naturally of the two womenfolk of the household. Their main supplier was Frederick Brigstocke, wine dealer of Carmarthen. Between January and April 1919 the household of four adults had ordered 2 bottles of whisky, 6 of sparkling wine, 15 of claret and 20 of burgundy.[66] On 20th May one Joseph Sharff collected 75 dozen empty bottles that the Greenwoods and previous owners had allowed to accumulate on the premises.[67]

Haigh also took a statement from Miss Phillips. He then took one from Hannah Williams and showed her a bottle to ask whether it was similar to the one that had been used at the lunch on 15th June. She thought that it was.[68] He was impressed by both of these witnesses. However, Haigh was concerned about the value of Dr. Griffiths, who was now retired from medicine saying, 'This gentleman will, I fear, be a very poor witness. He is not an old man by any means, and he seems to still bear strongly towards the opinion that the deceased suffered from some growth in the womb, which caused the original vaginal trouble … he is quite sure that his diagnosis of heart disease was quite accurate'.

As shall be noted, this was not the last time that the doctor's usefulness would be questioned. Meanwhile there was talk of a re-exhumation in order to check the muscles, hair and nails of the deceased for arsenic in view of Dr. William Henry Willcox's report and even calling in the eminent Dr. Spilsbury. This was reported in the press in early June. Neither of these possibilities occurred.[69] Dr. Willcox (1870-1941) had been junior scientific analyst to the Home Office from 1904-1908, Senior Analyst from 1908-1919 and was now Honorary Medical Adviser. He had given evidence at several prominent cases, including that of Dr. Crippen in 1910, Frederick Seddon, an arsenic poisoner in 1912 and the 'Brides in the Bath' killer in 1915, before seeing service overseas in the war.[70]

As to the other witnesses, Haigh was equally troubled, writing, 'Several of the witnesses were extremely careful to make their own lack of initiative, or even neglect, to appear in as favourable a light as possible with the result that points which would have told against the accused were either forgotten or so minimised as to render them of little value'.

There was one witness he spoke highly of, 'The best witness and one is undoubtedly best able to fix times and incidents is Miss Phillips who is an educated and intelligent lady'.[71] This tied in with the chief constable's assessment.

In the meanwhile, on 2nd June the coroner received the reports from the analyst. On the next day a date for the resumed inquest was given; 16th June.[72]

There was then a final interview Greenwood gave to the press before the resumed inquest. Greenwood and his second wife were interviewed together and they emphasised the first Mrs. Greenwood's illnesses and the remedies she took. Greenwood maintained the incredulous outlook he had always maintained:

> … what can I say, except the mystery seems to deepen every day. It is said that they have found arsenic in the body. That I cannot understand. I should not have been the least surprised to know that they found poison of some kind, for during the last two years of her life my wife took many kinds of medicine.
>
> They were treating her for catarrh, supposed cancer, her heart and her nerves and I understand that she had to take many kinds of medicine.
>
> There is one very important point which must be considered. Supposing I bought arsenic I should have had to have signed the poison book, and that would be traced at once. As a matter of fact I have not been beyond Kidwelly and Llanelli since October 1918, and then I went to Brecon on business for my present wife's firm. My first wife had been ill for upward of two years. She was wasting away and she knew it.
>
> She used to say 'I am dying on my feet' and to anyone who was associated with her it was quite obvious. I know quite well what the suggestion is, but it was so clear that my wife was

> dying and it was only a question of months at the outside that even supposing such a preposterous thing as I wished her to die, I had only to wait a few weeks.[73]

The journalist thought that Greenwood was 'much affected' by what he had just said and paused for a while before continuing:

> As a matter of fact we were very happy together. We were married for 23 years and I can honestly say we never had a quarrel. It was always give and take with us.

"And isn't that by far the better way?" said Mrs. Greenwood.

> My wife was so good, so kind, that it would have required a perfect monster to think harm towards her. She was very secretive, though, and many times I have come home from my office in Llanelli to find her out. Usually she would wait tea on me, but on these occasions I had tea by myself. When she came in I would ask her where she had been, but she would never say, but turned it off with a laugh. I never pressed her for explanations, as I knew she had been up to no harm. I do not know to this day where she had been to on these occasions.

"She was always having fainting fits, I am told," said Mrs Greenwood.

> Yes, I would be sitting here, smoking my pipe, and looking up would find that she had gone off in a dead faint, and it took a long time for her to come round.

Responding to the idea that the arsenic could have been self-administered, Greenwood said:

> I am sure she would not do it. She used to use a great many preparations for her face. Her drawer was full of cosmetics and face creams, but I am sure she never took any patent concoction to improve her figure or anything like that.

"Could paint have caused the poisoning [paint sometimes did contain arsenic]?" suggested Mrs. Greenwood, "At the time of her death this house was being repainted with white paint."

> Paint always upset her. On one occasion she had to leave the house in which we were living while it was being redecorated, the paint had such an effect in her.[74]

Greenwood was naturally painting a rose tinted view of his first marriage, that others would contradict. Nor did he relate, what he had done in private, about the doctor's pills being fatal, but that her patent medicines were to blame.

When Greenwood was told, no later than 9th June about the results of the exhumation, he spoke to a journalist in his Llanelli office, 'That beats me hollow. I cannot understand how they have found poison'.

On being asked if he had been told of this officially, he said:

> No I have heard nothing. Not a single thing.
> My wife was taking medicine before her death, but I don't know what was in it.
> No there could not have been that. If there had been she would have been writhing in pain, would she not? As it was, she died peacefully.[75]

Chapter Five

Adjourned Inquest

Once the results of the organ analysis had come through, the coroner could resume the inquest after a space of two months. He had suggested that a re-exhumation take place so that an examination be made of the victim's hair and nails (which would have given evidence of long term poisoning), after he had read the medical report, but this did not occur.[1] The inquest took place, once more, at Kidwelly town hall on Tuesday 15th June. Seward Pearce (1866-1951), assistant director of the department of the public prosecutions, was there on behalf of the police and Ludford, the fellow Llanelli solicitor who knew Greenwood, was there to represent Greenwood, who was not present on this occasion, and nor was Irene (both on Ludford's advice, but despite a subpoena). Nicholas told the jury of the new evidence he would bring to their attention and that he would be calling witnesses.[2] Accompanying her sister, Miss Bowater, was Sir Thomas Vansittart Bowater.[3] The jury was composed of local men, including Mr. Reynolds (a draper) and Mr. Shepherd (a baker whose shop was on the same street as Rumsey House). John Morgan, another juror, was the rate collector.[4] These were men who all knew the Greenwoods and thus represented local opinion and knowledge.

Police Sergeant Lewis and Webster, the analyst, briefly spoke in court about the despatch of the organs to London for examination. The latter told that arsenic had been found therein. There was no other indication of any other poison. Pearce asked Webster if he had heard of Cooper's weedicide. He had, and in response to questions, replied that it contained a high level of arsenic. Ludford then asked if it was possible to extract arsenic from this weedkiller. He agreed it might be and when asked if it was difficult to do so, answered, 'It would not be difficult for a chemist to extract oxide from these preparations, but it would be difficult for a layman'.[5]

Dr. Griffiths was the next witness to be called. He was asked about the deceased's medical history and what happened on the night of her death. He declared that the nurse claimed he visited between 10.00pm and 3.00am but he denied that this was true. He could not remember having done so. He was asked about any examination of the excreta. He had not carried one out but admitted if he knew then what he did now he would have done so. Likewise, with his current knowledge he would not have issued the death certificate that he had.[6]

He was then asked about the discrepancy between his and the nurse's recollections about his visits that night. He said that the nurse came to his house a few weeks ago and raised this with him then. He had asked her to enumerate his visits on the night of Mrs. Greenwood's death and of which he said 'I have no recollection and I told her so'. Pearce asked if the pills he had given Mrs. Greenwood contained arsenic and he said that this was not so. Ludford asked if he had ever kept white arsenic and if the nurse had hinted any suspicion about the death to him and he answered no to both questions.[7]

Miss Phillips, Mrs. Greenwood's best friend, was next and she gave a lengthy statement about her visit on the night of Mrs. Greenwood's death. She was then asked some supplementary questions. She was asked about a conversation between Greenwood and Miss Bowater and the former said how splendid the doctor had been. She was also asked if she knew that one of the servants had a partiality for burgundy; she did not know this. She was also asked if she had spoken to the doctor about the nurse's comment that Mrs. Greenwood's vomit had been white and flaky? She had not asked this of him.[8]

The district nurse, Elizabeth Jones, described her patient's symptoms. She had never seen such a state before. She was asked if the dying woman was groaning loudly because a servant had said she had heard her. No, this was not the case, the nurse answered. There were many questions as to the discrepancies for the times that Dr. Griffiths was at Rumsey House. She claimed he did not arrive until 11.00pm or afterwards whereas he had claimed he was there much earlier. She also said that he returned at 1.00am, which the doctor had denied. She agreed it was an unusual case but it did not occur to her that an irritant poison may have been administered.[9]

She was then questioned about her subsequent conversations about the case; to the vicar and to two ladies known to Mrs. Greenwood – Mrs. Meredith and Mrs. Smart. The coroner put it to her, 'You have been discussing this case a good while around Kidwelly?' to which she answered, 'No I have not'. She was then asked about various statements she had made to others after the death and concerning it. She was also asked whether she told fortunes and she said that she had told that of Greenwood at least once and possibly at other times. She was asked whether she said to Greenwood that if he knew what people were saying about him 'it would make his hair stand on end'. She did not recall saying any of this.[10]

Pearce asked her if there was anything that made her feel concerned about the death. She said that she had an uneasy feeling but that she could not express what it was. She could say no more than this. Ludford asked if she had spoken about yellowish green vomit and she replied that she had not. This was a suggestion made to her by the police. She was asked if the vicar had suggested the possibility of foul play and she said that he had at some stage. The coroner said that anything unusual should have been reported to the doctor, to which she responded by saying 'It was simply the diarrhoea that I thought was abnormal'.[11]

Miss Bowater then briefly told of her visits to see her sister. She added, 'Mrs Greenwood left no will. The principal part of her property was left in trust for children except for a small sum left to her by her mother. I do not know whether administration had been taken out'.

Ludford asked if there had ever been a suicide in the family and she said that an uncle of hers had died thus.[12]

Dr. Willcox stated briefly what the results of the organ examination had been; that there was arsenic in the body. He referred to what Dr. Griffiths and nurse Jones had said in court. There had been severe vomiting and diarrhoea in the six hours from 6.00pm to midnight and this would have led to 'the elimination of a considerable quantity of arsenic'. He was asked for his conclusions and stated that 'From the results of the analysis and the symptoms that have been described I think the case of death was acute arsenical poisoning. If the arsenic is in solid state the onset of the symptoms will be delayed. In this case the wide distribution of the poison indicates that it has been readily absorbed and had probably been taken in a dissolved state'.[13]

He was then asked as to 'What would be your view as to the time?' to which he answered that 'Taking into account the symptoms and the analysis, the arsenic was probably taken between 1.30pm and midnight. Most likely it was taken between 1.30pm and 6.30pm. From the evidence of the doctor and the nurse it is clear that Mrs. Greenwood suffered from abdominal pains, severe vomiting and diarrhoea, after which severe heart failure and collapse occurred, death resulting in about ten hours from the onset of the symptoms. The symptoms are typical of acute arsenical poisoning'.[14]

He was then questioned about the condition of the body. It was well preserved and there were no signs of any disease. There was a small tumour on the uterus but it was not malignant. The coroner then asked about the nature of arsenic. It was a white solid substance, in appearance like sugar or flour and was easily soluble in water. He was asked about arsenic in weed killer and said that a significant quantity of it was found in them. The next question concerned the symptoms of arsenic poisoning to which he replied that 'If the poison is taken in a soluble form the symptoms usually commence within an hour. They are nausea, abdominal pain, vomiting and diarrhoea, often of a severe type, usually occurs. These symptoms are sometimes associated with cramp in part of the legs, but this symptom is often absent'.[15]

The coroner then enquired, 'What follows the symptoms?'

Dr. Willcox affirmed 'Collapse and heart failure are likely to occur after the severe vomiting and purging, and if the person was previously suffering from a weak heart the collapse and heart failure would be likely to occur earlier in arsenical poisoning and it would be a more severe type. The stools are thin and watery and often have flakes of mucus present in them. In acute arsenical poisoning, inflammation of the stomach and intestines occurs, and if death results, signs of this inflammation, such as redness and congestion are found if the post mortem examination is made soon after death. If, however, several weeks or months elapse between the death and the post mortem examination, these signs will disappear owing to the putrefaction changes'.[16]

The coroner then wanted to know what was the normal medical dose of arsenic. It was between a sixtieth and a fiftieth of one grain. By way of summary be questioned 'Are you quite clear that this woman died from acute arsenical poisoning?' The reply was unequivocal, 'I have no doubt about it'.

Ludford then asked him about what would constitute a fatal dose. Very little in fact; it could be dissolved into a cup of tea. It was impossible to say how many doses would be needed, but it could be just the one. Ludford tried to pin him down which led to the following exchange:

> 'Two grains would be the smallest killing dose?'
> 'Yes.'
> 'Is it a favourite poison for suicide?'
> 'I should say it was not. It is taken by suicides moderately frequently. Carbolic acid and prussic acid are just as common.'[17]

The next witness of the day was housemaid Hannah Williams. She told how she had seen Mrs. Greenwood drink port wine – and she alone – at lunchtime, and that Greenwood had been in the china cupboard just before lunch and then spent a little time in the dining room alone. She replied in the positive about being asked about what Mrs. Greenwood drank. The cook, Margaret Morris, declared that all the household ate the lunch she prepared and that no one was ill. There was also discussion about whether any of the three servants heard Mrs. Greenwood groaning that night; Hannah said she had but fellow servant, Margaret Morris, said she had not. There was also talk about Hannah's leaving her job there. She said that she left of her own free will but Margaret said that she was under notice at the time of Mrs. Greenwood's death.[18]

The inquest was continued on the next day, Wednesday 16th June, exactly a year to the day that Mrs. Greenwood died.

Dr. Willcox was recalled to the witness stand. He stated that the symptoms of heart disease and valvular disease were similar. He also said that those of arsenic poisoning and food poisoning were, too, but that in the former case it was usual for several people to be afflicted by that. He reaffirmed his belief that the presence of arsenic in the corpse was without doubt.[19]

Margaret Morris was recalled and asked about her fellow servant, Hannah Williams. She had seen her tampering with the household's wine but not of drinking it. She said that another servant had seen Hannah drinking the wine. On being asked if she saw Greenwood in the china cupboard on the day of 15th June 1919 and she said she had not but later admitted that he might have done so, for she was in the kitchen and thus could not see the master's movements. There was also discussion about Hannah's leaving the service of the Greenwoods. Margaret said that Mrs. Greenwood had told her that she had given her notice because she stayed out too late, though Hannah said that she left of her own accord.[20]

Miss Griffiths, the doctor's sister, was the next witness and she was asked questions about Greenwood's visit to her house on the evening before Mrs. Greenwood died. The coroner asked about Greenwood's state of being when the doctor's sister saw him which led to the following guarded responses:

> 'In what frame of mind was he?'
> 'His usual frame of mind.'
> 'Was he in high or low spirits?'
> 'In ordinary spirits.'
> 'Was he jocular?'
> 'He is usually jocular.'
> 'Did he dance or jump around the room?'
> 'No.'
> 'Have you used the expression that he was perfectly happy?'
> 'He seemed to be quite alright.'

There was some question about fortune telling and did Miss Griffiths tell them; she did not and then Miss Griffiths was asked about the length of time Greenwood had been with them, when his wife was so unwell. She said that it had only been for a short time and later thought that 10 minutes might be right. Did Greenwood call again for the doctor that night? Miss Griffiths thought he did not. She did know about the 3.00am call, however. She did not know about any other calls made by her brother that night.[21]

It then came to a discussion about Greenwood's relationships with Miss Griffiths and Miss Jones which resulted in the following interchange:

> 'I do not want to be offensive, but you were on pretty intimate terms with Mr. Greenwood? You were on friendly terms?'
> 'Yes, on friendly terms.'
> 'Was he what one might call something of a flirt?'
> 'Always on pleasant terms.'
> 'Mr. Greenwood used to visit you frequently before his wife's death?'
> 'Yes.'
> 'Does he visit you now?'
> 'He does not come often since Mrs. Greenwood's death.'

There was then talk about Gwladys Jones' telephone calls being received at the doctor's for Greenwood. These calls persisted until 17th June and then not thereafter. Then questioning returned to the night of Mrs. Greenwood's death. Miss Griffiths recalled going to the drawing room to hurry her brother up into seeing Mrs. Greenwood. She did not know of any later visits.

'Was Mr. Greenwood distressed after the death of his wife?'
'I have been told he was not.'

Ludford brought up the matter if other visits by her brother after 1.00am but she did not know of any. This prompted the next exchange of words:

> 'There is no truth in the suggestion that Mr. Greenwood was dancing, but he is always inclined to joke, and is friendly with the ladies?'
> 'Yes.'
> 'As a matter of fact, he is always on good terms with the ladies?'

> 'Yes.'[22]

Hannah Williams was recalled again and was examined by Ludford about the bottle of port wine in the following dialogue:

> 'I suggest to you that there was never a bottle of port wine on the Greenwood table at all'.
> 'Yes, I saw the label. It was a red label.'

It was apparently three quarters full on the Sunday. Ludford accused her of drinking from it and that was why Mrs. Greenwood gave her notice. Once again, she asserted her innocence about that and about being given notice for either that or for once coming home as late as 11.30pm. Ludford then returned to the bottle of port wine, which he suggested was actually burgundy, but she refuted this and said that if Irene claimed otherwise, then she was wrong, as was the maid who said that Hannah was drinking the wine.[23]

The vicar was the next witness. He said he had seen Mrs. Greenwood on the Saturday, that she was well and that she had been spoken to by nurse Jones and Greenwood on the 16th June. The coroner asked him if Greenwood said anything about suicide. Apparently not on that occasion, but on the day of the exhumation, Greenwood had said to him, 'I wonder if she took something herself? There is nothing here. She was fond of staring at the water'. This prompted the question, 'What did you think about the suggestion of suicide?' to which he replied 'I cannot but regard any suggestion of that kind from whatever quarter it comes as an infamous slander on the character and memory of a deceased lady who is not here to defend herself'.

Ludford asked if it was slander to say that the deceased was depressed and the vicar said it was not but the suicide implication was.[24]

Annie Groves, Greenwood's office caretaker, was the next witness. She gave evidence of Greenwood and Gwladys Jones lunching together, of them being together in the back office and of Mrs. Greenwood's knowing that they were there. She was, however, contradictory whether there had been intimacy between Greenwood and Gwladys Jones prior to marriage. At first she said there had been but later she had said otherwise and this contradiction does not seem to have been resolved. Her last statements were that there had not been.[25]

[1] John Clifford Jones.

John Clifford Jones [1] gave evidence that in 1917 Greenwood had bought weed killer from his father's chemist's shop. Dr. Carl Edwards, B.Sc. and chief technical chemist of Cooper's Technical Bureau, stated that his company did produce weed killer that could be fatal if used on people and animals. He was asked if it would still be effective three years after purchase and said it would be so up to ten years later. Two single drops would be fatal.[26]

The next witness was Edward Roberts, a garage owner of Llanelli. He recounted that on 19th May Greenwood told him that his wife was very unwell. Greenwood then hired Roberts to drive him, Gwladys Jones and Llewellyn, a brother of hers, from Porturdulais to Kidwelly. When they got there they drove through the town and then back again, depositing Greenwood about a quarter of a mile from his house on the other side of Kidwelly. He then drove the Joneses to Llanelli. This occurred at about 1.30pm on that day.[27]

Gwyneth David, neighbour to the Jones family of Llanelli, was the next witness. She told about her learning of Mrs. Greenwood being unwell from Gwladys Jones and on writing to Mrs. Greenwood with her sympathy she received a sharp rebuke for Greenwood, accusing her of damaging his friendship with the Joneses. Gwladys Jones had accused her of being a liar. She was asked whether Gwladys Jones had spoken to her and she said she had. The coroner then called Greenwood as a witness but Sergeant Lewis could not find him.[28]

Lily Powell was another servant at Rumsey House at the time of the death. She said 'I had the same food as everybody else at the house on the Sunday before Mrs. Greenwood's death, and I did not feel any ill effects'.

Further she stated that the wine served at the meal was burgundy. She had rarely seen port wine in the house and would not know the difference between the two when served in glasses. She could say it was red wine, but thought it was burgundy because that was the wine that Mrs. Greenwood always took. However, she was not waiting at the table that day and so could not be certain what it was that Mrs. Greenwood then drank.[29]

The last witness was Martha Morris, an occasional help at Rumsey House, who recalled seeing Mrs. Greenwood on the Saturday before she was poisoned. She thought that she had seemed weak and was in low spirits, the latter being asked by Ludford.[30]

Mr. Nicholas, the coroner, now began his final address to the jury. He reminded them of the basic facts of the case, of Mrs. Greenwood being unwell, but was bright and active up to 14th June, that she was seriously ill on the Sunday and that she died in the early hours of the next day. He recounted how Dr. Willcox said that there was a significant amount of arsenic in her body, probably taken in a drink. He concluded, 'and it is for you to consider carefully how it came to be taken by Mrs. Greenwood'.[31]

There were three possibilities; she might have taken the poison accidentally; she might have taken it deliberately or someone else administered it to her. He thought that there was nothing to suggest that the first two possibilities were correct. Therefore, 'The crucial question is: was the poison administered to her, and, if so, by whom?' Dr. Willcox had stated that it was ingested between 1.30pm and midnight on Sunday, but probably before 6.30pm. 'The only people in the house were the children, the servants and the husband. You can eliminate the servants and the children'. It was Greenwood's actions that the jury must focus on. Were they merely suspicious or were they those of a murderer?[32]

Nicholas drew their attention to the second visit of Greenwood to Dr. Griffiths' house and the length of time he spent there; up to an hour according to the nurse, so long that his daughter went over to hasten the doctor back. 'This is a curious thing for a husband to do when his wife is in such a serious state'. He also referred to Greenwood's jocular demeanour at this time. Of course, some people were in good spirits at the worst of times, he observed, but 'I must, however, call attention to it and couple it with the fact that the Greenwood was so long in taking the doctor back to the patient'.[33]

He then referred back to the question of the bottle of wine. Hannah had put the wine out on the Sunday and the next day it was all gone. She had seen Greenwood in the china room and then to the dining room cupboard just before lunch. On the other hand, another servant could not support what Hannah had said. Nicholas said 'If he were there, you cannot say what he was doing there. That is only a matter of inference and surmise'. However, the wine was the only drink she was known to have had at lunch that no one else had, and her husband had been to the place where it was stored where he never was usually.[34]

Then there was the matter of Greenwood's relations with the woman who was now his present wife. Mrs. Groves had told how Greenwood and Gwladys Jones met when he was at work. Miss Griffiths told how Gwladys Jones telephoned Greenwood via the Griffiths telephone. 'All these things indicate that at that time he was on familiar terms with his present wife'. He also pointed out that Greenwood seemed anxious to portray his first wife as being ill.[35]

Finally, he referred to the purchase by Greenwood of weed killer in 1917. Any two drops of this could prove fatal. Arsenic is tasteless and it could have been put into Mrs. Greenwood's drink. He told the jury that Greenwood had the means and 'evidence of a motive'. On the other hand, 'Between that and coming to the conclusion that the arsenic was administered by Greenwood there is a considerable gap that needs other evidence to fill'. They had to decide whether Greenwood was responsible or not.[36]

It had been expected that Greenwood would have attended the inquest. A summons had been issued, but he ignored it 'contrary to general expectation'. A newspaper noted that 200 yards away from the town hall, Greenwood 'might have been playing croquet on the lawn of his house'.[37] It seems he ignored the subpoena because Ludford had advised hm not to attend. It did not look good that he had not done so, however and it meant that his version of events was not aired in court.

This was not a criminal court. More latitude was possible at the inquest because of that. However, if the jury found Greenwood responsible then the coroner would then issue an order for his arrest. The jury retired for 35 minutes, then asked the coroner additional questions before retiring for another 15 minutes. They finally returned to the court and he asked the foreman, George Jones, 'Concerning the death of Mabel Greenwood, are you agreed upon your verdict?'

The reply was concise 'That is the verdict of us all'.

A piece of paper was passed from George Jones to Nicholas, who read aloud: 'We are of unanimous opinion that the death of the deceased, Mabel Greenwood, was caused by acute arsenical poisoning, as certified by Dr. Willcox, and that the poison as administered by Harold Greenwood'.[38]

This result vindicated the gossips. It was a popular verdict. Some of those present in the town hall clapped the result of the inquest.[39] The court was crowded with locals, 'largely women'. Apparently they often 'broke into animated chatter in the Welsh language during pauses in the proceedings, and were frequently called to order for sudden excursions into laughter while the evidence was in progress'.[40]

That afternoon, Police Sergeant Lewis and Police Constable William John Thomas, in plain clothes, had been to Rumsey House, on Chief Inspector Haigh's immediate orders from the chief constable. They knocked on the door and were met by a maid. They entered the house and told Greenwood they wanted to see him on an apparently trivial matter. He was upstairs at the time when the maid brought him this news. Coming downstairs, the two policemen arrested Greenwood, who later recalled 'No sooner had I approached within a few feet of them than they both dashed forward and gripped me by the arms. Whether they did it in the excitement of the moment or from excessive zeal it is for them to say, but I can say without exaggeration that they did not err on the side of gentleness in the way they handled me. Telling me they had come to arrest me, they hurried me hatless into the street', taking him the 50 yards southwards to the police station at No. 36 Banc Pendre, Lewis' house; very few people were then around.[41] Greenwood later indignantly recollected the experience, 'I will leave it to imagination of my readers to picture to themselves the sensation of a man roughly torn from the comfort of his home and dragged like any common felon through the streets of the town in which he was a prominent and respected citizen, on a baseless charge'.[42]

At 4.30pm that afternoon, Haigh, who had been at the inquest, went to Lewis' house in Kidwelly (the town's police station), following the instructions of the chief constable. There, in the presence of yet another policeman, he addressed Greenwood. He told him that he was under arrest, owing to the verdict at the inquest against him for the murder of his first wife, and would be taken before the magistrates' court at Llanelli on the following day, before cautioning him. Greenwood merely replied 'All right' and then asked 'What was the actual verdict?' he was told that 'The jury unanimously found that your late wife died from arsenical poisoning, and that the poison was administered by you'. Greenwood simply said 'Oh dear'.

The police then took him to Llanelli police station, watched by his servants, where the charge against him was officially recorded and he was taken to the cells. Apparently, Greenwood 'looked pale and hung his head as if desirous of avoiding the observations or the attentions of the camera men, who had been haunting the village for several days'.[43] Superintendent Jones read the charge to him and cautioned him again, with Greenwood replying, 'I understand'.[44]

A crowd waiting outside the police station for his arrival there both hissed and booed him.[45] Later Greenwood claimed that the police warned him of the crowd's hostility but wrote 'there was not a voice raised either for or against me'.[46] Apparently Greenwood later recalled 'I was absolutely stunned, and for the moment felt helpless in the face of this blow when I heard the terrible text of the finding'.[47]

There was a formal appearance before the magistrates on the next day in which Haigh gave evidence of arrest. Greenwood was held over for another week as the police finalised their investigations. On 17th June he was incarcerated in the county prison. The prison, contained within Carmarthen castle which stands 20 metres above sea level, had been designed in 1789 by John Nash, with extensions in the 19th century. By 1920 it had only five years of its existence as a prison to run. He was visited on the Saturday by Ludford, his wife and two daughters. A crowd followed them from the railway station to the prison, but when Mrs. Greenwood and Greenwood's daughters came again on the Monday, the crowd was less interested.[48]

One important point that had been raised at the inquest was that the arsenic had been put into the wine that Mabel Greenwood had drank at lunch on 15th June. This was to be a key facet of the prosecution case. Whether it was taking a risk in placing the emphasis on this, and this alone, is another question; Dr. Willcox stated that the fatal poison was taken between 1.30pm and 6.30pm which would include the time of the wine being drunk, but he did not exclude the poison as having been taken later in a different medium.

Chapter Six

At the Magistrates' Court and After

Meanwhile, there were other further investigations, as Chief Inspector Haigh wrote 'with a view to obtaining some evidence to strengthen the case against the prisoner'. He and his sergeant spoke to many of the witnesses already interviewed by their Welsh colleagues who were 'extremely careful to make their own lack of initiative, or even neglect, to appear in as favourable a light as possible, with the result that points which would have told against the accused were either forgotten or so minimised as to render them of but little value.' Haigh added 'The whole case from the commencement of police action has undoubtedly been hampered by this feature, hence the importance of further strengthening evidence'.[1]

He went back to London on 17th June and had a meeting with the director of public prosecutions, returning to Wales on 22nd June. He investigated the purchases of wine for Rumsey House. The late Mrs. Greenwood had occasionally bought burgundy and port wine from Edwards' wine merchants in Llanelli. Unfortunately Hannah Williams, the former housemaid, could not identify the bottle labels. More importantly, whilst searching through these documents concerning wine purchases, he 'came across the delivery of a parcel of weedkiller on the 2nd of May 1919. He found that these had been taken to Kidwelly by train from a firm known as T. and H. based in Lincoln. Haigh wrote 'I recognised the importance of this discovery'.[2]

He then left Kidwelly and returned to London on 24th June, to confer with Pearce and Sims at the public prosecutor's office. He then went to Lincoln to trace the firm who supplied the weedkiller; Messrs. Tomlinson and Hayward Ltd., horticultural chemists. They explained they supplied such to Greenwood on an order from Messrs. Dobbie and Co., Edinburgh seedsmen. He found the weedkiller contained about 60% arsenic. The chemist who had compounded it was now working in Huddersfield so Haigh arranged for the police there to take a statement from the man, one Arthur Bell, whilst Haigh went to Edinburgh. There he found that the firm had a good reputation and they supplied him with the information he needed, and he interviewed the man who had dealt with Greenwood's order and found the papers showing Greenwood had bought Eureka weed killer. Returning to London he gave this information to the public prosecutor and then was back in Wales on 28th June.[3]

Following the finding of the arsenic and further statements 'it seems pretty certain that the woman died in consequence of arsenical poisoning and that the poison was administered by her husband, who within a few months of the death married a young woman named [Gwladys] Jones with whom he had been more than friendly during the lifetime of the deceased'.[4]

Before Greenwood could be put on trial, the prosecution had to present the case against him at the lower courts, often called, as they are in the newspapers and even the published trial transcript of the *Notable British Trials* case for this, 'Police Court proceedings'. This is a misnomer; they are not run by the police but by the amateur magistrates, or the justices of the peace (J.P.s), who deal with the vast majority of wrongdoers and usually hand out summary justice without a jury. In more serious cases it will be passed upwards and the verdict will be decided at the county assizes. These magistrates' courts are the stepping stone before the ultimate court of the assizes.

The magistrates here were Mr. Richard Harry Sampson, Mr. Daniel Ward (mayor of Llanelli), Dr. Owen Williams (1853-1924) of Burry Port (whom Dr. Griffiths had confided in about the cause of Mrs. Greenwood's death) and Mr. Frank Nevill (1851-1924), an engineer, of Llanelli. These men were J.P.s, who were used to dealing with the petty crimes prevalent in the district, such as animals straying, men getting drunk, vehicles without lights and parents failing to send their children to school.[5]

On Thursday 17th June, the day after the inquest, Greenwood appeared before the magistrates' court, at Llanelli town hall [1], which had been built in 1894 in the park, by a design of William Griffiths for the council, before two magistrates, Sampson and Nevill, but it was only to hear the formal charge and Haigh's describing his arrest of the previous day.

[1] Llanelli Court House.

A newspaper stated:

> He wore a grey suit, check breeches, brown boots and a puce tie, and was generally spick and span, although unshaven. He stood impassively with his hands clapped behind his back all the time he was in court, now and then directing his glance to the crowd which could clearly be seen outside the window.

This could have been because when he had been driven to court that morning it had been 'amid some booing'.[6] Hundreds of people had crowded the narrow thoroughfares near the police station, thinking that Greenwood would be taken from there to the town hall. Superintendent Jones told them that this would not be so and consequently they dispersed.[7]

Whilst in prison, Greenwood had his meals brought to him from a Carmarthen hotel. His wife visited him on 20th June, along with his eldest daughter, Irene and his solicitor, Ludford, who had taken the train to Carmarthen. A crowd assembled to watch them enter the prison.[8]

Greenwood was remanded until Friday 25th June and then, at Superintendent Jones' request, was remanded again until Thursday 1st July. It was only then that the proceedings began in earnest.[9]

At an early hour of the day a large crowd began to gather outside the town hall. This had been anticipated by the police who were there beforehand. Just after 8.00am, Greenwood, who had been brought by train from Carmarthen, passed through the main gates and was lodged in the cells beneath the court room. There was space in the latter for up to 50 journalists. The court room was spacious, and the gallery for the public soon filled up. Others early to arrive were the police officers associated with the case; the chief constable, Picton Phillips, Superintendent Jones, Haigh and Police Sergeants Lewis and Helby. Numerous solicitors were there, including Ludford, Mervyn Paton (1891-1966) from Llanelli whose firm held a watching brief for the Lincoln weedkiller company, Mr. Walter William Brodie (1864-1931), the magistrates' clerk and a solicitor by profession, and Seward Pearce, who would oversee the court proceedings as deputy public prosecutor.[10] Despite the drizzling rain outside, crowds had gathered, which was ascribed to 'The intense interest taken locally'.[11]

The session began at 10.30am. Pearce made the opening case for the prosecution, before calling on the necessary evidence to support the case he was making against the defendant. He outlined the main facts in a narrative that supported the case against Greenwood. He delineated Mrs. Greenwood's death, burial, exhumation and the discovery of arsenic in her corpse. The fatal dose had been given, he stated, on the afternoon of Sunday 15th June. Mrs. Greenwood had been the only one at lunch to drink red wine, and her husband had arsenic in his possession, ordered a month before his wife's death.[12] Following on from the coroner's conclusion at the inquest the prosecution saw this as categorically the medium for murder.

There was also evidence of motive, as Greenwood married his present wife only months after the death of his first. As to the evening of his first wife's death, though Greenwood went for the doctor at 6.30pm, thereafter he both delayed his further visits and gave the doctor misleadingly positive information about his wife's condition.

Pearce also referred to Hannah Williams' seeing Greenwood in the china cupboard prior to the lunch. Ludford clashed with Pearce over the intended inclusion of Greenwood's statement to Superintendent Jones (see pages 91-95) as it showed that Greenwood knew his wife was ill in the afternoon. It was allowed.[13]

It was now time for the witnesses to give the evidence. First was the undertaker and then Dr. Dick, the local police surgeon. The latter was asked as to the cleanliness of the jars into which he had placed the organs from Mrs. Greenwood's corpse and he was adamant that they were sterile. Police Sergeant Lewis told how these jars were given to Dr. Willcox.[14]

Dr. Griffiths was the next witness. He referred to the poor state of Mrs. Greenwood's health and what he had seen when he was called over by Greenwood on 15th June. He told of the two morphia pills, answering that these did not contain arsenic and would not be injurious to health. He was then asked what he now thought was the cause of death which brought about the following exchange:

> 'Arsenical poisoning.' [which was in contrast to his view at the time]
> 'Did the medicine you supplied in the six or seven weeks contain any arsenic?'
> 'None at all.'[15]
> 'And were they a family living on exceedingly happy terms?'
> 'Most happy terms.'

There was discussion about Mrs. Greenwood's health. The doctor stated that she had been in bad health and that he was not surprised to be called to see her on 15th June. Ludford asked if she had been poisoned by arsenic would the vomit that she was throwing up have been green? It would. He was then asked 'And there were no traces of colour of any kind?' to which the reply was 'None at all'.

He was asked about his visits and he stuck to there being none between 7.30pm and 10.00pm and none after the 10.00pm visit until the final one at 3.00am, despite what nurse Jones claimed. He did not remember making any other visits.[16]

He was then asked about the morphia pills and their effect on Mrs. Greenwood who had a bad heart. The doctor said that even if taken together, they would be safe, despite her medical condition. He had thought at the time that she was suffering from gastritis brought about by eating the gooseberry tart. He was asked about the symptoms of arsenic poisoning; pains in the abdomen, cramp, excessive thirst, and stated that none of these was apparent. Ludford was trying to make the doctor admit that this might not be a case of arsenic poisoning by saying 'Bearing in mind the small quantity of arsenic found in the body and Taylor's opinion, are now you still in doubt as to whether the death took place from arsenic or from the irritation she told you of, resulting from heart failure? Is that a difficult question?'. Dr. Griffiths afirmed that it was 'Very difficult'.[17]

The doctor then stood down for the next witness. Pearce then took Miss Phillips through her version of events on the evening of 15th June. She highlighted Greenwood's taking an hour to fetch the doctor from just over the road. Ludford then asked about relations between the Greenwoods, given her frequency of visiting in the previous decade 'And therefore you had ample opportunity upon what terms Mr. and Mrs. Greenwood were?'

She agreed that this was so. Ludford pressed her to state whether there were arguments but Miss Phillips was halting and hesitant in her replies, when she replied to the questions at all, as often she did not. She agreed that there were domestic disturbances, 'Mr. and Mrs. Greenwood had tiffs and brawls about women' was the most that Ludford could elicit from her. The discrepancies between the time that the doctor was present were also discussed.[18] Miss Phillips was clearly reticent about discussing her late best friend's innermost concerns in a public venue, despite Ludford's insistent questioning for her to do so.

Nurse Jones was next. Again she said that Greenwood took an hour to fetch the doctor between 9.00pm and 10.00pm, and that Dr. Griffiths returned at 1.00am. She was asked about the morphia pills and she replied that Greenwood gave them to his wife. She talked of attending two of the Greenwood children for their ailments. Ludford asked about relations between the Greenwoods and she replied, 'I always found Mr. and Mrs. Greenwood on very good terms'.[19]

Miss Griffiths, the doctor's sister, was then asked about the evening of 15th June and she recalled Greenwood coming over at 9.00pm, in a seemingly good temper, and then Miss Greenwood later visiting but that she went to bed at 10.00pm and could tell no more about her brother's visits, if any; until that of 3.00am. She agreed that Greenwood was usually in a cheerful mood. She answered questions about calls being made to him using the Griffiths' telephone.[20]

Hannah Williams was a crucial prosecution witness as the Greenwoods' former housemaid. She stated that she had poured out the wine for Mrs. Greenwood and put the bottle out again in the evening but next day it was nowhere to be found. The questioning continued:

> 'On the Sunday morning did you see Mr. Greenwood about?'
> 'Yes.'
> 'Where did you see him?'
> 'In the china pantry.'
> 'How long was he there?'
> 'About a quarter of an hour.'
> 'Have you ever seen him there before?'
> 'Not to my knowledge.'[21]

She said that all the family, servants included, had some of the gooseberry tart. Ludford tried to suggest that she might not have remembered all the details after so much time, but she said she did. Ludford suggested that the police had put these details into her head, with their frequent meetings with her in the previous months. He then suggested that it was usual for Greenwood to go to the china cupboard, where there was a sink, to wash his hands and that others might say so.

> 'I am going to suggest to you that you never at lunch on the Sunday in question, nor on any other day, poured wine for Mrs. Greenwood.'
> 'That was the only time I did it. I only waited on them on Sundays. Mrs. Greenwood asked me to do it.'

> 'If Miss Greenwood says you did not pour the wine, what would you say?'
> 'Well, I did. I am here to tell the truth.'

There were questions about Irene taking wine prior to that Sunday (the first time this suggestion had been aired in public) and whether it was burgundy or port wine that Mrs. Greenwood had drunk on that occasion, but Hannah stuck to Irene not drinking wine to her knowledge and that it was port that was then consumed by her mother. Ludford then questioned her about her alleged dismissal and her alleged drinking and Hannah said she was asked to leave by her aunt for farming work and that the only time she had drank when at work was when Greenwood gave her whisky.[22]

The vicar spoke next, to say how Greenwood made a suggestion to him about the possibility of his wife's having committed suicide. Gwyneth David, the second Mrs. Greenwood's former neighbour, told about the letter Greenwood had sent her about his first wife's illness. Then there was evidence of Greenwood's purchase of weedkiller because the garden was overgrown with weeds. That was the end of the first day in court.[23]

Greenwood was thus described in court in that day:

> [Greenwood was] a type of country sportsman rather than an astute lawyer. He listened with intent as the prosecution unfolded the case, but throughout he was cool and collected and during a drab stage in the proceedings he used a paper to make sketches; he was alert, when, with a rapier directness his solicitor submitted witnesses to a keen and stern cross examination'.[24]

After the formal hearing of that day, Greenwood revealed a rather unpleasant side to his character. After shaking hands with two of his Kidwelly friends, perhaps the doctor and the vicar, he went to the ante room. There he saw Miss Griffiths. He spoke sharply to her, a former friend, 'You ought to be in quod [prison] for giving such evidence'. Apparently 'Miss Griffiths was very perturbed, and hysterically cried to the police 'Cannot you take care of that man without allowing him to insult me in this fashion?'.[25]

Greenwood was the subject of interest for the press and it was stated that at Llanelli railway station:

> ... there were several press photographers there to meet him. Their efforts at getting a good snap of the prisoner, were, however, fruitless, because one of the two warders stepped between him and the cameras, and Greenwood made good use of the screen. When he was seated in the safety of the motor car in waiting outside the station, Greenwood laughed without restraint of these photographers, who were good sports enough to acknowledge their defeat.

Apart from the photographers at the station awaiting his arrival from Carmarthen there was also a small group of women.[26]

Local interest in the case was still high, 'The queue of waiting people outside the court this morning was greater than ever, and when the building was opened there was an exciting rush for seats'. Inside, Greenwood was seated behind Ludford and 'has frequently given him whispered instructions as to the evidence, and when not so occupied would occupy himself in drawing caricatures of the witnesses and sketches. He was as bright and as alert as usual when he was ushered into his place by two policemen this morning, despite his early morning journey from Carmarthenshire'.[27] Greenwood had arrived at the court at 7.30am and so had two and a half hours to wait for the hearing to begin. He spent some of it reading the account of the hearing in the edition of *The Western Mail*.[28]

The local newspaper also described the situation in court after proceedings began at 10.00am:

> The history of the case was continued in an atmosphere of tension, and the punctuated murmurings from the back of the court brought rebukes from the chairman. Outside the town hall, the crowd, increasing in numbers as the hours passed, took the cordon of police by surprise. The main gates were rushed and many gained admittance. The proceedings, which

> were not without sidelights of humour – the cook's comments were a source of amusement to the prisoner.[29]

Evidence for the prosecution was continued on Friday 2nd July. The cook, Margaret Morris, 'a small frail figure, she gave her evidence very quietly' and described the lunch on 15th June and declared that none of the others who ate it had any ill effects from having done so. She was asked about how relations were between the family and about Mrs. Greenwood's health; she said that the former were good but her late mistress' health was not. It was asked of her if Irene and Miss Bowater drank wine and she said they did; it was burgundy. She was asked about Hannah's drinking and her notice to quit, but she had never seen her under the influence but thought she was told to leave and did so a week after Mrs. Greenwood's death.[30]

> 'Have you ever seen Mr. Greenwood going into the china pantry for that purpose [hand washing]?'
> 'Yes, he was very often washing his hands there. There was no other place downstairs for the purpose.'
> 'Have you seen him go there hundreds of times?'
> 'Hundreds of times and more.'

This caused 'laughter, in which the prisoner joined in'.

The Greenwood's other servant, Lily Powell, 'a trim figure, neatly dressed' stated that she had eaten of the same lunch but had not been involved in making or serving it. She added that Mrs. Greenwood, Irene and Miss Bowater sometimes drank burgundy but not port and it would come from a decanter not a bottle. She had also seen Greenwood in the china cupboard often on other occasions.[31]

Annie Groves, Greenwood's office caretaker, stated that Gwladys Jones and Greenwood often met but, in contrast to previous statements, that she had never seen anything untoward between them, but admitted that she had lied as to her boss' whereabouts to Mrs. Greenwood on the Wednesday before her death. She referred to a partly burnt letter received by Greenwood on the day of his wife's death in which the words 'It will be nice when I am your wife' had been written by Gwladys Jones, but Ludford undertook to question the day when this letter was received; it might have been a month later, at the same time that Greenwood bought a ring for his fiancee.[32]

Mary Morris, whose mother worked in the telephone exchange, recalled telephone messages between Greenwood and Gwladys Jones, which referred to a future holiday and buying chocolates for Easter, in the period of March to June 1919. James McPhee, employed by the Edinburgh horticulturalist firm, stated that Greenwood had asked about buying seeds and weedkiller in February 1919. There were other witnesses to testify about Greenwood purchasing weedkiller; the type he bought in 1919 was red and which colour could not be altered. It had been delivered to Greenwood on 2nd May 1919.[33]

Evidence was then given of the empty bottles of burgundy, port and others taken from Rumsey House in May 1919 and of Greenwood's buying a ring in July of that year. William Gould had worked in the house's garden in May 1919 and said he had never seen or used any weedkiller there. Benjamin Williams had done odd jobs in the garden and might know more, he said. The court was then adjourned for the day.[34] It was noted by a journalist that Greenwood made frequent notes in pencil and occasionally consulted with Ludford.[35]

Although this was not recounted in the account of the hearing as appeared in Duke's transcript, a newspaper reported this exchange, about Greenwood:

> The intuitive sagacity of the lawyer was manifest … a tall, commanding personality, he challenged the correctness of the book containing his statement to Superintendent Jones, 'I want to see the book' [and then in being shown it] 'This is not the book'.[36]

This was discussed later in the trial.

The final day of the hearing was on Saturday 3rd July. A reporter noted that Greenwood was 'well groomed, looked a trifle paler, but seemed quite at ease' and asked for sheets of paper.[37] Thomas Evans, a saddler in Kidwelly, recalled Greenwood and Gwladys Jones in his shop in December 1918 and he bought her a dressing case for £15.

Edward Roberts stated taking Greenwood, Llewellyn and Gwladys Jones in his motor car to Kidwelly in May 1919.[38]

There was then a lengthy examination and cross examination of the two scientific witnesses; Webster, the analyst, and Dr. Willcox. After giving an account of the examination, Webster was asked about the taste of the arsenic solution when put into wine, and then the same question as regards tea. There would be no taste, he said. What of the difference in colour to the drinks? There would be a slight difference in tea but hardly any in the wine and these would not be noticeable to most unless they were scrutinised and compared with one another.[39]

Ludford asked for more details about the examination that Webster had undertaken and stressed that accuracy was of crucial importance in the case. He thought that a second opinion should have been available.[40]

The principal scientific witness was Dr. Willcox. He was asked about organic disease and heart problems, to which he stated that Mrs. Greenwood suffered from neither. He was asked about the cause of death: arsenic. Its effects would take an hour on an empty stomach; longer if with a meal and longer if taken in solid state. A minimum fatal dose would be two grains and the distribution of the arsenic suggested that it had been taken several hours before death and by mouth. That she suffered from nausea, vomiting and diarrhoea was additional evidence of arsenic poisoning.[41]

There was some discussion about weedkiller and arsenic, and Dr. Willcox agreed with the previous witness. Ludford tried to suggest that heart problems were a realistic alternative cause of death and evidenced the fainting that the deceased had been known to suffer from. He also suggested that arsenic from weedkiller would leave a burning sensation. There were then questions as to when the arsenic was taken and Dr. Willcox could not commit himself to be definite that it had occurred at lunchtime, only that it was in the afternoon of the Sunday. There was also questioning as to whether Mrs. Greenwood could have been walking around the garden after having been poisoned at lunchtime. Dr. Willcox seemed to think this would not have been possible. However, some signs of recovery were possible. Reference was made to Dr. Spilsbury's expert testimony in a similar matter in the 1912 Seddon case.[42]

Ludford asked about the symptoms of arsenic poisoning. Were they all present in this case? There was no cramp in the legs or burning stomach sensations. What of excessive thirst which was not experienced by Mrs. Greenwood. This would not necessarily be the case, the doctor stated. Again Ludford cited Dr. Spilsbury as differing from him on this matter. Dr. Willcox thought that if the deceased had lived longer or had been given a bigger dose then that symptom would have been apparent. 'I do not consider that a very large dose was taken on this occasion'.[43]

Ludford then laid great stress as to the amount of arsenic found and whether this was the cause of death. He cited medical textbooks. Dr. Willcox recalled that the patient's symptoms must also be taken into account as to whether or not she died of arsenic poisoning. Pearce re-examined the witness to recall that someone physically weak would need a smaller dose than a completely healthy human. He also cited Greenwood's statement about his wife being unwell in the afternoon as evidence of arsenic poisoning at lunchtime. He closed with the question 'Taking into consideration all the knowledge you have acquired in this case, have you any doubt that the cause of death was arsenical poisoning?'[44] The reply was a simple 'No'.

The summing up by the chairman was brief. He read the charge out to Greenwood and asked him if he had anything to say. He 'in a voice that bore a tremor of agitation, and with face slightly flushed' said 'I am not guilty of this charge and I reserve my defence'.

Ludford did not address the Bench and so Greenwood was committed for trial at the next Carmarthen assizes without further ado. Ludford was then congratulated by Dr. Willcox for asking so many intelligent questions during the presentation of the medical evidence. [45] At the apparent end of the proceedings, one of the prison officers tapped Greenwood on the shoulder and beckoned him to follow. They left the court, but he was recalled by Superintendent Jones, 'Bring the prisoner back'. He did so and stayed until the witnesses had been bound over to appear at the assize and other formalities were completed.[46]

A crowd waited for the train at Llanelli which would take Greenwood to Carmarthen. He was escorted, as always, by two prison officers. That morning he had asked for a copy of *The Western Mail* and appeared 'keenly interested in the reproduction of his own sketch'. He wore the same navy blue lounge suit that he had worn on the previous day. In court 'He seemed somewhat paler than on the previous day. Otherwise he appeared quite sprightly and followed the evidence closely'. On his leaving, 'There was a considerable amount of booing on the part of the great crowd which had assembled to witness his departure' on the 4.10pm train.[47] He confidently said 'I shall be back in the office before long'.[48]

The train stopped at Kidwelly on its way back to Carmarthen. Greenwood's elder son, Ivor and his younger daughter, Eileen, were there, waiting for their father. The prison officers allowed Greenwood to go to the window and there he leant out and talked to his children for a few minutes. 'As the train moved away father and children waved their hands in a farewell'. It was 'an affecting scene' wrote the journalist.[49]

Haigh made his report on 5th July. He commented on the recent hearings, that 'it was perfectly apparent that the important witnesses (Dr. and Miss Griffiths and nurse Jones) were on the defensive others were decidedly actuated by feelings favourable to the prisoner'. He added that Ludford 'severely cross examined most of the witnesses including the analyst, Mr. Webster and Dr. Willcox'.[50]

He additionally noted that many of the witnesses had been evasive. He noted his concern over 'the easy manner in which the weedkiller can be acquired, and I suggest that some steps should be taken to bring to notice the provisions of the Poison and Pharmacy acts, which in the case of Messrs. Tomlinson and Hayward Ltd. have been, and in very many instances, entirely ignored'.[51]

He also noted the memorandum[52] from the public prosecutor, stated in chapter four:

> This condition, I am sure, operates in this case against us. And in this way. I was offered an opportunity to interview the accused, and I know now from a conversation with me by the solicitor Mr. Ludford, that Greenwood would have made a definite statement denying emphatically that he had ever purchased arsenic in any form, which statement would have been so palpably untrue that his conviction would have been almost certain.

Criticism has been made of the Welsh police by those in London. In turn, Superintendent Jones was critical of the Scotland Yard men when he made a report to the county police committee. He said that his officers 'had undoubted advantages over the strange detectives, however skilled'. He stated, though, that he appreciated their services.[53]

Greenwood returned to prison and later wrote at length about his time there. He was visited daily by his family but recollected, in retrospect, 'I can see the picture now of my wife and my children endeavouring from the other side of those terrible iron bars, to hold conversation with me while two warders were within earshot. Every word of endearment, every word of encouragement spoken to me was in a sense public since it was not private'. Newspapers chronicled his visits by family and Ludford, even his visits to the chapel.[54]

Greenwood claimed that his time in prison was even worse because of his usual lifestyle:

> I have led a life in the open. I have hunted with the pack. I have been fond and a constant user of the gun from boyhood, and one day I find myself confined to a prison cell with but an hour and a half for exercise on week-days and curtailed above all days, on the Sunday to an hour. Even this was not one good hour in the open air, but an hour divided between the fore and the afternoon.[55]

He had other complaints about his incarceration:

> Days became months and months years. I had but one thing to look forward to, and that was the visits of my family ... Then for the wretched day and the awful night. My only respite was to read, and all the sporting magazines and illustrated journals dealing with the healthy life in the open that I was now deprived of I devoured. I am not complaining of my keepers, who were gentlemen, but of the system ... I received no favours, but I suffered not any added harshness ...[56]

At least he was able to have food from the outside brought into him. 'I dare not give thought to the condition of the wretch in my position who possessed not the means that are so necessary these days to provide him with food and had to suffer the diet of the prison'.

Apart from this small consolation it was grim:

> Through the long summer months I was in close confinement in Carmarthen Castle, shut off from the beauties of the outside world.
>
> Remarkable though it may appear, wet days brought with them a strange relief. On these days exercise was confined to the precincts of the inner building. Along these corridors with their unsavoury histories, we used to parade.
>
> From the uppermost one, through a small window, a glimpse that was maddening of the wondrous vernol beauty of Carmarthenshire's wooded slopes could be had. As a son of the open, I sometimes felt that I could have jumped through that window so that I might embrace the intoxicating freshness of the scene.
>
> I was allowed to wear my own clothes, with certain restrictions. All clothes had to be put outside the cell at night. I was not allowed to retain my braces. All this was part of the prison regulations devised in order that those within those gloomy walls should not defeat the ends of justice.
>
> I had nothing in my pockets. The very dishes from which I took my food were enamel, the plates and dishes on which my wife brought my food from home being retained at the gates. Neither knife nor fork was permitted to me. I ate my food with a spoon of formidable dimensions.
>
> During the first week of this durance I could not read. The prison library had neither newness or variety and its contents offered but few attractions. My thoughts were in monotonous reverie.

He was even denied his pipe. He made an appeal to the Home Secretary though the Reverend Towys Jones (1858-1925), Liberal M.P. for Llanelli in 1918-1922, but in August learnt that there was no way that a relaxation in that rule could be made in his case. 'Everything tends to intensify the agony of those either incarcerated or awaiting as in my case, to prove their innocence. Oh the iniquity of it all'. He wondered if he was losing his reason by trying to work out the evidence that the prosecution would use against him.[57]

> Through a wretched little window (as compared with those of my home) the light of day and the air I had to breathe were permitted to enter my cell. At night, through a small pane, artificial light streamed into my cell, until dimmed by the light of day. I knew solitude, but not privacy.
>
> There were official ears even for conversation with my counsel. These restrictions are probably very necessary in the case of the guilty, but terrible for the innocent to endure.
>
> A clanging bell aroused me each morning at half past six. Breakfast of porridge without milk, bread and margarine and tea was at 7.20am. An hour later we were paraded for chapel, for service of half an hour's duration.
>
> Followed the governor's round of the prison and then an hour's parade in the yard. So small was the course round which we were marched that we had to be reversed so as to prevent dizziness.
>
> Dinner was at 12.30pm, but of prison fare I cannot speak because I had the good fortune not to have to eat prison food. At 1.30pm we went out for half an hour's exercise in the yard, and at three o'clock came the only high point of the day.
>
> It was at this hour that my wife paid her daily visit. We were allowed to converse for a quarter of an hour. Again we were conscious of official ears.
>
> 'Tea' consisting of bread, butter and cocoa was served at 4.30pm, and then, until the prison curfew tolled at eight, I was left to my silent meditations.
>
> Sunday was the worst day of the week, for them there were not even visits from the outer world to break the terrible silence within those grey walls.
>
> Had it not been for the unremitting care of my wife, I could never have borne the physical and mental strain which sometimes even the promptings of hope failed to relieve.

> Every day my wife visited the prison, bringing me dainties which she had cooked at home, she had often to run the gauntlet of curious and even hostile onlookers of her own sex in the streets of Carmarthen.

Women and girls criticised her dress, her appearance, her looks and her manner 'as though she were something not of her kind'. Once she was late to the prison, but when she met Greenwood 'it was to greet me with her usual cheerfulness and courage'.[58]

Greenwood did not comment about his fellow prisoners, but he would have had to have mixed with them, even if only for a limited degree. He would have found little in common with them. Some of his fellow prisoners were labourers, tin plate workers, a hawker and three soldiers. Some of these men had previous criminal records and all were in gaol for theft or robbery with violence. Socially speaking, he was even more of an outcast.[59]

In 1922 he wrote of his ordeal in retrospect:

> To be arrested, safely caged up, to become the centre of universal comment, to know that one's business, built up with such care, is daily falling to ruins, to be cut off from the world of home and friends … is sufficiently agonising.[60]

Meanwhile, on 21st July, Police Sergeants Helby and Lewis went to Rumsey House and made 'a thorough search of the house, the stables and outhouses adjacent, with a view to discovering anything of an incriminating nature'. Helby found three bottles of colourless liquid; these turned out to be photographic mixtures. A spirit flask was found in the cupboard in the dining room, possibly the one Greenwood had drunk from on the 15th June. In Greenwood's bedroom were found three small bottles marked 'POISON'; these were lineaments. Letters and bills were found, but nothing relevant to the case. Mrs. Greenwood was present throughout the search. One item found was a receipt for a fur coat that had been bought for her from a Birmingham furrier prior to the marriage, but she told him it had been bought with her own money.[61]

One of the last witnesses to be interviewed was Benjamin Williams, and this was on 10th August. Williams said that he helped to sprinkle weed killer on the garden path in 1919. Prior to this it would be mixed in large tins, each holding four gallons. He had never seen Greenwood use such, however. Nor had he seen anyone else to do so. He could not recall whether it had been in liquid form or powder before dilution. He did not recall seeing weedkiller tins there, whether full or empty. He had mixed it near to the stable and poured out water into it many times.[62]

There was discussion as to where the trial was to take place and one suggestion that it was to be at the Old Bailey in London. This was because it was feared that there might be bias against him if it was held in Wales, as seen at the inquest hearings and in the 'demonstrations inside and outside the courts'. If it was in Wales then a Welsh barrister would have the prosecution brief.[63] Haigh thought that this would be the case, too, writing on 5th July, 'In the district of Carmarthenshire this case has aroused intense feeling, mostly against the accused, and I understand that in all probability steps will be taken to transfer the trial to London'.[64] This was almost Haigh's last act as a serving policeman as he retired on 12th July 1920, though his involvement in this case was not entirely at an end, as we shall see in the next chapter. However, no such application for trial elsewhere was made.[65]

Initially it was thought that Sir Gordon Hewart (1870-1943), the Attorney General in 1919-1922 and a Liberal M.P. for Leicester, would be the principal barrister for the prosecution.[66] He would be supported by Wilfrid Lewis and Sir Edward Marley Samson, but by early October, his name was dropped and the two aforesaid Welsh barristers would deliver the case for the Crown.[67] Meanwhile Ludford, as soon as the magistrates' court proceedings were over, made overtures to Sir Edward Marshall Hall.[68]

Leading the case for the Crown, then, was Sir Edward Marlay Samson C.B.E. (1869-1949), a K.C. since 1919 **[2]**. He was a judge of the South Wales circuit and was also a justice of the peace and a deputy lord lieutenant in Wales. From 1918 he had also been recorder of Swansea and Lord Lieutenant of Carmarthenshire. He was also organiser of the Welsh National Fund for ex-servicemen and had worked for the Ministry of Pensions.[69] He was aided by Mr. Wilfrid

Hubert Poyser Lewis (1881-1950), who had been called to the Bar in 1908 and served as a captain in the Glamorganshire Yeomanry in the Great War. He had chambers in the Temple (London) and in Cardiff and was a familiar figure in the South Wales circuit and the Cardiff and Swansea sessions. He was grandson of the bishop of Llandaff and was married to a daughter of Lord Justice Bankes.[70] The prosecution case, they decided, 'It is not thought the financial aspect has any bearing upon the crime is alleged ... but that motive is to be found in his attachment to Miss [Gwladys] Jones during his wife's lifetime'.[71]

[2] Sir Edward Samson.

The police were concerned about the forthcoming trial succeeding against the defendant for two reasons. Lewis thought that the defence might be one of suicide.[72] His superiors were concerned about the evidence that Irene might bring for the defence and that they had been unable to take a statement from her.[73]

[3] Edward Marshall Hall.

Ludford was successful in his aim in his choice of barrister. Sir Edward Marshall Hall (1858-1927), K.C., was the principal barrister for the defence **[3]**. His first prominent success was to reduce the charge of murder to one of manslaughter in the case of Marie Hermann in 1894. He had many notable triumphs for the defence, including of men who were probably guilty, such as Robert Wood in the 'Camden Town Murder' of 1907 and Ronald Light in the 'Green Bicycle Case' of 1919. Yet despite his great reputation as defence counsel, he had his failures too, as with poisoner Frederick Seddon in 1912 and serial killer 'Brides in the Bath' murderer George Joseph Smith in 1915. His first murder case of 1920 had also been a failure for the defence. His father had been a doctor and his son was medically literate, which assisted him in his cases. He was known to use moral blackmail in his defence of clients. Yet his reputation stood high.[74] Assisting him was Mr. Trevor Howard Hunter (1877-1960).

His father was a Welsh magistrate and he himself had been admitted as a solicitor in 1899 and had been a barrister at the Middle Temple since 1911, joining the South Wales and Chester circuit. He had served as a second lieutenant in the third battalion of the Royal Welsh Fusiliers in the recent war, though on home service, in 1917.[75]

Ludford went to London to consult Marshall Hall.[76] On 12th October, Marshall Hall and Ludford visited Greenwood in Carmarthen for a lengthy consultation.[77] However, Greenwood later wrote, 'I was racked with anxiety as to how the ways and means of my trial could be found'.[78]

William Cooper Hobbs (1865-1945), once a solicitor's clerk and accountant, later alleged that he played a key part in the defence case. He was later gaoled for blackmail, so perhaps his comments should be dealt with cautiously. In 1934 he claimed in print that Marshall Hall approached him and said 'The man is innocent – but how to prove it? There must be some spot somewhere where we can begin to demolish their case. If I could only find it. Now you think it over. Where is the weak spot in the prosecution'. Cooper read through the case notes and he thought that the morphia pills were a possible source of Mrs. Greenwood's death and therefore it could be successfully suggested that Greenwood was not guilty. Marshall Hall was told of this, 'It would shake the prosecution. But there is the analysis'. Cooper went to Kidwelly and investigated, telling the barrister, 'We're on the right track'. He then introduced the barrister to a Dr. Toogood and Cooper claimed that he 'knows more about poisoning than any man', a somewhat dubious proposition to say the least.[79]

Because of his lack of ready money for legal costs, Greenwood put Rumsey House up for sale, probably because he needed to raise money for his defence. It would not be easy or quick to sell. The mayor and corporation of Kidwelly entered into negotiation for its purchase.[80] He was said to be in good health and had daily visits, each lasting the allotted 15 minutes, with his wife, there. She also brought him changes of clothes at regular intervals. He also received a copy of the *Western Mail* every morning from a nearby newsagents.[81]

The leading figures for the prosecution also had conferences before the trial. Sir Edward Samson and Wilfrid Lewis met Dr. Willcox, firstly at No. 3 Paper Buildings, the Temple in London on

21st October and then again at Carmarthen on the day before the trial began.[82] Picton Phillips contacted Pearce on 20th October to note his concern about the defence calling Irene as a witness and he suggested the poison 'might well have been put in the medicine' and he would investigate this.[83] The trial was fixed for 30th October.[84] There would be no female jurors. Despite recent changes in legislation to allow women on juries, the earlier list of jurors was to be retained to the year's end.[85]

Just before Marshall Hall went from London to Carmarthen, he visited his favourite silversmith. The man, knowing what Marshall Hall was about to do, remarked, 'I'm surprised at you, Sir Edward, for defending that blackguard Greenwood. You must see he's guilty yourself. However, I suppose it's your job'. Marshall Hall replied 'Guilty, indeed. The man's innocent, and I'll get him off – you'll see'.

Unconvinced the silversmith showed the barrister an 18th century silver tankard saying 'Very well, whether you get him off or not, if you convince me that man's innocent, I'll make you a present of this'.[86]

Marshall Hall, Dr. Willcox and Samson all stayed in the same hotel, The Ivy Bush, Spilman Street, in Carmarthen. The former confided in his confidential clerk, Ernest Harvey, 'I cannot make up my mind about calling Greenwood [as a witness in his own defence]. I am afraid he will make a bad witness, and everything will turn on the evidence of his daughter and the cross examination of Webster and Willcox'.[87]

Chapter Seven

The Case for the Prosecution

The trial took place at the Carmarthen guildhall, as part of the bi-annual assizes for the Carmarthen circuit. The guildhall had been built between 1767 and 1777 from a design by Sir Robert Taylor in a neo-Classical style and extended since. From 1906 there had been a war memorial outside to commemorate local men killed in the second Anglo Boer war, a war in which Greenwood's elder brother had fought.

[1] Judge Shearman.

The trial was billed as being of national interest, with a Welsh newspaper stating, 'No trial since the Crippen case [of ten years earlier] has stirred interest in London more than that of Harold Greenwood at Carmarthen. Every evening newspaper devotes pages to the first day's proceedings and one of them has a number of photographs developed in an aeroplane cabin on the way to Carmarthen'. The case was discussed in clubs and even the House of Commons.[1]

The judge was Mr. Justice Sir Montague Shearman (1857-1930), who was also a co-founder of the Amateur Athletics Association [1]. He had been called to the Bar in 1881 and became a K.C. in 1903. He was appointed as a judge to the court of King's Bench in 1914. One of the first cases he oversaw was that of Nicolaus Ahlers, for assisting the flight of Germans from Britain in August 1914. He was found guilty but the case was quashed in appeal. He was accused of misdirection in the case of Dr. Bateman shortly afterwards.[2]

The trial was major national news for a fortnight. As Duke wrote in 1930:

> Exactly a decade ago, Carmarthen, a small township in south Wales, was the spot upon which the attention of the entire British Isles was focussed throughout one breathless week. Harold Greenwood's trial at Carmarthen assizes for he alleged poisoning of his first wife, the probing into the supposed taking of a single life just after the conclusion of four years' wholesale murder, distracted the public attention from anything else of moment or importance.[3]

It should be recalled that there was much of moment occurring in the world at this time to distract the average news reader. Despite the end of the First World War in 1918 there was little sign of a new dawn of universal peace and security. The new Bolshevik regime in Russia was waging war against Poland and its own people and was progressing towards dominion in the former Russian empire. Turkish atrocities against the Armenian people led to appeals for help. Closer to home there was violence in Ireland as nationalist terror was met by counter terror on behalf of the state. Starvation and misery lurked in parts of the defeated lands in Europe. Yet perhaps all this was deemed too far away and too impersonal that it was difficult for many to relate to; individual domestic drama was something they could relate to, however.

Public interest was high, 'the town tonight is in a state of great excitement in consequence. The movements of all the persons concerned in the case are watched with unstinting interest. Little else than that will be placed before the jury has any place in conversation. Throughout the day large crowds of people have waited in the neighbourhood of the guildhall, but nothing has happened to satisfy their curiosity'.[4] However, another journalist thought that the journalists were more interested in the trial than the public and that the latter were more interested in observing the activities of pressmen and photographers.[5]

One reason for such an interest was that this case was literally a matter of life and death. Capital punishment by hanging was the penalty for a defendant found guilty of murder. This did not mean that everyone found guilty would be executed. Cases after the trial could be heard by the court of criminal appeal. There could also be substitution of hanging with imprisonment. Yet the possibility that Greenwood would hang three weeks after the verdict did exist.

[2] Carmarthen Guildhall.

The bi-annual Carmarthenshire assize was dealing with ten serious criminal cases. These included three murders and one manslaughter, but the Greenwood case was the one that was predominant. On the last day of October, a Sunday, the judge, along with the county officialdom, such as Mr. H. J. Read, the High Sheriff, William Brodie, clerk of the court, along with Andrew Fuller Mills, the Mayor of Carmarthen and Henry Brunel White (1853-1942), a solicitor employed as the Town Clerk, attended a civic service at St. Peter's church, as was customary prior to the assizes, on Sunday 31st October. The first day of the assize was Monday 1st November.[6]

The trial began on Tuesday 2nd November 1920. Greenwood was brought to Carmarthen guildhall [2] from the prison (which was not very far away) in a closed carriage drawn by two horses. He was sat therein between two prison officers and the coach was escorted by two mounted policemen. He was out of sight of the crowd and on arrival the carriage went to the Hall Street entrance, and there was then only six feet of space to traverse before reaching the court house. He arrived prior to the legal dignitaries, the judge entering to the customary fanfare of trumpets.[7] Another journalist noted 'Greenwood's demeanour, as he sat in the dock, was that of a cool, clear headed man, active in mind and body'.[8]

A newspaper described the scene on the first day of the trial:

> Picture a finely proportioned hall, with a domed ceiling, decorated in green and white, walls panelled in light cork, with seats and dock to match, huge windows looking out onto a square, with a statue in the foreground, the bright sun streaming in, and you have the setting, as Harold Greenwood, stepped into the dock at the Carmarthen assizes, to take his trial for his life. Well groomed, and apparently in excellent health, he looked all over the country lawyer, and emphasised this by carrying in his hand a sheaf of blue and white foolscap paper. He faced the court calmly, even confidently. Directly in front of him sat the judge in a high backed chair upholstered in red, and over his head, a very fine picture of General Picton, who died so gloriously on the battlefield of Waterloo, and who was a native of Carmarthen – and on either side of the picture the royal arms and those of the county blazoned in the heraldic

colours. Slowly the names of the jurors are called. In a steady voice Greenwood challenges three of them and they are rejected The panel is quickly formed and sworn to 'well and truly try' and then Sir Marlay Samson rises to outline the case.[9] Greenwood later wrote dismissively of the court room, 'the still more vilely ventilated and poky assize court in Carmarthen Town'.[10]

[3] Jurymen walk to Carmarthen Guildhall.

The jury [3] was all male (the first female jurors appeared at a murder case in Buckinghamshire in 1921). Their foreman was Mr. E. Willis Jones, a chemical manufacturer of Lanelli. There were five farmers, and another two men employed in allied businesses. Then there was a tailor, a grocer, a publican, and a retired bank manager. Three were from Ammanford and the others from other villages in the county. None were, naturally, from Kidwelly.[11] During the time not spent in the courtroom, the men were kept together and away from anyone else in order that they might not be influenced by those outside the courtroom.

'A feature of the proceeding outside the court has been the way in which the jurymen have been marshalled and marched to and from the court in double with a policeman before and behind them. Special arrangements have been made to entertain them during the week end. The weather keeps bracing and fine, and the programme includes a long motor trip in the country tomorrow.'[12]

The first day of the trial began with the formal indictment being read out; to which Greenwood answered 'Not Guilty'. After that pronouncement 'Greenwood sat in the dock with an absolutely nonchalant air. He was as impassive as a statue'.[13] Then Samson had all the witnesses save Dr. Willcox and Webster, being removed from the court until they were called to give evidence. The judge agreed and so this was done. In retrospect, Greenwood wrote, 'I took my place in the dock before a battery of curious eyes'.[14]

Samson began with the opening speech for the prosecution. He stated that Mrs. Greenwood had died at 3.15am on 16th June 1919 and that Greenwood had been arrested at 3.30pm on 16th June 1920. He then pointed out that 'The crime of administering poison is almost always a crime done in secret and the evidence in regard to it is as a rule indirect evidence'. Rather it is the circumstantial evidence of what happened at the time of her death and afterwards that he would use to show that Greenwood was guilty.[15]

As ever, he asked them to dismiss anything they had heard outside the court room and consider only the evidence they would hear within it. They had to decide if Mrs. Greenwood was killed by arsenic and if so was it an accident or deliberate? And if it was the latter, did Greenwood do it? The jury must consider both his opportunity and his motive and what was his conduct before, during and after his wife's death. He briefly described the household and noted that Mrs. Greenwood was unwell, being treated by Dr. Griffiths.[16]

Then, he described the events of Sunday 15th June, referring to the housemaid Hannah William's recalling that Mrs. Greenwood drank wine, Greenwood drank whisky and the children drank water. Later the wine bottle disappeared. Samson declared that Greenwood had the opportunity of poisoning the wine prior to the lunch. That afternoon, she began to suffer from diarrhoea and that is a symptom of arsenic poisoning. She had very little afternoon tea and by 6.00pm was increasingly ill. She was given brandy by her husband and was then sick; which are signs of being poisoned by arsenic.[17]

Dr. Griffiths was summoned but Greenwood did not tell him that his wife had had diarrhoea. The two men whiled away an hour playing clock golf in the garden and Samson suggested that this was a way of preventing medicine from being brought to his wife. Vomiting and stomach pains continued for Mrs. Greenwood; further symptoms of arsenic poisoning. Greenwood's failing to summon the doctor between 7.30pm and 10pm and then his delays in fetching him after 10.00pm were highlighted. Samson concluded 'as a result of Greenwood's action there was an obstruction to Mrs. Greenwood's receiving medical aid with the speed which she should have had it'.[18]

Samson was fair to point out that there were disagreements over times and with what Dr. Griffiths knew of Mrs. Greenwood's symptoms. Throughout, Samson observed that Greenwood played down to the doctor the seriousness of his wife's condition. There was also digression on the doctor's later visits to Mrs. Greenwood. As to the murder, Samson summed up the evidence that Greenwood had the opportunity to do so and then deliberately obstructed medical aid.[19]

The crux of the case was summarised thus:

> There will be evidence suggesting that poison had been put in the wine; there is the disappearance after supper of the bottle of wine; there is the evidence of the first symptoms of diarrhoea and the first symptoms of arsenical poisoning; there is the brandy given to her by Greenwood; and there is also the remarkable statement he made to Miss Griffiths, and I suggest there was deliberate obstruction against medical aid being given to the dying woman at the earliest possible moment.[20]

Motive was then discussed. Samson pointed out that the friendship between Greenwood and Gwladys Jones (now the second Mrs. Greenwood), dated back to at least 1918. There had been quarrels between the Greenwoods over his friendships with other women. He pointed out Greenwood's relations with Miss Griffiths, the doctor's sister. Finally, he said 'He had formed an intimacy with a much younger woman ... Within three months [of his wife's death] he had married Miss Gladys Jones'.[21]

Then there was the matter of arsenic in his wife's body as proved beyond doubt. He told how Greenwood had purchased arsenic rich weedkiller in 1917 and 1919 and so 'The Crown alleges that that was the form of arsenic used by the prisoner'.[22]

He concluded with reading the statement that Greenwood had made to Superintendent Jones on 24th October on the events of 15th to 16th June 1919. This has been related on pages 91-95. Samson regarded it was 'inaccurate as to many details'. For example, he had suggested that his wife had drunk whisky not wine at the Sunday lunch. Greenwood had given himself a far more proactive role in summoning medical aid which was contradicted by other witnesses. He had suggested heart failure as the cause of death and then mentioned morphia pills as being crucial and suggested his wife might have committed suicide. Finally, he told the jury that they must listen to the evidence and do their duty.[23]

Ex-Chief Inspector Haigh was the first witness to be called and Samson's junior, Wilfrid Lewis, examined him. He was asked about the details of Greenwood's detention and arrest by the police on the second day of the inquest. The vicar was next, recounting his conversations with Greenwood in 1919 and 1920; in the former, Greenwood stating that his wife died from heart failure and in the second, at the exhumation, that perhaps she committed suicide. He agreed that she was very much beloved by her family and others.[24]

Mrs. Sarah Edwards, of the Phoenix Stores in Kidwelly and a wine dealer, was the next witness and again Lewis examined her. The Greenwoods bought wine from them and on 14th June a bottle of burgundy had been purchased by Mrs. Greenwood. Marshall Hall elicited from her that a bottle of burgundy and one of port could not be confused, that Mr. Bowen was the previous owner of Rumsey House and that there were many bottles in the Greenwoods' summerhouse.[25]

Thomas Foy, the manager of the local cinema, was next and he was asked by Marshall Hall that if Greenwood and his daughter had said that he was at Rumsey House on the 8th June, would he still say it was a week later and he said he would. On being asked when Greenwood was with him in the garage on the 15th, he thought it was between 11.00am to 11.30am and about 12.00pm to 12.30pm. Miss Phillips was the next witness and Samson then took over the examinations from his junior as he was to do for the rest of the day's hearing. She was asked about whether Greenwood asked her to fetch nurse Jones on 15th June and she said it had been on her own initiative. She agreed that the nurse later suggested calling for Dr. Griffiths and that Greenwood volunteered to do so, though an hour later Irene had to fetch both.[26]

Marshall Hall asked if she knew anything about Mrs. Greenwood having heart problems and she said she did not. She was asked when she first suspected poison and she said she could not recall this. She was also asked about whether there was wine on the table that evening and she thought there was none. He also asked if Greenwood was affected by his wife's death and she said he was. She also agreed that Irene was considerate to her mother on the last night of her life.[27]

District nurse Elizabeth Jones was the next witness. Samson established from her that Mrs. Greenwood's hands were cold that last night. She confirmed that there was vomiting and diarrhoea that night. She was asked whether Mrs. Greenwood improved that night or not and she said not. The judge had to intervene into some of Marshall Hall's cross examinations, when he was asking her about her departure between 9.00pm and 10.00pm. Marshall Hall was citing what she had said on previous court hearings and 'You should not put too much upon her'. She told him that she had to briefly leave as she had two family members at home who needed attention.[28]

She was asked about previous times when she had been asked about the events of that night, but she could not always remember what she had said on these occasions. She denied making several statements to Greenwood. Marshall Hall then asked about the pills she gave Mrs. Greenwood, 'which contained a whole grain of morphia'.

> 'If you had known that the pills contained 1 grain of morphia, would you have given them to her?'
> 'No, I would not.'

But she did not know that when the doctor told her to give them to the patient. She was also asked if the police had been threatening her and she said no. The last question 'If the accused says that Mrs Greenwood was much easier between 10.30pm and 11.30pm, was that true?' was answered concisely with a 'No; there was no time between the time when I arrived and the time of her death when she was really better'.[29]

Dr. Griffiths was then called upon. After briefly relating Mrs. Greenwood's medical history prior to 15th June 1919, Samson asked 'During those last four or five weeks that you prescribed different medicines for her. Did any of these medicines contain arsenic?'

'None at all' was the reply.

Marshall Hall objected to the question because 'there are so many things that contain arsenic'; this is true but in most cases these are the merest traces. The doctor said then that to the best of his belief this was so. He was then asked about his actions on the fatal night. He recounted what he witnessed and what he prescribed, first brandy and water, then a mixture containing bismuth and finally two *opium* (author's italics; previously he had described these as morphia pills) pills. He claimed he knew nothing about the patient suffering from diarrhoea, only that she was vomiting and was very weak.[30]

When he was asked about the contents of the pills and replied 'Each pill contains half a grain of opium. It is known as 'Pll Opium'. It means that there was one fortieth of a grain of morphia in each pill'.

This led to a chance for clarification 'In your opinion would it be correct to say that those pills were too strong to give to the patient?' to which the reply was 'No, not at all'.

Marshall Hall then made a strong protest at what had just been said:

> I protest, because the evidence the witness is now giving is entirely different from that which he has sworn at the previous hearing. Here is a doctor who has sworn on three previous occasions that the pills contained half a grain of morphia each, and Dr. Willcox has been examined from that point of view. I have got experts down from London to prove that 1 grain of morphia would be a dangerous dose, and now at this stage,

> without having given any notice, they have taken the evidence of the doctor, which is quite different.

The judge intervened with 'Don't get excited' and added that 'There might have been a mistake honestly made'.

The question here must be why did the doctor state something differently to what he had at both the inquest and the magistrates' court hearings? It was no small detail as morphia was deadly while opium was not and thus a new avenue of how Mrs. Greenwood died was closed off for the defence to exploit. Ludford nor anyone else had picked up on the potential importance of the morphia pills but Marshall Hall with his medical knowledge did. It can only be assumed that Dr. Griffiths was wrong on the earlier occasions (because no evidence of morphia had been found in Mrs. Greenwood's corpse) and now he was putting this right, but his earlier errors now rebounded against him.

Samson resumed his examination of the witness.[31]

He was asked about his actions late on the night of 15th June and when asked about the nurse's recollection of him returning to Rumsey House at 1.00am, he said 'I have no recollection of the visit' and when pressed added 'I don't say I did not make it'. He confirmed he had been present at Mrs. Greenwood's death and at the subsequent post mortem. With the knowledge he had learnt there his opinion of cause of death was different. Marshall Hall ended the day in court with another question 'If you had given her two half grain of morphia, you would not be surprised that she died at 4 o'clock?'

'Yes I would' was the reply.[32]

The second day of the trial was Wednesday 3rd November. Dr. Griffiths resumed his place in the witness box for the cross examination by Marshal Hall. He began by asking about Mrs. Greenwood's health problems and elicited that 'her heart was distinctly bad' and that gooseberries would possibly have been bad for her. He emphasised this point constantly, with questions such as 'Whatever caused the vomiting was also a danger to the heart?'.

'Yes' was the reply which led to 'The danger to the heart, in your opinion, was a very grave danger of death?'. Again it was affirmed that it was 'A very grave danger'.[33]

Questions were made about the relationship between Dr. Griffiths' sister and Greenwood, and the sister delaying Greenwood when he visited that night, with the former replying 'Only a very ordinary friendship'.

He was also asked about the letter Greenwood had sent to his sister, but he claimed to know nothing of this. Marshall Hall then returned to the strictly medical matters of the case in the following exchange:

> 'Now, Dr. Griffiths, there is an enormous difference between morphia and opium?'
> 'I know that.'
> 'Morphia is ten times as strong as opium, is that it?'
> 'Yes.'
> 'You said that, in your opinion, there would have been no danger in giving this woman two half grains of morphia?'
> 'I meant two half grains of pure opium.'
> 'I asked you the question last night purposely before the court rose. I asked you if it would have been safe to give this woman two half grains of morphia, and you said it was perfectly safe. Did you think I meant opium then?'
> 'Yes.'
> 'Have you the smallest doubt whatever that if you, as a medical man, were accurate when you said you gave her two half grains of morphia after 10 o'clock she would have been dead before 4 o'clock?'
> 'If I had given her morphia she would, but I did not give her morphia.'[34]

Marshall Hall hammered the point home by asking him if he had not known that Ludford had meant morphia pills not opium pills when cross examining Dr. Griffiths at the magistrates' court and the latter maintained his position before not giving answers. Marshall Hall then asked about the arsenic that the doctor had in his possession in a medical capacity. He stated that he had, in liquid form. He was then asked 'What tonic did you give Mrs. Greenwood?'

Dr. Griffiths produced a paper which had been copied from his prescription book. He was then asked to bring the entire book with him tomorrow and he said he would. The judge thought it would be better if it could be brought along later that day.[35]

The doctor's sister was the next witness for the prosecution. Samson asked her about how Greenwood seemed to her on the fatal night and she said that he seemed to be in good spirits and that he talked about a fortune teller saying he would be going on a honeymoon soon. She was asked about the telephone calls to Greenwood made to her house. They were fairly frequent. Marshall Hall asked her about her knowledge of the rumours about Mrs. Greenwood's death but she could not be precise, except that some were heard before Greenwood's second marriage. He asked her about her relationship to Greenwood and she replied, 'I was a personal friend of the family'.

She was then asked about the letter Greenwood wrote to her on 26th September. She agreed that after seeing the letter she asked him if he was to marry Gwladys Jones. She was also asked if the contents of the letter were public knowledge and she said that that was not so until the inquest.[36]

Other questions asked where whether she delayed Greenwood from fetching her brother on the fatal night and she said not. Did she ask Greenwood to write the letter to her; she said not. She was asked about her knowledge of the marriage licence that Greenwood had applied for and she claimed she only knew about that in retrospect. The letter was the first that Greenwood had ever sent her.[37]

Margaret Ann Morris was the cook at Rumsey House and she was asked if the servants had the same food as the family, which she said they did. Samson then asked 'Did you suffer any ill effects from eating the lunch?' to which the answer was 'No sir'.

Marshall Hall asked her if Mrs. Greenwood frequently drank burgundy at lunch and she said yes, as to Irene drinking the same she replied that 'Sometimes she did so'.

Marshall Hall then asked 'Did Mr. Greenwood use that pantry sometimes?' to which she affirmed 'Yes, very often'.

This was followed by 'Was the china pantry the usual place for him to go to wash his hands after he had been working in the garden?' and again the answer was 'Yes sir'.[38]

Lily Powell was the next servant to be examined and this time by Lewis. She stated that she had eaten of the lunch and was not ill because of it. Marshall Hall asked similar questions to those he had just done so and elicited the same answers, that both Mrs. Greenwood and her daughter took burgundy and that Greenwood often washed his hands in the china cupboard. However, Samson was able to establish that it was Hannah Williams, not her, who had served the lunch and waited on the family as they ate.[39]

Hannah Williams was next and again Lewis undertook the examination – his final one for the day. She stated that she poured out wine for Mrs. Greenwood and that the others did not drink it. She had had one glass and she had put the bottle out again for the evening meal, but when asked if it was there on the next day she said it was not. She was also asked about Greenwood's being in the china cupboard before lunch and had been there for a quarter of an hour. Marshall Hall then spent some time asking her about the numerous statements she had made to various policemen after Mrs. Greenwood's death. She could not remember them all and when asked about what Mrs. Greenwood drank was sure that it was port. She was not sure about the writing on the bottle label and Marshall Hall tried to suggest that she was confused between burgundy and port.[40]

Hannah was asked about Irene's drinking habits and she replied that she had never seen her drinking burgundy. Questions were then asked about Greenwood's visit to the china cupboard prior to lunch in the following exchange:

> 'Do you mean to say that you have never seen Greenwood in the china pantry before?'
> 'I have never seen him.'
> 'I put it to you that every Sunday when he was at home, or after every time he was in the garden, he did go there to wash his hands at the sink?'
> 'No.'
> 'Hundreds of times?'
> 'No sir. He used to go upstairs to wash his hands.'
> 'Are you telling the truth?'
> 'I have come here to tell the truth.'

She was asked about whether Mrs. Greenwood was about to sack her and whether she drank her employers' wine and she answered in the negative to both.[41]

The judge then intervened because of Marshall Hall's method of dealing with this crucial witness:

> 'You were getting rather excited just now and shouted at the witness ... It was very difficult for the witness because of your emphasising. I have to see that the witnesses are not addressed in a vehement way.'
> 'Why not?'
> 'Because it confuses them.'
> 'Why, it is my duty to be vehement.'
> 'Have you finished speaking? Now let me have my say. I trust you as you are trusting me. It is my duty to see that witnesses are not upset.'

Marshall Hall later said to the judge that 'if he raised his voice somewhat it was owing to the strain that he was under in such an important case'. It was also decided to not recall the witness until all the statements she had made had been made for those in court.[42]

It was now after lunch and Dr. Griffiths returned to the witness box and brought his prescription book with him. Marshall Hall asked him for the entry concerning the pills. The doctor said that 'The entry is not in it. I kept it in an old prescription book, and the old book has been destroyed. I thought I had copied it into this book'.

The doctor added that the prescription had been entered into the old book. Returning to the morphia pills, Marshal Hall reiterated:

> 'You sent over to Mrs. Greenwood two pills which contained a half grain of morphia. Is that true?'
> 'No, it is quite untrue.'
> 'What do you say they contained?'
> 'I say that each pill contained half a grain of powdered opium.'[43]

There were other questions about Mrs. Greenwood's ailments. Samson brought him back to the question of arsenic being fatal to her when he asked 'Assuming that he had a fatal dose of arsenic, was there anything inconsistent with that in the symptoms she showed that night?'

Marshall Hall tried to intervene but the judge forbade the question because Dr. Griffiths had only seen one arsenic poisoning case in his life. Marshall Hall asked next about the prescription book:

> 'Why sir, after you made that copy, was that book destroyed?'
> 'It was destroyed at the same time as I destroyed other things.'
> 'That is no answer … it must have been destroyed since June 1920?'

Dr. Griffiths could not say why he had done so. Marshall Hall then hypothesised on his behalf:

> 'Why was it destroyed? You were in a state of great agitation. You knew perfectly well at the inquest that the suggestion was made that this lady died from morphia, and you never corrected that mistake. May not you in your anxiety have made a mistake and given her morphia?'
> 'I must have made a mistake.'[44]

The effect of this witness on the jury was unfavourable as was later reported 'The unfortunate vacillation, and the obvious reticence of the Doctor in the witness box, and especially his confused statements regarding the Morphia or Opium pills given to Mrs. Greenwood when she appeared to have been in extremis left a grave doubt in the mind of the jury as to the real primary cause of death'.[45]

Mrs. Annie Groves, Greenwood's office caretaker, was next and Samson asked her about Gwladys Jones' visits to see Greenwood at his office in Llanelli. She agreed that they occurred there since the end of 1918. He asked her about the day of Mrs. Greenwood's death when Greenwood went to his office. She recalled that she handed him a letter and it was thought to have been from Gwladys Jones. As it was destroyed it could not be further discussed. She had also found a receipt for the £55 ring in the grate in July 1919. Marshall Hall queried how she knew Greenwood and Gwladys Jones had lunch and she admitted he had not told her nor had she followed him.[46]

Mary Morris briefly replied that Greenwood had used the telephone exchange to ring the office of *The Llanelli Mercury* for a woman but could say no more. Gwyneth David, neighbour of the Jones' family in Llanelli, recalled a conversation about the first Mrs. Greenwood's illness and Greenwood writing to rebuke her about such. She was asked if she was a gossip, 'Is it true that you spread malicious gossip about other people at Llanelly?'

'No; quite untrue' was the reply.

Pressing the point he continued 'So gossip is pretty rife down in that district and in this case. Has it maligned you?'

She answered 'Yes'.[47]

Other witnesses made very brief appearances; to relate how Greenwood and Gwladys Jones bought a dressing case in 1918 at a shop in Llanelli; how Greenwood bought a £55 ring from a London shop, and how in 1917 he had bought weedkiller in a shop in Kidwelly. The suppliers of weedkiller from Edinburgh who used a Lincoln firm to deliver it to Greenwood also made brief statements. The chemist who made up the weedkiller was also examined as was the railway employee who had it delivered to Rumsey House.[48]

William Gould, employed as a gardener at Rumsey House, asserted that 'During the whole time I was there I never saw any weed killer used there. The gardener who was there before might have done so, but I have never seen any signs of it'.

Both Samson and Marshall Hall examined him and he said the same, as to the latter 'Between April and June, 1919, did you see any signs of weeds having been killed in any way on the path?' to which the reply was 'No way at all'.

There were another few witnesses who had but brief times in the witness box. John Sharff attested to having taken away empty bottles of all types from Rumsey House. The registrar said that Greenwood notified him of his second marriage. William Morgan spoke of the burial of Mrs. Greenwood and its disinterment. Dr. Dick, the Carmarthenshire police surgeon, witnessed the removal of the corpse and in carrying out the post mortem and removal of organs.[49]

Superintendent Jones was the last witness of the day. He was asked about the statements he took from Greenwood in October 1919, which Greenwood had questioned in the lower courts. Marshall Hall wanted to know how accurate a recording of Greenwood's words the written statement had been. He also asked about the veracity of a number of comments allegedly made by both parties, such as Jones declaring the purpose for which he was asking the questions he did. Jones refuted all Marshall Hall's allegations.[50]

A newspaper reported about Greenwood on that day:

> 'Greenwood, who came into court clad in an apparently new light cloth chesterfield, which he did not discard, maintained his calm demeanour, except on one occasion, the gruesome details of his wife's death agony were being related. He bent his head, buried his face in his hands, and for some minutes his frame was shaken with sobbing'.[51]

Another newspaper referred to the scenes of the onlookers:

> 'This is early closing day, and the court, especially in the afternoon, was crowded to its utmost capacity. Again, the majority of the spectators were women. Many hundreds of people were unable to secure seats, but they congregated in groups outside, and when Greenwood was driven back to the gaol this evening, the streets through which the closed carriage passed from the Guildhall were lined with dense crowds'.[52]

Public curiosity was also substantial as it had been in the previous hearings in the summer. As one journalist wrote:

> 'The public interest in the trial deepened every day. The crowds who assemble are kept at some distance from the court by mounted policemen and all that the majority of the people can see is the arrival and departure of the principal actors in the drama ... each morning and evening there is an excited rush to watch the arrival and departure of the prisoner. He is

> conveyed to and from Carmarthen Gaol little more than a hundred yards away, in a close cab guarded by three warders and the vehicle is attended by mounted police.
>
> Today, as before, there was a great struggle for admission as soon as the little court opened. Greenwood entered the dock with his usual quick step. He looked better, for he had lost the flush of the last two days. Before taking the seat he had a few words with his solicitor.'[53]

The third day of the trial was Thursday 4th November. Superintendent Jones was further cross examined. There was much discussion as to whether pages had been removed from Jones' notebook in which he had recorded Greenwood's statement. Marshall Hall stated 'I am not suggesting that this witness tore it out, but that a leaf has been removed from that book'.

He also claimed that he was being blamed for having done so 'After what has happened, my lord, I shall have to be allowed to go into the box myself. I have never had such an experience as this before'.

The judge assured him that such an allegation was not being made. Marshall Hall resumed his cross examination 'Now, on your oath – a man is on trial for his life – have not ten pages been taken out of that book?'

He replied 'Not a single one, sir. I may say that I am not used to such dirty tricks as to cut leaves of statements by prisoners.'

He was asked if he had been in charge of the case and he replied that he had been to an extent, but so had Haigh. There was discussion as to who had taken various statements from witnesses and Superintendent Jones said that the work had been divided between himself and Sergeant Lewis. Inspector Nicholas verified that he had been with Jones when the statements were taken by Jones from Greenwood. He could not say anything conclusive about the note books.[54]

Hannah Williams was recalled, her previous statements having been made available to the court. Samson asked her about her recollections of 15th June 1919. She was asked about and read the statements she had made about having seen Greenwood in the china cupboard for a quarter of an hour before lunch and then putting a decanter of whisky and a bottle of wine on the luncheon table. She was asked about the colour of the glasses and other details but could not remember these. She was asked about how much wine had been drunk and whether the bottle was on the table in the evening. There was a discrepancy in her statements as to whether the bottle was half or three quarters full. Marshall Hall also quoted one of her statements to say that Greenwood went into the china cupboard on two occasions before lunch, but she could not remember having said so. She now said that it was only once that he had done so. Samson re-examined her in the following exchange:

> 'Can you remember how many wine glasses had had wine in them?'
> 'There was wine in only one wine glass and whisky in the other.'
> 'Do you usually speak in Welsh?'
> 'Yes.'
> 'Do you understand Welsh or English better?'
> 'Welsh.'[55]

Sergeant Lewis was next. Marshall Hall asked him about the interviews he had had with a number of people in Kidwelly. He emphasised how important a witness that Irene would have been.

> 'Did it occur to you that in the interest of justice you should take a statement from Miss Irene?'
> 'She was not at Kidwelly.'
> 'There are trains. Did you not know where she was?'
> 'I believe she was in London.'
> 'Have you ever made the slightest attempt to interview Irene?'
> 'No sir.'

He was then asked about Williams' statement as to the weedkiller and whether that would have been relevant. He said he thought not.[56]

William Bell, former manufacturing chemist of Eureka weedkiller, was then examined. He was asked by Marshal Hall about how deadly weed killer would be to animals in the garden and how long it would retain its strength. He agreed as to its potency and risk to animals. Mrs. Groves was recalled, about the letter that she had passed to Greenwood on the morning of his wife's death. Samson asked if she could see anything written in it and she replied 'It's nice when I will be your wife!' or words to that effect.

Then there were the questions to when it was passed to Greenwood and Marshal Hall suggested that it was a month later than what the witnesses claimed.[57]

John Webster was the next witness and he explained how he had arrived at the figures he had for the amounts of arsenic being in different parts of the organs. He stated that he had found no morphia there, thus negating Marshall Hall's comments over Dr. Griffiths. He was asked if he had ever sipped port wine with weedkiller in it. He had. To the question 'Is there any difference in the taste?' he answered 'No; by sipping the port there is practically no difference to be detected'.

Marshall Hall had Webster admit that he was a chemist not a toxicologist and he agreed. He then questioned Webster about the calculations and the possibility that the results might be incorrect due to contamination. He had Webster state that the distribution of poison in the organs was not uniform. He asked about there being arsenic in the human body naturally and he said it was minimal. Arsenic was found in many products in common use. Webster was noted as an experienced chemist and he said he did not think he had made a mistake.[58]

Dr. Willcox was next. He stated that the organs he had been presented to investigate were in good condition and if they had not been he would have thought that it was probably not a case of arsenic poisoning. Samson then went through the various alternate possibilities as to the cause of death.

> 'Could the cause of death have been valvular disease of the heart?'
> 'No; there was no valvular disease.'
> 'What do you say as to the uterus … Was it a condition which would cause pain and suffering during lifetime?'

> 'It might have caused a certain amount of pain, and possibly a little tendency to haemorrhage, but it would not in any sense be dangerous to life.'
> 'Having regard to all circumstances of the analysis of Mr. Webster, what in your opinion was the cause of death?'
> 'Arsenical poisoning.'[59]

He was asked about how arsenic was administered and he replied that it would have been by the mouth and this was because of the arsenic being found in a number of organs. That there was little in the stomach was indicative of the poison being taken several hours before death, some having been vomited out. It was probably taken between 1.00pm and 6.00pm. He was also asked about the symptoms of arsenic poisoning. These, Dr. Willcox said, were nausea, diarrhoea, cramp in the legs, stomach pains and sickness.[60]

The fact that Mrs. Greenwood had a weak heart meant that she was more vulnerable to heart failure. The latter was caused by 'prolonged diarrhoea and vomiting, due to the effects of the poisoning. Samson also asked how much arsenic had been taken. Willcox thought that the unexamined parts of the body; skin, muscles etc., would mean that the true amount would be as high as three quarters of a grain to a whole grain of arsenic.[61]

Marshall Hall began his cross examination. He ascertained that the doctor had given evidence in many poisoning cases. He was asked if he still thought that death was due to arsenic and he agreed with this. The barrister then went in to suggest that diarrhoea could well be a symptom of other health problems and to this Willcox had to agree, leading Marshall Hall to state, 'Oh, Dr. Willcox, so many things are possible'. The fatality caused by morphia pills was mentioned; a null point as already stated. He asked if it were possible for a doctor to fail to differentiate between opium and morphia and he said it should not be the case. This was a red herring; Webster had already stated that there was no morphia in the corpse. Marshall Hall asked 'When Dr. Griffiths says that morphia pills are often called opium pills, that is news to you?' to which the reply was 'Yes'.[62]

Arsenic in the weedkiller used at Rumsey House in the garden was then discussed. After asking questions about its application, he asked

'Would it be possible for a person to absorb poison by walking about the garden?'

He did not think that arsenic could have been inhaled or if it did it would not be fatal. Marshall Hall asked if Irene drank the same wine that Dr. Willcox had claimed was poisoned, would she have not been very ill. He agreed that this would have been the case. Marshall Hall carried on in this vein. He also focussed on the weakness of her heart and how gastric disturbances caused by eating could be important. Symptoms were discussed, but Willcox replied that 'the long continued vomiting and diarrhoea for several hours would be more consistent with arsenical poisoning'.[63]

Marshall Hall raised the possibility of food poisoning or gooseberry skins which had been contaminated by weedkiller in the garden. Dr. Willcox was dismissive of such theories, stating 'Gooseberry skins would cause the intestinal irritation, but it would not produce a condition similar to the symptoms of arsenical poisoning'. They would also have harmed other members of the household, too. Marshall Hall then turned to the amount of arsenic and used text books to state that at least a grain would have to be in the body for it to be fatal. Willcox countered this by replying, 'in this case the great vomiting and diarrhoea would account for the elimination of considerable quantities of the arsenic'. Marshall Hall asked about other possible causes of death from natural diseases and these were rejected.[64]

The fourth day of the trial was Friday 5th November and Dr. Willcox returned to the witness box. The subject of the minimum level of arsenic in the body was returned to and the text book was again referred to. At least one grain, said the barrister. Although Dr. Willcox was in general agreement with that which was quoted, he added 'that is subject to qualification I have made'.

Marshall Hall countered with 'But the qualification is as to vomiting and diarrhoea?' to which Dr. Wilcox replied 'Yes, but in this case there was sufficient length of time for the greater part of the arsenic to be evacuated from the stomach and intestines'.

Marshall Hall referred to the Seddon case but was increasingly annoyed and said 'Dr Willcox, try to get rid of what I call the lecture room style' to which the judge exclaimed 'Oh no!'[65]

Greenwood later noted his feelings on hearing these witnesses:

> 'I cannot forget the deadly effect of the evidence of the Home Office experts. These men seemed so sure, so terribly sure, so calm and detached. They had found arsenic. They described their wonderful scientific tests. How must this impress the audience, I thought.
>
> What did it matter that I knew nothing about any arsenic? The arsenic was there. Only my word could be given that I was innocent.
>
> That long scientific evidence appalled me. Why, until after I was arrested I did not even know that weed-killer contained arsenic. I thought what destroyed the weeds was some compound of copper and sulphuric acid.
>
> And there on the judge's bench was a weed-killer tin. The scientists had talked about tiny fractions of poison – quantities too small to weigh or handle.
>
> This was something that everybody could see. It was only a small tin, just like a tin of baby food. If only it had been as harmless! But it seemed to me as big as a mountain, which might fall on me at any moment.
>
> I had had enough arsenic in my possession, said the counsel, to have poisoned the whole town of Carmarthen. It was true, though I had not known it. But who would believe that?'[66]

Had Greenwood but known it, these two witnesses did impress the jury as a memorandum later made clear:

> 'Satisfactory and conclusive proofs of the administration of a dangerous dose of arsenic, either wilfully or inadvertently, were given to the court.
>
> The jury were satisfied that the expert witnesses for the Crown had succeeded in presenting irrefutable evidence of this fact. Sir William Willcox and Mr. Webster placed this matter beyond a doubt'.[67]

Greenwood later wrote, perhaps at this point, 'The jury of necessity are swayed backwards and forward by the skill of contending counsel. I remember that when a telling point was made by the Crown against me, I simply dared not look at the jury'.[68]

Marshall Hall then went on to ask about the effects of arsenic on different parts of the body. He also suggested that someone else should have examined the organs taken from the body, someone acting on behalf of the defendant. He now showed the doctor two bottles of red liquid, one containing a bismuth solution and the other liquid arsenic. He said that Dr. Griffiths had these in his surgery and so suggested 'If by some unfortunate mistake he, in the anxiety and hurry, gave her four teaspoons of Fowler's solution, you would have got all the arsenic you found, or more than you found?'

Following an affirmative reply he continued 'And there would be practically no distinction in colour in the mixture, whether the mixture were bismuth or a solution of arsenic?' to which the answer was 'No. They resemble one another'.

This was another of Marshall Hall's red herrings; nurse Jones had stated that she had tasted the said mixture and nothing untoward had happened to her. The judge tried to sum up what Marshall Hall was implying when he stated 'It is suggested that Dr. Griffiths, having these things in his surgery, sent over something which poisoned the lady, and did that by mistake. It is a shocking blunder'.[69]

Marshall Hall then discussed other cases in which arsenic had been found in people either naturally or might be found in glucose and cited a case in Manchester where this had occurred. He returned to the possibility that arsenic in the weedkiller might be breathed in. Gooseberry skins were once again mentioned as a possible source of the vomiting and diarrhoea, and again the doctor tended to disagree with these suggestions.[70]

Three earlier witnesses were recalled. One was Superintendent Jones to state that the new note book, like the old one had the same number of pages and so the imputation of pages being removed from the latter was voided. Dr. Griffiths was asked whether there was a possibility that he had dispensed arsenic instead of bismuth and he replied 'Quite impossible'. Miss Griffiths was also recalled and was asked about whether there was 'a strained relationship between you and Mrs. Greenwood'. She replied that the two had worked together on various committees and at various charitable events such as a flag day on 7th June at Kidwelly. Miss Griffiths said that they were on speaking terms but a letter was produced from the deceased to state that 'We are still only on bowing terms'. Miss Griffiths said that they were on amicable terms and did she did not know whether Mrs. Greenwood was jealous of her.[71]

That was the end of the case for the prosecution. Marshall Hall had certainly dented it with his cross examination of Dr. Griffiths and to a lesser extent that of Hannah Williams and the two scientists. He then had further opportunities as he could then go over to the offensive.

Chapter Eight

The Case for the Defence and the Summing Up

In the afternoon of Friday 5th November, the trial proceeded with the case for the defence. Marshall Hall made the opening speech. It was necessary for the defence to sow as much doubt in the minds of the jury in their faith in the case for the prosecution and this he had already begun by his cross examination of the prosecution's witnesses. He addressed the jury to tell them that he would bring medical witnesses to assert that death was not due to arsenic and that another person drank the same wine as Mrs. Greenwood. He reminded them about the weakness of housemaid Hannah Williams' evidence. He stated that a defendant is innocent until proved guilty and that was what Greenwood's position was as matters now stood. The prosecution had to prove that Mrs. Greenwood died of arsenic and that Greenwood gave it to her. No jury would convict on the evidence put before them, he asserted.[1]

Marshall Hall then spoke sympathetically of Greenwood; imprisoned for over four months, with limited access to his family and the victim of gossip and prejudice, adding 'Trifles as light as air are confirmation as strong as Holy Writ to jealous people'. That he did not apply for trial in London was surely a sign of his innocence not his guilt because he felt confidence in the former to face his fellow countrymen, though of course Greenwood was English not Welsh.[2]

The value of Irene's evidence was that if she thought her father had killed her mother she would not testify for him, which she was to do in due course. He questioned the worth of the testimony of the academic experts from London brought by the prosecution and claimed he detected a shade of hesitancy in one of their answers and that the symptoms of food poisoning and arsenic were similar. A recent medical text book buttressed this view.[3]

He would bring forth Drs. Toogood and Griffiths – the latter from Swansea (thus implicitly commending him to the Welsh jurors) – 'and they will tell you that in their opinion, this death was due to gastric irritation produced by gooseberry skins'. Arsenic from weedkiller used in the garden could have led to this. Mr. Webster might not deliberately err, but to do so is human, he reminded the jury. Marshall Hall stated that many diseases and poisons had the same symptoms. Then there was no motive – Greenwood stood to lose financially and his wife was the best of women. Surely if he was guilty he would have had cremated her to avoid arsenic that he knew was there being found?[4]

Then there were the gossips who gave Greenwood's desire to marry Gwladys Jones as the motive. He said that marrying her was a great give away, as was the buying a large tin of weedkiller; no guilty man would have done that because it would seem far too suspicious. The principal witness was weak, 'Do you believe a word of Hannah Williams' evidence? The girl contradicted herself'. Her evidence about Greenwood's going into the china cupboard was contradicted by other servants.[5]

Dr. Griffiths was also savaged. He had said that the morphia pills were safe and also claimed he had not given these to Mrs. Greenwood. The missing prescription book was noted as another sign that the doctor was not to be entirely relied upon. He suggested that 'Don't you think it is more than possible that this man might have given morphia pills, and that it might be that death was caused by giving the morphia?' He reminded the jury that the doctor and nurse were in disagreement about the former's visits to Mrs. Greenwood. These were unreliable witnesses, therefore.[6]

Marshall Hall concluded that a medical error might well have occurred and it was that which killed the unfortunate woman. He did not suggest that the doctor definitely gave her arsenic in error but that he might have. Bottles of the same colour liquid might be confused in the excitement of the night in question. He then said: 'I am here fighting for a man's life. It's not for us to prove his innocence … unless you, each one, is prepared to stand up in that box and put your hand in your heart and say "I believe and am convinced that Harold Greenwood poisoned his wife and that she died from the poison that he administered" ... it is not the benefit of the doubt I ask at your hands, but we will demand an acquittal'.[7]

The address over, a plan of the house and grounds was shown to the jury and then the first witness for the defence was called. This was Dr. Frederick Sherman Toogood (1862-1958), Medical Superintendent of Lewisham Infirmary (ironically only two miles from where Greenwood once lived in Forest Hill) who had some experience of arsenic being used against humans. He agreed to the examination hypothesis that morphia could have killed Mrs. Greenwood. To one question he replied, 'Taking the gastroenteritis from swallowing gooseberry skins, and assuming that a grain of morphia was given, the actual cause of death was morphia poisoning'.[8]

Marshall Hall continued to emphasise that the gooseberry skins were laced with arsenic. He asked about its symptoms and Dr. Toogood said that diarrhoea would be one. Vomiting was another. Tomato skins could have the same effect on a weak heart, as the doctor could personally testify. If she had died of morphia, as the doctor stated, there would be no evidence of that when her body was examined 10 months later (though Webster had stated otherwise). Would weedkiller used in the garden have led to Mrs. Greenwood inhaling it to deadly effect? 'I will not say it was impossible'. She could have breathed it in just as artists inhale deadly lead. Arsenic was not the cause of death the doctor concluded.[9]

Samson then cross examined. He asked Dr. Toogood whether his attention in the case was wholly directed on the subject of morphia from the outset. He agreed that it was and that the possibility of arsenic wafted into the lungs was only a very recent suggestion of his. He pressed on the question of arsenic and said 'Is this the first occasion in which you have given evidence in a criminal arsenic case?' to which he was forced to answer 'Yes'. He then had to agree that Dr. Willcox was an authority on the topic and that the last time Dr. Toogood had dealt with a case of arsenic poisoning was in 1905. He had to agree that he was not an analytical chemist and he also agreed that such an expert would have been useful for the defence.[10]

He then cross examined Dr. Toogood about his knowledge of arsenic and how the amount in the body was calculated. He could not always answer the questions put to him and had to allow that Samson was sometimes in the right. He had to agree that the poisoning could have been due to arsenic. He tried to suggest that the strain on the heart led to death, not poison but had to admit that the latter would cause greater strain. Marshall Hall briefly re-examined his witness to ask him if his diagnosis of the death had changed after the recent exchange and he said it had not.[11]

The doctor later wrote about his impact: 'I think I succeeded in putting a doubt into the minds of the jury. The face of Webster was a picture. When I attacked him for not calibrating his mirror slides and not using the whole organs. I am afraid we rather slapped it on the poor doctor'.[12]

Dr. William Layard Griffiths (1871-1935) of Swansea was the next medical witness brought forward to cast doubt in the prosecution's case: 'I think that the finding of a quarter of a grain of arsenic in the viscera of a corpse is by no means conclusive evidence that the person died of arsenic poisoning'.

This was because he claimed that a human body could have anything between a quarter of a grain of arsenic and up to five grains without any loss of health. Finding a quarter of a grain did not mean that two grains had been definitely administered.[13]

He was asked how frequently it was that arsenic was to be found in drinks and foodstuffs. Yes, it could be there and also in tonics and even bismuth. On being asked about contamination from the weedkiller used in the garden he answered that it could not be ruled out. As with Dr. Toogood, he agreed that Mrs. Greenwood could have died of morphia poisoning, especially as she had a weak heart. The morphia pills, on top of everything else would have led to death. Gastroenteritis was another possibility.[14]

As before, Samson cross examined the doctor about his relevant experience. He had to admit that he had never seen morphia and opium tablets being mixed up. When asked about his experience of examining a corpse who died of arsenic he had to reply that he had no experience whatsoever. He did think that the presence of a quarter grain of arsenic was not conclusive that she died from it. Morphia poisoning was probably to blame for the death. Marshall Hall drew out of him that it was not unknown for doctors to give the wrong medicine or even deadly poison in error; a case occurred in Swansea in the early 1890s for instance.[15]

The next witness was perhaps the most important of all – Greenwood himself. A journalist described the scene: 'The most dramatic moment of the Greenwood trial arrived at five minutes past three this afternoon, when the prisoner himself entered the witness box, and prepared to defend himself against the charge ... wearing a lounge suit of blue with a thin white stripe, Greenwood walked briskly from the dock in the centre of the court to the witness box beneath the Bench, and as he arranged a bundle of papers on the ledge before him, every spectator in a crowded court turned towards this little grey haired man, who looked rather more than his forty six years'.[16]

Greenwood, writing later, noted:

> It is an ordeal that can never be realised except by those who have been through it. After been worn out with some days of unparalleled strain in the earlier stages of the trial, the prisoner 'goes into the box'. The eyes of the crowd watch every motion, the twitch of his face, the fluttering of his hands. He knows that he will be exposed to a pitiless hail of questions from an expert in the art of interrogation ... I was on the verge of a breakdown, only sustained by the knowledge that if I did not keep my head, I was lost. For weeks after I felt the strain of that ordeal. It was, of course, a perfectly fair cross examination'.[17]

It is not necessary or even desirable to put the defendant in the witness box to give evidence. A poor witness, as in the Seddon case in 1912, can help convict himself by his manner and his answers in cross examination. However, a good defendant can help his case considerably. It is thus a calculated gamble.

He answered that he and his wife lived happily; that she provided £900 per year to the household budget and that his new wife had no such income. All his first wife's money went to her children. The financial motive having been disposed of, the following exchange took place:

> 'Now, Harold Greenwood, did you, directly or indirectly, administer or cause to be administered, to your wife any arsenic at any time in your life?'
> 'I have not.'
> 'Had you anything to do with your wife's death?'
> 'Nothing whatever.'

He again sought sympathy for his client by reference to his being in prison for four and a half months.[18]

The cross examination then began. After having Greenwood repeat that he was very attached to his first wife, Samson then asked about the purchase of an engagement ring just a few weeks later:

> 'If you had such great affection for your wife, why within a month after her death should you gave Gladys Jones a ring?'
> 'I do not know how your remark applies at all.'
> 'Please answer my question …'
> 'I considered the matter … I felt so hopelessly out of it – it was not like a home.'[19]

Then there was questioning about his feelings towards Gwladys Jones. He denied he had been fond of her in his first wife's lifetime, though he had known her and her family for 20 years. He denied that the dressing case he had bought in her company in 1918 was for Gwladys but for one of her sisters. Miss Bowater was briefly discussed. He was asked whether he had ever bought any wine, in Carmarthen or Kidwelly and he said that his first wife and her sister had bought wine, but never port.[20]

Samson returned to the subject of Gwladys Jones:

> 'You were fond of her, were you not?'
> 'I was not at that time [of his first wife's life].'
> 'When did you become fond of her?'
> 'I did not become fond of her until 12th July.'
> 'It really dawned on you all of a sudden?'

> 'All of a sudden.'

Fortunately he had an engagement ring to hand at the time.[21]

There was then discussion about Greenwood talking to Gwladys Jones on the telephone at the Griffiths house and he said he did so occasionally. He denied meeting her in his office and having lunch with her often. Greenwood emphatically denied that he was on close terms with her in his wife's lifetime. His first wife's health was then discussed. He agreed that she often took medicines and tonics to counter her worsening health in the last six months of her life. They then got to the lunch on 15th June. On being asked about his going into the china room, Greenwood said he probably did so as he did every day. Samson asked 'I suggest you went into the china pantry that particular Sunday and were there about a quarter of an hour, and then you were in the dining room?' to which Greenwood retorted 'Pure imagination'.[22]

He then answered about drinks and said that his wife often drank whisky and soda. He was asked about the afternoon tea and was vague and forgetful. He did recall that she had been unwell and complaining about her health. He agreed that he gave his wife brandy to ease her state. He was then asked questions about the first of Dr. Griffith's visits that evening and his giving Mrs. Greenwood the medicine. Greenwood said he did not think the situation was serious and at times recalled thinking that his wife was getting better.[23]

On being asked about his visit that night to the doctor's, and was tasked with his conversation with the doctor's sister, Miss Griffiths, in which he said that he thought his wife would not recover he replied 'That is a pure invention' on the part of Miss Griffiths. Samson then asked:

> 'Was your wife jealous of Miss Griffiths?'
> 'Yes; she was jealous.'
> 'Was she jealous of your present wife?'
> 'Not a bit. It was only of Miss Griffiths that she was jealous.'[24]

The statement that Greenwood had made to Superintendent Jones was scrutinised and Greenwood claimed that some of it had been taken down in error. Samson asked him about his wife being given the two pills and it was to those that Greenwood now ascribed his wife's death, 'She would not have died if she had not had the pills'. He was convinced that these were two morphia pills not two opium pills and that they had been told to give Mrs. Greenwood both at once. There was a discrepancy over when the pills were given; the doctor had said 10.00pm and here Greenwood said it was at 1.00am.[25]

The letter that Greenwood wrote to Miss David was then enquired about. Greenwood had resented that Miss David, his second wife's former neighbour, had stated that his wife was not ill, but that she later apologised. Greenwood was then asked whether there was any communication between him and Gwladys Jones on the day his wife died and he denied there had been. It was suggested that Greenwood had also proposed to Miss Griffiths as well as being engaged to Gwladys Jones in the summer of 1919. Greenwood spoke of his meeting Miss Griffiths prior to his second marriage and that the letter he wrote to her was merely to assuage her feelings and to counter gossip against her and Greenwood and to show that it was she who had refused him.[26]

Greenwood said that most of what Miss Griffiths had said was untrue. He said 'That is what I cannot understand about it all. I think she has been got at' (presumably by the police). He was then asked about the statement he made to Superintendent Jones in October 1919. Greenwood claimed not to know that he was then possibly facing a criminal charge though the policeman had cautioned him. He thought that nurse Jones had talked about the morphia pills and that was what the police were asking about. He had hitherto heard no rumours about the possibility of his wife's death being due to foul play. He also said that the statement had been added to. He alleged that the policeman accused him of insuring his wife's life for a large sum and he recalled stating that an exhumation might be beneficial.[27]

The court then adjourned. Saturday 6th November was the fifth day of the trial. A reporter observed:

> There was again a rush for seats this morning, and despite all the elaborate arrangements made by the court officials, the gangway and every portion of the court became crowded.

> Accused, on arriving at the court, used one hand to hold up his coat collar and the other to hold a newspaper before his face. Apparently, among those in court were the present Mrs. Greenwood's sister and her two brothers.[28]

Greenwood again entered the witness box. He was first asked about his engagement to Gwladys Jones. He agreed that he first bought a cheap ring to ascertain the size of her finger and then bought a more expensive one after that had been ascertained. Greenwood then wanted to discuss the further visits that Superintendent Jones had made to him in late 1919. He said that hundreds of statements there were incorrect, such as stating that his wife suffered from diarrhoea. 'I say that he put it down wrongly' Greenwood told Samson. He added, among many other errors in the document that he had not signed it. Samson clarified and summed up 'Do you suggest that he wrote the statement and brought in matters you never said, and left out matters you have said?' to which Greenwood affirmed 'I do'.[29]

Then there were questions about the 10 gallon tin of weedkiller. Greenwood said that it was all used up in the same day. This was on the Saturday after 22nd May and in the presence of Ben Williams, employed as a gardener. The other gardener was one Gould but he was not there when Greenwood and Williams distributed the weedkiller in the garden. There was also discussion about mixing the weedkiller powder with water in order to make the liquid.[30]

Samson then asked Greenwood about his opinion that the morphia tablets had killed his wife. He replied that that was what nurse Jones told him. He later tasked the doctor about this but he denied that the pills were too strong. Samson thought Greenwood was being evasive and said as much to the judge, who had also noticed that. Greenwood admitted that he had told his daughter and a brother-in-law about the morphia pills being deadly but had not told the police so.[31]

Greenwood was asked about his dealings with the vicar and the press in his alleged comments about how his wife had died. Again, he claimed to have been misrepresented by them and never claimed he suggested that it was suicide. He was asked about the ring he gave to his daughter, and then to Gwladys Jones and another he gave to

Irene. He was then asked about his relationship to the Jones family and in particular Gwladys:

> 'Had there ever been any affection, any passages of love, between you and Gladys Jones until after you proposed to marry her?'
> 'None whatever.'
> 'Was there ever any thought of improper relationship between you and Gladys Jones before the marriage?'
> 'None whatever.'[32]

A newspaper commented on this stage of the trial:

> This has been, perhaps, the least interesting and sensational day of the trial. Greenwood ... seemed mentally alert, but physically weary. He leaned heavily upon the low rails of the witness stand, and spoke in a faint voice that often failed to carry far beyond his lips. To counsel and the press men his replies were quite inaudible. Occasionally, especially when pressed hard on some point, he stood erect, and threw his head back, a favourite gesture of his, and addressed his explanation to the jury'.[33]

Dr. Griffiths was recalled. He was told about the answers that Greenwood had given about him telling the doctor about the morphia pills being the cause of his wife's death and that he had told the doctor this, which he agreed that he had used such pills but that they were not injurious. Was there any conversation of this sort?' he replied 'I never remember any conversation of that sort'.[34]

Nurse Jones was recalled and asked similar questions. She was also clear that Greenwood had not discussed with her about the alleged fatal nature of the morphia pills. Martha Morris was examined by Hunter, Marshall Hall's junior, on the first time he spoke in the trial, about the Greenwoods' domestic life.

> 'Have you ever seen Mr. Greenwood use the china cupboard for any purpose?'
> 'Hundreds of times.'
> 'What for?'
> 'To wash his hands.'

She added that after Miss Bowater left in April to go on a holiday and then Mrs. Greenwood became worse, health wise, with diarrhoea and was thinner. She seemed in low spirits on the day before her death when Martha had seen her.[35]

The final witness was Irene, who was also examined by Hunter. A newspaper described her thus, 'a frail little gentlewoman giving evidence in defence of her daddy'. Before she took the customary oath on the Bible, she looked across at her father. Apparently, 'she just nodded gracefully how pathos can be expressed in the simple lowering of the head and over her face there was a sweet, sad smile'. She had come into court 'in a smartly tailored dark costume, wore upon her shoulders a heavy fur cape, and upon her shapely head a rather large hat of greyish silk … a strangely impressive figure'.[36]

Another journalist noted 'Irene is a slim girl of 22. Over a black coat and skirt with a thin white stripe, she wore heavy furs and held in her hand a small lace edged handkerchief. A light fawn hat covered a mass of very dark hair. She gave her evidence quite firmly, but her voice, in which there was a distinct trace of the musical Welsh accent, was so low that she was frequently inaudible'.[37]

She was asked about the last day of her mother's life, which she was able to recall in detail. However, she was not audible in all of what she said and had to be told to speak up on occasion. She referred to Greenwood as Daddy on several occasions, which could have been a sign of affection or of middle class affectation. After describing her actions on that Sunday, leading up to the lunch, Hunter then asked:

> 'At lunch on Sunday, what did you have to drink?'
> 'Daddy drank whisky and soda. Kenneth had soda water. Mother and I had burgundy.'
> …

> 'It has been suggested that you never drank burgundy. What do you say?'
> 'I always did on Sundays, and three or four times during the week'.

She was able to describe the wine, the bottle and the glasses used. She then described the afternoon and her mother becoming unwell by its end.[38]

Then she was taken through the evening and the arrival of Miss Phillips and the nurse. The sickness of her mother and her eventual death was described. Then she was asked about her drinking habits and those of her mother. Irene replied that she drank port, burgundy and Beaune; her mother drank port as well, but usually Beaune. She was then asked about her whereabouts after her mother's death and about Gwladys Jones' visits to Rumsey House when her mother had been absent in 1918.[39]

Samson tried to unsettle her definite statements about what had been drunk at lunch, asking her if she kept a diary; she did not. If it was a warm day would she still have drunk wine; yes, if she was advised to. She was asked if her father had told her about the morphia pills being the cause of her mother's death and she replied that this was so. She was also asked about the afternoon tea on the Sunday and she described what her mother had and how she became unwell. She was asked about her mother's final illness and death.[40]

A newspaper commented, 'Next to her father. Irene Greenwood has attracted more attention than any other person in the case. She alone, of all those who could throw light on the mystery, had remained in seclusion until today. Her narrative was clear and connected, and was unshaken … At one stage, in her examination, Miss Greenwood broke down for a minute or two'. At one point, her father reacted to her by bowing his head and then drying his eyes with the back of his hand.[41] Once she left the court room, she fainted in the arms of Mr. Eustace Hazzel Vant (1887-1947), a solicitor of Settle and the Greenwood family legal trustee from Yorkshire (the Greenwoods were still listed as one of the principal landowners in Ingleton). Vant was clearly a trusted family friend as Greenwood's other daughter resided with his family in 1921. Irene later said 'I do not remember what I have said ... I do not know whether my evidence has saved or hanged my father'.[42]

Greenwood later wrote, 'Of my daughter I cannot speak too highly. She has behaved splendidly, and I cannot forget her brave bearing in facing the ordeal of cross examination'. Irene added, modestly, 'Too much has been made of my part ... I was doing right in telling the truth' and that 'I know my father better than these people can know him'.[43]

Once Irene stepped down, the case for the defence was over. The judge then decided that the day's hearing would end there, with the final witness. He declared that he hoped the trial might be concluded on the Monday. For him there were two main questions that needed answering.

'The first question will be, was there arsenic in the body? Next, was the accused man intentionally responsible for introducing it there? If the jury are satisfied he was not responsible for introducing the arsenic there, then that is the end of the case'.[44]

Another important development was that Greenwood signed an agreement with *The Illustrated Sunday Herald* that he would write his story for them for publication after the trial. They would pay him £3,000. Cheque book journalism of this type was very common with tabloid newspapers often competing for the life story of a person accused of a heinous crime; not just any murder but one that was attracting mass press coverage. Earlier in the court that day it was noted 'Greenwood again looked pale and wore a rather anxious look'.[45]

Greenwood had noticed that from the onset of the trial, he had seen a lady sitting on the left of the judge, 'of mature years dressed as though in deep mourning'. It was the judge's wife (Mary Louise Long, once of New York). However, on the day just passed she had not appeared there. He later wrote 'It sent me cold. I thought I could but read into it that the judge believed the evidence was so much against me that he would have an awful duty to perform, and so that she might be spared the none too pleasant experience of seeing a man sentenced to death he had advised her not to attend'.[46]

Meanwhile, as a newspaper noted, 'Carmarthen today was like a fair without the roundabouts'. It was market day in any case, but those attending it had the court case as an added interest.[47]

Every night when Greenwood was back in his cell, he went over what he had heard in court that day. He wrote 'As my eyes became sore for sleep I would endeavour to snatch a little rest. But the mind refused'. He analysed the pros and cons of 'The evidence' until the clock tolled six.[48]

Meanwhile, the jurymen, who had been secluded socially, had enjoyed evening motor trips to neighbouring towns. On the Sunday they had their first daylight trip. Two were ill and so could not do so. Those who did made 'a journey of about 50 miles through the fine scenery of Carmarthenshire, heightened at this season by the wonderful autumnal foliage'.[49]

The penultimate day of the trial was Monday 8th November. As on previous occasions, Greenwood arrived in a horse drawn carriage for 9.00am, an hour before the trial began. He was described thus:

> Appeared in the dock looking as smart and spruce as usual ... sat in the dock twirling his moustache and apparently unconcerned. He looked around the court, seeming, for the first time in the long trial, to take no interest in the proceedings. He was so indifferent in what was going on that he closed his eyes as if in sleep for a while. At other times he sat with his right hand to his cheek and turned his eyes to the ceiling as though in introspective mood. Only very occasionally did he glance towards the judge'.[50]

There had been concern about Marshall Hall's health in that week. Dr. Willcox, who he had cross examined in the previous week, had been administering to his health needs. There was, however, concern that Sir Edward would not be able to attend the court on this crucial day.[51]

It began with the closing speech for the defence. Marshall Hall began by telling the jury that his illness meant that he would be obliged to leave the court after his final speech. He emphasised that it was their responsibility to find Greenwood guilty or not guilty and reminded them that he had said in court 'I have never given arsenic to my wife'. He said that the prosecution's case was that Greenwood had introduced arsenic to the wine that his wife then drunk at Sunday

The Case for the Defence and the Summing Up 197

lunch on 15th June. He added that the prosecution had all the advantages of the chemical experts, the detective force and 'whole of the machinery of the law'.[52]

Yet in spite of all this, he argued that 'the case has gone into thin air'. He emphasised the role played by Irene Greenwood, 'a young woman standing in the witness box in a trial of her father for his life … if she loved her mother, as it is admitted she did, she would be hardly likely to have a kindly feeling for her father whose hand had done to death the mother whom she loved … If you believe this witness, the case is at an end, because she swears that she drank the red wine'.[53]

He argued that 'there was not one title of evidence' that Greenwood gave his wife any arsenic, though it is almost unknown for poisoners to be witnessed poisoning their victim's food or drink. He had five points to be made in Greenwood's favour. Firstly, there was no motive; there was no case that Greenwood was in love with Gwladys Jones or had made her pregnant. There was no financial motive; Marshall Hall said that Mrs. Greenwood had an annual income of £900 but none of this went to Greenwood. He discussed the rings and Greenwood's engagement. As to the weedkiller, 'the accused has legitimately accounted for it, and no inference from that is to be drawn against him'.[54]

As to opportunity, the only point against Greenwood was the evidence of Hannah Williams, dismissing her as being a 'poor little frightened thing'. He inferred that her evidence had been drawn out of her by the police. He spent some time attacking her evidence and stated that it was contradictory and changing. She was unclear about the glass that it was drunk out of or whether Mrs. Greenwood had one glass of wine or two. He cast doubt as to whether Greenwood would have poisoned the wine and then risked one of his children then present of drinking it as well. As to his spending time in the china cupboard, other witnesses said he went there often to clean his hands. The morning of the alleged crime saw Foy working in the garage with Greenwood. He added that the disappearance of the bottle of wine was irrelevant.[55]

Then there was Greenwood's behaviour of the night of his wife's death. If he was a killer, would he have gone for the doctor? He said that if this were so, would he have had nurse Jones and Miss Phillips present with his wife on her deathbed. He then discussed arsenic and how widespread it was. Could such a small dose of arsenic have killed her? He questioned the accuracy of the medical witnesses and their calculations.[56]

Medical evidence was also questioned. Mrs. Greenwood was unwell, he reminded the jury. He recalled that the doctors called for the defence suggested that morphia, not arsenic was the cause of death. 'If you believe that, then the case for the prosecution fails'. The judge intervened to state that this was putting it too far. Marshall Hall then claimed that Dr. Griffiths might have given Mrs. Greenwood arsenic rather than the bismuth, given the similarity in appearance of them both. 'I contend that I am justified in suggesting that Dr. Griffiths made an unfortunate mistake that was colossal in its results'. This was an error on his part.[57]

Greenwood's innocence was stressed. It was argued that he would know the symptoms of arsenic and thus would not be likely to use such. He reminded them that there was no reason for him to have killed his wife. He used moral blackmail as he began to sum up, referring to the fact that if they found him guilty 'you would draw the lever to launch him into eternity … Your verdict is final, necessarily final'. They must also consider his children and their reputation if their father was found guilty of murder. He cited a passage from *Othello* and added 'Are you by your verdict going to put out that light? Gentlemen of the jury, I demand at your hands the life and liberty of Harold Greenwood'.[58]

Marshall Hall was indeed an unwell man. Aged 63, he suffered from phlebitis and varicose veins, worsened after falling through a cucumber frame at home. A habitual smoker of cigars his lungs were in poor shape. He had stage fright and was stressed.[59]

Archibald Edgar Bowker (1884-1966), later wrote of his master's performance 'it is an education in the marshalling of facts in clear and telling phrases, but I who knew him well and knew just what an artist he was in the timing of a point, and how he could use an inflexion in that marvellous voice of his to emphasise some argument can well imagine how he let himself go in a case of this nature'.[60]

It was now Samson's turn to speak for the prosecution. He complimented both jury and Marshall Hall and sympathised with the latter's illness which forced him to withdraw. He drew the jury's

The Case for the Defence and the Summing Up 199

attention to three issues. Was there arsenic in the body, did Greenwood administer it and was there enough to be fatal? He stated, as to the first 'it is a physical fact beyond all dispute that arsenic was there'. Was it there by result of accident or because it naturally exists in the body? Samson reminded them that Webster claimed that 0.275 of a grain found in June 1920 would equate to the fatal two grain dose ingested in the previous year. He spent time justifying the validity of the evidence given by Webster and Dr. Willcox and casting doubt on Drs. Toogood's and Griffiths' assertions, neither of whom had much relevant experience or knowledge.[61]

The next question to deal with was how was the fatal dose of arsenic administered. He argued against the accidental theory as proposed by the defence. Had it been an accident, then it was odd that no one else had been affected. Mis-administering of medicine and gooseberry skins were also disposed of. Poison in the food was impossible because all had eaten it and not suffered ill effects. It therefore had to be in one of the drinks she had; wine, tea or brandy even (given Irene's evidence he could no longer definitely state that the arsenic was in the wine). He also reaffirmed the essentials of Hannah Williams' testimony that she had seen Greenwood in the china cupboard. Hunter intervened on two occasions during this part of the speech.[62]

He then addressed Irene's evidence, which he said was in part contradicted by Miss Phillips' evidence about there being no wine at table in evening whilst Irene said there had been. He drew the jury's attention to Greenwood uncorking a new bottle of brandy to give to his wife in the afternoon. Why did he do so when there was a bottle of brandy partially drunk.[63]

Motive was next. Samson said that the ring given by Greenwood to Gwladys Jones was bought prior to him proposing. He asked why Greenwood's present wife was not brought as a witness. 'Why is it that my learned friend has not got Gladys Greenwood to give testimony in this crucial point? The whole crux of the case is this – what was the relationship between this man and that woman? The accused was animated by desire of Gladys Jones, and it was to consummate that desire that he removed Mabel Greenwood from this life'. No one else had reason to administer the poison. It was recalled that there had been a length of time in Greenwood's bringing the doctor over. This suggests 'a very grave matter'.[64]

He also doubted whether morphia was in the pills given to Mrs. Greenwood. First, both the nurse and doctor denied telling him about morphia pills. Dr. Griffiths had asserted that these were opium not morphia pills that he had given out. He had sworn this under oath.[65]

As he began to conclude, Samson stated that arsenic was the cause of death, that there had been sufficient of it to have done so and that Greenwood alone had opportunity and motive. He said that Marshall Hall had used eloquence and moving speeches, but he appealed to the jury to listen to logic and reason. He asked for sympathy towards the life of 'that poor soul who lies in Kidwelly churchyard'. They owed a duty to the defendant but also to the victim. His final words were, 'I can only hope in this solemn matter that Almighty God, in whose hands are all our destinies will guide you a conclusion that is both just and right'.[66]

It was later said that 'the jury were all greatly impressed by the Prosecuting Counsel's scrupulous fairness in presenting the case for the Crown, and also in his searching cross examination of the witnesses for the defence. The defending Counsel was also splendid. His rhetoric, however, did not deflect to the slightest degree, the mind of the jury in their endeavour to find the truth in the case as it was presented to them. The exhaustive and clear summing up of the judge was greatly appreciated by the jury'.[67]

It was probably this which upset Irene, who was in court with her younger sister. Irene later wrote, 'it was a terrible thing for me. As I sat there listening to all the counsel's insinuations against my father who has been to me all that a father could be ... it is as though all the vicissitudes of the prosecution were so many stabs at my heart'.

To her father was the man who had played with her as a child in the garden and had kissed her goodbye when she left to go to London from the railway station for the first time.[68]

Finally, it was the turn of the judge to address the jury. His speech that afternoon was very short indeed, compared to that of many judges at this stage of the trial. It was a simple task for the jury; they had either to declare the defendant's guilt or if they were very doubtful they would declare him being not guilty. He reminded them that 'motive is not evidence'. They must not be distracted as to

The Case for the Defence and the Summing Up 201

whether the police had tampered with the evidence or whether Dr. Griffiths had erred in giving medicine. This was not what they had to dwell on. The jury were now the sole 'judges of facts'. They must not be influenced by popular opinion. They must not judge Greenwood about whether they liked him or not but whether he was guilty or not. He would go through the evidence with them on the next day.[69]

The final day of the trial was Tuesday 9th November. The trial had been expected to have lasted five days but now it was in its seventh. As ever public interest was high, again there was a rush and again the police had a difficult task. 'Greenwood had borne the strain of the trial well, but there were signs of fatigue in his face as he sat in the dock today'. Marshall Hall arrived early 'and seemed somewhat better in his health'.[70]

The judge carried on with his charge to the jury. As he began, 'It now becomes my duty to sum up the evidence'. They had to judge the facts only, not acting on suspicion or anything they had read. Were the witnesses correct in what they had said? Memories might be hazy after so long and the witnesses need not be perjured.[71]

The first question to answer was, was there sufficient arsenic in the body to kill. Webster and Dr. Willcox, experts both, thought so. Then, if they agreed on that, who administered it. 'That is the real difficulty in the case'. Then there was motive. He reminded them that there was no pecuniary reason for Greenwood to do so. Then there was passion though Greenwood had denied this. The judge personally disregarded Mrs. Groves' evidence about an association between Greenwood and Gwladys Jones prior to the former's wife's death but the jury need not do so.[72]

The prosecution stated that the arsenic had been in the wine drunk by Mrs. Greenwood at lunch. There was the alleged opportunity for Greenwood to have done this. Witnesses, however, were contradictory. Likewise, the possession of arsenic by Greenwood could have been merely to dispose of the garden's weeds or to kill his wife. The gardener's evidence was not conclusive either way. The judge reread some of the witness statements to remind the jury of them.[73]

He then reminded them of the evidence of Hannah Williams but cautioned them about the accuracy of her recollections. The jury must not draw any inference from the lack of the second Mrs. Greenwood as a witness (she could not be called anyway as a spouse could not then testify against their spouse, and as Marshall Hall rightly said his opponent should not have made the suggestion she should be). There was discussion about whether the same wine bottle that was allegedly poisoned was on the table in the evening as well. The judge thought not. He then said, 'The accused and his daughter say it was there, and the daughter says she partook of it. If the daughter partook of the wine, then there is an end to the case'.[74]

The judge then said that Mrs. Greenwood exhibited the symptoms of arsenic poisoning; such as diarrhoea and vomiting, but these could be symptoms of natural illnesses. Gooseberry skins did not have the same effect, he also stated. The evidence of Greenwood's activities and his alleged delays on the fatal night were recalled. Dr. Griffiths' prescriptions were discussed as was the possibility that he had inadvertently given her a solution of arsenic rather than bismuth. The judge thought the latter unlikely. Whether the doctor gave morphia pills instead of opium ones was another matter; again the judge thought on balance not.[75]

Finally, he told them that the defendant might have killed his wife deliberately with arsenic and that was murder, or he may have given her arsenic to shorten it and that this was fatal because of the addition of morphia, that was manslaughter. His final instruction to the jury was 'I now ask you to consider this case with courage, earnestly and honestly, desiring to do what is right and just. That is the last assistance I can give you gentlemen. You will have to retire to consider your verdict'.

They did so and Greenwood was also removed from the court. It was adjourned at 2.15pm.

The twelve men of the jury were of a range of ages and occupations, all drawn from parts of the same county. It was said of them 'Like all citizens who take a serious view of their duty to the State, they gave their concentrated attention to the evidence during the eight days of the trial, and fearlessly delivered their unbiassed finding in this case'. The facts as presented did not satisfy their opinion that the accused was guilty beyond all doubt.[76]

We do not know the nature of the jury's discussion, but Greenwood later wrote at length at this period of suspense from his viewpoint:

The Case for the Defence and the Summing Up 203

I will now tell you of my experience while waiting, with my life suspended by a thread, below the court, while the jury were arriving at their conclusion.

In the long, narrow cell, with its barred windows and precautions against anything a man on trial for murder might do to defeat the demands of justice, I paced up and down, as if in a cage. Moments in the trenches when the watch had been set for an advance, were mild in comparison. In that case, at least, every man would have some opportunity to shoot, to strike a blow in defence.

I had to go up and 'over the top' to be shot at with my eyes blinded and my arms pinioned. I might have shouted, screamed or hit out – but without avail.

A warder, and a gentleman, too, tried to shunt my thoughts into more cheerful channels by telling me Army stories. Even in my extremity my heart was bursting in gratitude to him but I am afraid my ears were deaf and my mind careless of his efforts. I could see those twelve men in my mind's eye, under lock and key, zealously guarded, debating the points for and against me.

I had the fortification of my innocence, but there was the natural and awful thought 'Will they make a mistake?'

As the minutes ticked away, my mind underwent the agonies of Hell. Then I found the terrible influences of the mind dominating the body. My knees shook, my body vibrated as there came to me the picture of the consequences if those twelve men were mistaken.

'Put out the light'. Those words!

They burn into my brain now, just as they blinded me with tears when they fell from Sir E. Marshall Hall's lips a few hours before.

Outside that barred window leading to the main street, a thousand voices buzzed in opinions on my chances. That sheet of glass, those iron bars might have forever cut off my freedom on earth.

I had spent an hour thus, but my trial had not ended. Another half an hour, and yet another had to be endured.

> I prayed for the suspense to end. Was the life I had been reduced to worth fighting for? In truth, I had ceased to live as normal beings understand life.
>
> Then like a flash came an awful picture before me.[77]

It was just over an hour and a half later, at 3.53pm that the jury returned. This suggests that the decision had not been initially clear cut and that there had been discussion. The officials resumed their seats. Greenwood later noted:

> The jury had been back in their places some moments before the judge had returned from a case which I hear since, he had begun in another court – a case of alleged murder, too.
>
> And the judge settled down to perform his office, people crowded in from the passages to the court. I saw them collectively, I recognised some of them individually. And all this whilst wildly anxious men and women breathed faster in the tense atmosphere of expectation.
>
> I regarded them all in these few moments – the faces of the jury. I felt in a moment that they gave no reflex of a verdict that would carry with it my doom.
>
> But my mind was seized with the fear of the dread alternative verdict which the judge had mentioned at the close of the evidence.
>
> As a lawyer I realised what would happen if this substituted the one of 'not guilty', which was mine by right. Prison walls would be my bondage for years.
>
> But this was not the worst.
>
> Suppose these twelve men disagreed! Suppose there had to follow in consequence a second trial over interminable days!
>
> The horror of it. I could not stand it. I had reached the limit of what a human being can endure.
>
> For seven days I had been in that dock, and a Sunday had intervened. This reads like a seven day trial, but to me the trial lasted the while of the twenty four hours of the clock – except the night before the final day …

> Had this to be re-endured? Good God, it could not! I should be beyond hope, and would end my days in an asylum.
> The Clerk of the Arraigns rose to his feet. The great question was now about to be put. It was put in dead silence.

He also later wrote, 'How slow, how impossibly deliberate he seemed!'[78]

The clerk of the court then asked the foreman of the jury: 'Gentlemen of the jury, have you agreed upon your verdict?'

The answer was 'Yes'.

The clerk continued 'Look upon the prisoner at the bar and say whether he is guilty or not guilty'.

The foreman stated 'Not guilty'.[79]

A journalist reported the scene, writing that 'He [Greenwood] stood, pale certainly, but without any sign of agitation'. On hearing the verdict a man ran across to Greenwood and shook his hand. Then, for Greenwood, 'A smile in which there was something of sadness and of gladness spread over his pale face'. The man who had rushed to him was Hubert Jones, a brother-in-law of his, and he said 'I congratulate you, Harold, old man'. He did not leave the court house immediately but went to the cells below for a drink and to discuss the situation with the newspaper that was buying his story.[80]

Apparently 'Mr Greenwood pulled himself together, and with a smile and a heave of his shoulders expressed with a movement of face and body that must have been to him the most intense relief that possibly have come to him after the terrible strain of the past seven days'.

Women in the public gallery clapped him; in contrast to how he had been dealt with after the inquest and earlier court hearings. 'Mr Greenwood was sufficiently self conscious and composed to turn round and to smile again his pleasure and relief in being a free man'. Vant brought Greenwood's two daughters to meet him and to take him by car home.[81]

It was reported that 'Mr Greenwood turned around sharply, but before he could move a step the governor of the Gaol [David Johns] smiled, said something to him, and shook him by the hand. As he reached the head of the stairs, which led from the dock, and to liberty and freedom, a burst of subdued applause came from the public gallery', which the judge condemned and warned against any repetition.[82]

[1] Harold Greenwood, a free man, leaving court for the final time.

The Case for the Defence and the Summing Up 207

Greenwood later wrote 'Freedom! An innocent man! [1] It was as though I had taken a great draught of wine. My excitement was terrible, and it was rising still with the applause that crashed out – sternly stopped by the judge'.[83]

Authors on the case often state that Marshall Hall left after his summing up speech and whilst it is true that his junior made comments about the prosecution's summing up the trial transcript makes it clear that Marshall Hall spoke during the judge's words to the jury.[84] He actually caught the 6.37pm train from Cardiff that evening.[85] Whilst awaiting his train a porter came up to him and said 'I see you got him off, Sir Edward'. On his return to London he visited his silversmith friend who presented him with the silver tankard with the inscription, 'I dared you to do it and you did it'.[86]

Mrs. Greenwood had remained at home that day, with her sister, Mrs. Gertrude Johnson. When news of the trial's verdict reached Kidwelly, Mrs. Greenwood learnt the news of her husband's acquittal by telephone. Hundreds gathered outside Rumsey House. It was towards 7.00pm that he arrived home.[87] She later wrote that on hearing the news, 'God be thanked a thousand times. I knew he was innocent, but I had a terrible fear that he should not be able to overcome the prejudices against him'.[88]

Greenwood later recollected the journey:

> Before very long I was speeding along the road in the motor car to my home, where my wife's brother, Hubert, who dashed over to me in court on hearing the verdict and shook me by the hand, had preceded me to inform them of the actual time of my arrival.
>
> It was a beautiful sight. I passed by the house [Broom Hill] I used to live in, and as we swept round the bends in the road to Kidwelly I remembered that the last time I took my late wife out for a motor ride it was in a little Calthorpe along that very road …
>
> The next moment the lights of Kidwelly could be seen, and in a few minutes we had crossed the bridge by Rumsey House, and, the chauffeur having given the agreed signal on the klaxon we swung in, through the carriage entrance, to my home.

> It was just as though I had returned from an exile abroad covering many years. I felt that half my lifetime had passed since the day when I was arrested in the very portals of that door, the day the coroner returned the verdict that became one of the milestones in my life.[89]

Once at Rumsey House and the gates closed behind the car, he alighted and went in. Apparently 'Mr. Greenwood was in the highest spirits and there was an affectionate scene when he met his wife in the hall … He spoke in the warmest terms of appreciation of the way in which Sir Marshall Hall and Mr. Ludford had fought for him'. He had never doubted the verdict, so he said.[90]

[2] Percy Greenwood. (Jonathan Hewlett's collection)

All of Greenwood's children were there; Eileen and Irene came over after having stayed at a hotel in Carmarthen during the trial. His younger brother Percy **[2]** was there, as was the family solicitor, Vant.[91]

What was not published until another decade was the content of the note that Mr. E. Willis Jones, a Llanelli chemist and jury foreman, had passed to the judge, which showed that the jury's verdict was not unequivocable:

> We are satisfied on the evidence in this case that a dangerous dose of arsenic was administered to Mabel Greenwood on Sunday, 15th June 1919, but we are not satisfied that this was the immediate cause of death.
>
> The evidence before us is insufficient, and does not conclusively satisfy us as to how, and by whom, the arsenic was administered. We therefore return a verdict of 'Not Guilty'.[92]

In Scotland this would have been a verdict of 'not proven'; that the jury thought the defendant was guilty but that they thought the evidence presented was insufficient to prove this beyond doubt. Greenwood's innocence was still not clear to all.

Chapter Nine

Aftermath

On the day after his acquittal, Greenwood, never shy of potential good publicity, entertained a reporter from the *Western Mail*, the Cardiff based newspaper that he had enjoyed reading during the trial, to lunch at Rumsey House. He joked with the man to say that he was unable to offer him any burgundy.[1] Others were less sanguine.

There was a brief flurry of correspondence between some of the officials involved in the case in its aftermath. The judge was concerned that the jury denying that arsenic was the cause of death might be taken as a precedent. However, it was decided to keep the confidential note passed from jury to judge secret. The judge had had a talk with the jury foreman (a chemist) 'that he had some doubt whether the dose was given on the Sunday was itself a fatal dose' and he added 'It may have occurred to you – the theory of cumulative poisoning in smaller doses over a period. There were indications of that here and there in the non-medical evidence'. Dr. Willcox replied, 'There was no evidence for the fatal dose given in the Greenwood case – no doubt full doses of poison had been taken in the previous few days. I have no doubt about arsenic being the cause of death and appreciate that the jury have not. I do not think that any other verdict was possible on the evidence given'. We shall return to this point later.[2]

Samson, who had led for the Crown in the trial, made an interesting remark in January 1921 about the case, 'Everyone I have met in South Wales seems satisfied as to whom administered the poison and the findings of the jury is now commonly known in S. Wales'. He noted that the jury foreman was vexed about the contents of his note being suppressed 'as they took so much trouble to come to that conclusion'. Samson was unhappy about this decision to officially conceal it, 'It is very unfortunate and contrary to the jury's wish and from our own point of view leaves undecided the question of supreme interest'. He recalled the 1886 Adelaide Bartlett poisoning case in which the defendant was found not guilty of spouse poisoning but the general opinion was that of guilt yet the method of administration was unknown.[3]

Dr. Willcox never spoke about the case in public but his biographer son wrote:

> There is no doubt that he shared the Judge's opinion that Mrs. Greenwood was the victim of cumulative poisoning over a long period. The medical history of the case is strongly suggestive ... impaired appetite, weight loss, debility, a tendency to faintness and recurrent attacks of gastroenteritis which had always, according to her doctor's account, cleared up until the last attack on the final Sunday. A clear picture of arsenical poisoning could not have been proved by the Crown in court because no specimens of hair or nails or skin were kept for analysis.[4]

There was also discussion among the police about what had gone wrong. As with the jury, Dr. Griffiths was singled out for comment, as Sergeant Helby wrote, 'The evidence of Dr. Griffiths was most unsatisfactory and it would appear that the doctor really did not know what he prescribed ... The evidence and dejected appearance of this witness no doubt had a great impact on the jury'. The fact that his prescriptions book had been destroyed was another problem because the conundrum of whether opium or morphia pills was given could never be resolved.[5]

Then there was the issue, already noted, about witnesses not been questioned. Helby wrote 'There can be no doubt that a grave mistake was made in not taking a statement from Miss Greenwood'. Superintendent Jones put this down to the fact that 'I left the Kidwelly people to Sergeant Lewis'. There was more to it than this, however, as another officer wrote 'I was strongly of opinion that she should be seen and a statement taken from her at once'. However, as a senior officer at the Yard stated 'We however, received explicit instructions in writing **not** to interview her'. A memorandum that had been drawn up (stated on page 110) of what to and what not to do stated 'Take no statement at present from the Greenwood family'.

Therefore, 'Chief Inspector Haigh was greatly handicapped in this case. He had an extremely difficult position to fill and the way he carried out his duties reflects great credit on him'.[6]

The newly appointed bishop of Durham, Hebert Henson (1863-1947), wrote in his diary on 17th November 1920 about a conversation he had had with a judge at the Athenaeum that evening:

> He told me that he was himself persuaded that Greenwood was guilty, and that five judges discussing together the case took the same view, though one doubted. He admitted that the evidence was inadequate, and that the case for the Crown had been badly handled. The LCF [Lord Chief Justice?] thought that the judge should have directed the Jury to bring in a verdict of attempted poisoning. For arsenic had been given, and probably by the prisoner, but the woman may have died from the morphia pills.[7]

There was an alternative theory to account for the death of Mrs. Greenwood and that was put out by Mr. George Sims (1847-1922), an amateur criminologist, who had posited solutions to the mystery of Jack the Ripper of 1888 and to that of the equally unsolved murder of five year old Willie Starchfield on a train in 1914. He wrote that there had been two deaths in Llanelli in 1892 which were attributed to inhalation of arsenic from the ground. Given the amount of land used for industrial and mining purposes, which involved arsenic, this could have led to her death, though if this was the case the question should be why was no one else afflicted thus.[8]

One of the myths of the case, repeated as recently as 2021, originated in 1929 in the first biography of Marshall Hall, who had died in 1927. His biographer wrote:

> The verdict was an exceedingly popular one; but although Sir Edward probably received more congratulatory letters and telegrams on this case than any other, none came from the prisoner himself – the only one of all his prisoners who never thanked him by word or letter. Perhaps his counsel's absences were still rankling Mr. Greenwood's mind. It is certainly a fact

> that he refused to pay him his fee, for 'refresher' for the last day of the trial. As Marshall Hall was there for such a short time, he was perhaps within his strict legal rights.[9]

Duke and others refuted such in the press and in her volume on the case, published in 1930, so quite why there is such repetition when the refutation features in the one crucial text on the case is a mystery. Ludford, too, stated that this was the case. Greenwood's legal costs were 200 guineas for the brief, plus 100 guineas special fee and 50 guineas a day refresher. With a trial of six days, the refreshers cost a total of 300 guineas. There was another £67 10s. for a consultation fee. The grand total was stated as being £759 15s. (though a calculation of these sums actually adds up to £667 10s.; (possibly there were other fees payable not listed separately). This was promptly paid (it should be recalled that Greenwood received £3,000 for the newspaper articles).[10]

The origin of the myth seems to be that after the acquittal, Marshall Hall's clerk suggested that a refresher be paid for the Sunday on which the barrister was not in court but was subject to strain and having to refuse other briefs during the period of the case. The matter was dropped. Apparently Greenwood objected to paying additional fees. An examination by Edward Marjoribanks into Marshall Hall's fee books does not support what he alleged in his book and he promised to delete the passage from subsequent editions of the book.[11] However, Herbert Bottomley (1860-1933), M.P. for Hackney South from 1918-1922, claimed in the House of Commons that Greenwood had had to find £2,000 in total for his legal costs and would these be defrayed from the public purse? He was told that this would not be so.[12] This figure does not seem to relate to that quoted above about the barrister's fees; and in contrast the cost of the prosecution was £853 3s., so Bottomley (a fraudster) may be exaggerating.[13]

The press were critical of the investigation and trial, applauding the verdict. According to *The Times* [1], 'It ended, as all sensible persons and all lawyers anticipated, but there were a great many incidents in the proceedings which were not creditable to our system of administering justice'. They claimed that from the outset the prosecution had a weak case. Greenwood having to wait four months for a trial was due to defects in the circuit system as 'To a prisoner who is not guilty, that must mean torture'. The evidence was flimsy and this reflected badly in the public prosecutor who had allowed it to go ahead. It should not have been allowed to proceed; even with better preparation the outcome would have been the same.[14]

> **The Kidwelly Trial.**
>
> The acquittal of MR. HAROLD GREENWOOD, who was tried at Carmarthen on the charge of murdering his wife, should stir feelings of relief in the public mind. The trial lasted seven days, and it was followed with the interest and speculation which such cases invariably evoke. It has ended as all sensible persons and all lawyers anticipated, but there were a great many incidents in the proceedings which were not creditable to our system of administering justice. From the outset the prosecution had a weak case. It does not seem to have been recognized that to place a man in peril of the hangman's rope is one of the heaviest responsibilities that the State can undertake in the cause of the community. The defects of our circuit methods unhappily led to the imprisonment of the accused man for more than four months, with the capital charge ever in his contemplation. To a prisoner who is not guilty, that must mean torture, although our law presumes innocence until the contrary is proved. That was bad enough. But when we read the flimsy evidence we marvel that the indictment was ever proceeded with, and that the DIRECTOR of PUBLIC PROSECUTIONS had the temerity to put MR. GREENWOOD in the dock. The subordinates of that official have proved to be utterly incompetent in this case, and even the leading counsel whom he instructed committed an error of which we should hardly have suspected a junior, through forgetting the provisions of the Criminal Evidence Act and commenting on the absence of the second MRS. GREENWOOD from the witness-box.

> When the trial stage was reached it was found that the prosecution had given no notice for the production of essential documents, and that the police had ignored MISS IRENE GREENWOOD, whose evidence went far to establish the innocence of her father. She swore that she had drunk twice from the bottle which was supposed to hold the poisoned wine. In conflict with her oath was the hesitating and indefinite evidence of the parlourmaid. Then came the evidence of DR. GRIFFITHS, who had attended MRS. GREENWOOD for sixteen years, and had signed a certificate that she died from heart disease. He swore on three occasions that he had given his patient two morphia pills, but at the trial he admitted that that was a mistake. He confused morphia with opium in his evidence, and he said finally, in cross-examination, that if he had given morphia it would have caused death. He was unable to produce his prescription book. These are but a few of the surprises in a surprising trial. We do not suggest that had the CROWN been competent in the preparation of the case the result would have been different. Far from it. But the DIRECTOR of PUBLIC PROSECUTIONS should not have launched these proceedings without the inquiries which are ordinarily expected of his office.

[1] Newspaper cutting concerning trial verdict.
(Courtesy of Fr. Jim Flanagan)

There was an analysis of the verdict. It was imagined that the jury might have been unsure whether a crime had even occurred. The evidence for Greenwood's guilt was there but the jury may have found it insufficient or unsatisfactory. Marshall Hall was praised, his conduct of the defence is admitted on all sides to have been of a brilliant and decisive character seldom excelled in the criminal courts of the country. Justice was deemed to have prevailed, 'We have more cause for pride that a case in which sentiment might have ruled has been tried with such calm and care and in the last decided on principles so sound'.

Greenwood, in his fifth article for the press, also gave his opinion on the law as it now stood. He began, 'I want to take the opportunity of making a few comments on the course of judicial procedure in criminal cases. Writing both as a lawyer and as a man who has suffered under the law, I want to protest, as strongly as I can, against the system which compels an innocent man to go through the ordeal from which I have just emerged'. He stated that bail was never allowed in a murder charge. He did not see why a magistrate may not use his discretion in allowing it in cases where there was doubt. He said that he had been tried three times, at the inquest, at the magistrates' court and at the assizes. He wrote 'the delay involved in judicial proceedings resulted in my spending four and a half months in gaol. Why should I, an innocent man, have had to endure that agonising wait?'

It had been suggested that even if he had applied to be tried at the Old Bailey that the trial would have been much quicker because of the Long Vacation; so a three months wait. The stronger reason why not to apply would be that it would have suggested that he dare not face his fellow countrymen in south Wales and thus a pointer to his guilt.

What he suggested was a judicial Home Rule, with three or four High Courts sitting continuously in the provinces to which cases like his could be referred to. Then 'A man against whom a grave charge is preferred ought to be able to have the matter settled within three or four weeks'. There could be a High Court sitting in Cardiff, one in the Midlands and at least one in northern England. He also suggested that there should be an Office of Public Defender. The prosecution had all the resources of the state and this was lacked by the defendant and so was not a case of fair play.

He concluded this and all his public articles thus:

> My trial is over. Whatever improvements may be effected in judicial procedure as a consequence of the public conscience being aroused. But my case cannot benefit me. But there may be others in like case to myself. I am not the first, nor I am afraid, am I likely to be the last, to suffer under our judicial system. It will be some consolation to me if my case leads to

> improvements that will lighten the burden that other innocent men may be called upon to bear'.[15]

The Nation newspaper took a rather different angle. Thereced was criticism that this was a very suburban and apparently trivial case yet it had absorbed all the newspapers, popular and high brow. More weighty subjects such as the death of the Greek King (King Alexander had died on 25th October 1920), massacres in Ireland and Armenia, starvation in Russia and diseases in Austria were neglected as being minor matters in comparison. It stated 'The first impression is of disgust. The spectacle is one of febrile decay. A nation with desperate realities and concentrating on a trivial and irrelevant issue is a nation, which on the first indignant verdict, seems not worth preserving'.[16]

Yet there was a counter argument. First, this was a real life drama, a problem with evidence that was uncertain and complex, concerning 'Death and Eternity'. Second. It was a story of a man fighting for his life 'against the enormous resources that a Government could bring up against him. The appeal was therefore to an elemental sporting instinct'. Most important was that this was 'the revelation of a commonplace life is in the main that it is commonplace. Every incident was read as the incident of every man's life'.[17]

Meanwhile, the council of the Pharmaceutical Society met a few days later and they discussed an aspect of the business. They were concerned about the fact that the composition and dispensation of drugs was often by the same hand, and that the sale of weedkiller was so easily made. Better regulation was the answer, they concluded.[18]

Greenwood's articles for the newspaper, most of which has already been cited in this narrative, were published in November and December 1920. He covered the last part of his first wife's life, his trial and his imprisonment. He wrote about his wife's illnesses and her death. He naturally painted himself in as glowing a light as possible, innocent of the charges of adultery and murder, a victim of evil gossip and a prison and judicial system that was hostile to the innocent man. Quite some time was spent on denying that he had poisoned the wine drunk at lunch, claiming that had he done so he would have risked killing not only his wife but his children as well. He said virtually nothing about his life prior to 1919. According to

Duke, 'It threw no new light upon the case'.[19] It is full of self pity in the same vein that Annie Hearn was to compose her life story for the press 11 years later after she, too, had been acquitted of arsenic poisoning.

He spent a lot of time attacking those who had thought him to be guilty, condemning them as:

> ... lying and malicious enemies suggested I had cunningly and wicked murdered.
>
> And just as the law has accepted the truth of my plea, I pray that God may forgive those who would have had me die in the ignominy of the scaffold.
>
> For nearly 5 months they have had me nailed to the cross of suspicion: not dead and benumbed, but alive and sensitive to its anguish.
>
> I can see evil faces now rejoicing as the points of the prosecution were brought out by the powerful address of Sir E. Marlay Samson.
>
> I can see the same people who tried to encompass the ruin for me they had often threatened to bring about, gloating over the scientific evidence of Mr. Webster, the analytical expert, and Dr. Willcox, the pathologist.
>
> In the name of God, was not my ordeal terrible enough without enemies mocking me in my fight for life? A dog dying by the roadside will find sympathy in the most hardened felon, but these thought they saw me going to the scaffold, and the journey occasioned them rejoicing.[20]

He added:

> [that apart from the] little handful who tried to bring about my downfall and death; who tried to visit my children with a murderer as a father.
>
> On the other side is the great multitude, many of them entire strangers, who followed my case with their sympathies on the side of the prisoner, who rejoiced when justice was vindicated,

> and who lost not a moment in expressing to me their joy at my deliverance.
>
> I have received hundreds of letters and telegrams overwhelming me with good wishes and congratulations. I thank their senders from the bottom of my heart.
>
> I have endured so much and I am well nigh drained of emotion, but I should indeed be heartless and ungrateful if I did not, both for myself and my wife, avail myself of the opportunity in these columns to express, however feebly, what such messages have meant to us.
>
> For this experience has shown me my enemies. Far better than this it has also shown me my friends. It has introduced me to new friends and strengthened the old ties of existing friendships. I have had much trouble, but out of this trouble I have got many blessings, a greater appreciation if possible of my wife and my family, a greater exultation in freedom, a keener sense of the worth of an unsullied name.[21]

Apart from the story over the five issues of the newspaper, another newspaper, *The Empire News*, from the same owner, published a booklet titled *Greenwood's Thrilling Fight for his Life*, published later that year. It is an account of the trial, allegedly written by Greenwood, and it is well illustrated with pictures of the key legal figures, witnesses and others involved. It is 55 pages long but does not add to what is already known in its account of the trial at Carmarthen. It sold for sixpence.[22]

Despite the hitherto amicable relationship between Greenwood and Dr. Griffiths, the two fell out over money at the onset of 1921. Greenwood owed the doctor £45 in unpaid fees going back to 1915. The doctor had Mr. Paton take his case to the Llanelli county court to recover his money; as ever Ludford defended Greenwood.[23] There is no further reference to this business, so perhaps Greenwood settled out of court. Duke claimed that Greenwood was obliged to pay up.[24]

Meanwhile, in 1921, Greenwood, described as being a solicitor (although no longer listed in *The Law List* from this year onward), continued to live at Rumsey House. Just after the trial he declared that he wanted to live in peace with everybody for his children's sake. His wife wondered if they might have to move to make a fresh start but she put this decision in her husband's hands.²⁵ With Greenwood at Rumsey House was his second wife, his 17 year old son Ivor, having taken an engineering course in 1920, his occupation described as 'nothing at present', and two general servants, Lily Powell, aged 21 years, who had been with the family since 1918, and a new servant, Annie Wilkins, aged 18 years. Greenwood's other three children lived elsewhere. John Kenneth, then aged 11 years, was at a small boarding school for boys at St. Andrew's Tenby, run by John Burleigh, Irene worked as a governess in Cheshire and Eileen was employed as a clerk in Settle, Yorkshire.²⁶

Waxwork museums often capitalised on sensational trials by making effigies of notorious murderers. Madame Tussauds in London was the most famous of them all in Britain, but other cities had them as well. Most usually wait until after the execution or at least after the prisoner has been found guilty, but in the waxworks at St. Mary's Street, Cardiff, one William John D'Arc acted most unwisely by putting an effigy of Greenwood near Charlie Peace (1832-1879), a Victorian burglar and murderer who was hanged. It was next to Katie Whistance, a 15 year old who killed her aunt at Llanvetherine in 1920, on one side. On the other was Terence McSweney (1879-1920), Lord Mayor of Cork and who died in a hunger strike for his Sinn Fein beliefs. These figures were naturally in the 'Chamber of Horrors', for which visitors paid an additional three pence. The figure showed Greenwood in a striped suit and a green cloth cap. Greenwood himself later said it was 'clumsily made' and was not an accurate resemblance to him. Benjamin Williams, a former gardener at Rumsey House, saw this in December 1920, after seeing on a revolving sign 'Harold Greenwood now showing' and brought it to Greenwood's attention. It was not listed in the exhibition catalogue and was later moved to another room to stand by Captain Matthew Webb, a famous swimmer, and Sir Thomas Lipton, a well known tea merchant, and close to two noted Liberal prime ministers, Lloyd George and Herbert Asquith.²⁷

Doubtless realising the legal possibilities, Greenwood sought damages. A writ was issued in February 1921.²⁸ At the Glamorgan assizes on 7th March 1922, before Justice Sir Rigby Philip Watson and a jury, 'Harold Greenwood, solicitor of Kidwelly' was the plaintiff. D'Arc said that he had meant that the effigy be placed in the famous people gallery, not the 'Chamber of Horrors' and so had not meant to cause any distress. Greenwood attested 'My personal reputation suffered' and 'I felt very hurt indeed' at the 'cruel and palpable wrong'. It was said that he had gained £3,000 from a newspaper for his notoriety. Another newspaper alleged 'Mr. Greenwood who looked older than he did when he was so prominent a figure, his hair being wholly silver grey, was in court wearing a navy blue suit'. D'Arc lost his case and Greenwood was awarded £150. The matter was widely reported nationally in many newspapers.[29]

Another woe was that in August 1921, five panes of glass in the garden's greenhouse at Rumsey House were broken. The culprit was one George Trembeth, an unemployed man of no fixed abode. He was arrested and given 10 days in prison.[30]

[2] The one who did not get away: Major Herbert Rowse Armstrong. (Wikicommons)

In 1922 another English solicitor in Wales was charged with murdering his wife, Katherine, with arsenic. This was Major Herbert Rowse Armstrong (1869-1922) of Hay-on-Wye [2]. As with Greenwood, his wife's death in the previous year was initially deemed to be due to natural causes and she was buried in the churchyard without investigation. Suspicions arose as time went on as it seemed that the major attempted to poison his rival solicitor, Oswald Martin. There was an exhumation and arsenic was found in large quantities in the corpse. Unfortunately for Armstrong, he did not have the good fortune to be defended by Marshall Hall when it came to trial at the Hereford assizes and the investigators were rather more competent. Armstrong was found guilty and sentenced to death. He was executed on 31st May at Gloucester prison; the only solicitor in Britain to have been hanged for murder; Greenwood having been saved from that dubious distinction. The press were quick to scent the comparison between the two cases, following as they did so quickly after one another. Some of the same men were involved in each case; Dr. Willcox (by now Sir William) and Webster for the prosecution; Dr. Toogood for the defence.

Apparently Laura Davies, the chemist's wife in Hay-on-Wye, in 1922 recalled reading about Mrs. Greenwood being ill prior to her death and likening it to that of Mrs. Armstrong.[31] It has also been argued that, in the words of one author, 'I am quite sure that if Harold Greenwood had not been acquitted Herbert Rowse Armstrong would never have been tried. Whether the two men ever met we do not know. But their oddly dissimilar fates notwithstanding, they will be together in the minds of criminologists for many years to some'.[32] It has also been suggested that Armstrong was inspired to murder his wife by the same method as Greenwood is alleged to have done because Greenwood was found not guilty. Because one solicitor had been found not guilty of murder, it provided some kind of immunity to another doing likewise. It seems that Armstrong, on hearing of Greenwood's acquittal, talked at great length on the topic. Willcox wrote 'It cannot be doubted that the sensational report of a noted case of arsenical poisoning (the Greenwood case) led to the selection and use of this poison in these two cases [Pace and Armstrong]'.[33] Yet as one author on the Armstrong case has put it, this does not hold water because Armstrong had been poisoning his wife prior to

Greenwood's acquittal.³⁴ Perhaps, though, when he resumed poisoning his wife in January he had been emboldened to finish the job by Greenwood's escape.

Greenwood was prevailed upon to write an article for publication about his experiences in 1920 and was doubtless glad to do so for the money. He wrote:

> Only those who have been the man in the dock can realise the awful sensation … a helpless, suffocating sense of impotency and doubly so when the prisoner is a lawyer. It sounds black – black to the point of certainty … I know what the prisoner felt! Helpless, trapped, overborne. He steals a glance at the jury and sees that every word is telling … It is a fearful, unbelievable thing to be tried for your life. But terrible though the ordeal was, I am perfectly certain British justice is scrupulously fair to the accused. Nevertheless, only those who have been charged with murder can realise the exact nature of the ordeal'.³⁵

A contemporary journal referred to this article, titled 'Armstrong's fight for life', as being in 'bad taste' and 'revealing as to the mentality of the writer'.³⁶

The Greenwood case was commented upon during this investigation by various officials. Archibald Bodkin, director of the public prosecutions, commented that Webster should check for other poisons, not just arsenic, as in the Greenwood case.³⁷ Armstrong's legal defenders were aware of the precedent and considered putting Armstrong's 14 year old daughter in the witness box after seeing how effective Irene had been for her father. They decided not to and Armstrong said 'A little too like the Greenwood case'.³⁸ 'The failed Greenwood case hung over the entire prosecution' as Armstrong's recent biographer has noted.³⁹

As in 1920, Greenwood tried to sell Rumsey House. There was a public meeting at Kidwelly town hall in March 1923 to discuss his offer to sell it for £1,800. One Mr. H. G. Edwards said that it was one of the finest monuments in the town and that it could be utilised to the local war dead and so be sponsored by the Royal British Legion.

It was also said that a grant of between £500 and £1,000 could be obtained from the Miners' Welfare Association. However, no decision was reached at the meeting because of the large sum involved which would need a ballot of ratepayers before it could be accepted.[40]

[3] Rumsey House in 2024 still exhibiting the 'Chapel Sul' sign over the front entrance. (Author's photograph).

The council did not go ahead with the purchase and Greenwood was forced to drop his selling price. That August he did find a buyer; the Capel Sul, the independent Presbyterian chapel in the town. They agreed to pay £1,525 **[3]**. They planned to convert the house into a chapel.[41] It is not known how much of this went to Greenwood who badly needed money; the house was probably mortgaged and so the sum accruing to him was certainly less than the sale price. The contents of the house, 'a sale of household goods' were also sold. This occurred at the end of November 1923 and lasted two days. It was arranged by Messrs G. G. Anes and T. L. Stewart. Many people came and good prices were reached.[42] A note which was found in Dr. Willcox's file after his death in 1941, which makes interesting reading. A vase at the house was bought by a curate. Inside the vase was a broken packet of greyish powder. The buyer threw this on to an open fire and it caused a violent flame. Some of the powder remaining in the vase, he sent it to the Chief Constable who sent it to Webster who found a high proportion of arsenic in it.[43] It would seem that someone in the household was using the poison for purposes other than killing weeds.

[4] The Paddock. (Jonathan Hewlett's collection)

The Greenwoods left Kidwelly in 1923. He sold his practice, which had collapsed to nothing since 1920, to his articled clerk, Richard John Roberts.[44] They travelled first to the adjoining county of Breconshire, then rather further afield to Norfolk and finally settled in the little village of Walford, near Ross-on-Wye in Herefordshire. A county directory stated that the place was 'a large parish and small village, amidst beautiful scenery, on the river Wye, about one mile north from Kerne Bridge station'. It had a population of 1,080 in 1921 and many of the locals worked in farming.

Greenwood was almost a recluse and was known as Harold Pilkington (it is noteworthy that many who change their names retain one of their former names), being listed by that name in the commercial section of the county directory as being a farmer. His home was The Paddock, Great Howle in the hamlet of Coughton and he had a 90 acre farm [4].[45]

Mr. Albert Edward Morgan of Ross, a friend, described him and his life there:

> I called him 'Pa'. I can say that I never met a finer gentleman, yet there was something over which he was brooding and which made him sorrowful and sad. I used to accompany him on shooting expeditions, and we went ferreting together. On occasions I found him in tears. Now and then he referred to the late Mrs. Greenwood, but it was only in terms of endearment and respect. Sometimes he would mention the trial, but he would always protest his innocence. During the latter days of his illness his mind would wander a good deal.

He was engaged in farming and gardening and was a frequent visitor to the local market. He would travel by horse and gig to Ross. He was universally respected by those he met but people thought that his spirit was broken. 'He was always a charming companion and his whim of always being faultlessly dressed he preserved to the last'. Another report, a year later, was that he was 'courteous and amicable to a degree'.[46] Another journalist wrote that he was 'a tired, worn out man, who took no interest in anything except his wife and his pony'.[47] In 1925 Gwladys gave birth to a son, Gerald, named after Greenwood's half brother who had been killed in the war. It seems that his surname was registered as both Pilkington and Greenwood. Also living with them was his son John Kenneth, presumably having left school.

There was one final attempt at re-establishing a legal career. He sought the post of town clerk for Ross-on-Wye urban district council in August 1928 when the vacancy arose, but was unsuccessful. His health was poor and he suffered from a stroke in May 1928. He was stricken with paralysis on the right side and there was another stroke on Boxing Day. Thereafter he could only walk on crutches and with a stick and then only the 50 yards down the drive of his house to the gateway. The last two months of his life were dominated by illness. He died peacefully in his sleep on 17th January 1929, aged 55 years.[48]

[5] St. Michael's and All Saints' church, Walford-on-Wye.

Details of his funeral, which was 3 days later, were kept from the public. The service at the parish church, St. Michael's and All Saints, Walford-on-Wye, was officiated by a friend of his, the Reverend Albert Henry Bromfield (1884-1957), vicar of the neighbouring parish of Bishopwood [5]. Both his older sons attended as did two of his brothers-in-law. One of the wreaths read 'In loving affection from a devoted wife and Gerald'.[49] His grave was at the end of the churchyard's Road of Remembrance, which formed part of the war memorial.[50] There was no gravestone (as with his first wife); clearly finances were limited. Duke refers, in 1934, to his resting place as 'a nameless, neglected looking mound'.[51] As with the waxworks episode, his death was widely reported, though deep within the newspapers, and they referred to his being involved in the poisoning case of 1919 and subsequent trial. It does not seem that he left a will; perhaps there was so little to leave.

The press seemed largely sympathetic, as had been the case in November 1920 after the acquittal. One referred to him as being 'hounded by gossip from place to place', that he 'led a life of torture', 'the victim of malevolence and slander'. Apparently he 'was barely 60' on death, 'he had grown white haired with worry, financial worries and the mental strain'.[52]

His last years were spent under a cloud. So great had the unwelcome spotlight been on him in 1920 that he clearly desired to be forgotten. Yet he had maintained the love of his second wife, who, as we shall see, was concerned about his reputation almost two decades later.

Later that year Messrs. Watson and Sons, ironmongers of Ross, brought a civil suit against Greenwood's widow. They alleged she owed them £34 17s. 6d. for work they had done on the house, Paddock Farm. In court she declared that she was not responsible for this bill because it had been taken out by her husband. The case went in her favour.[53]

Mrs. Greenwood's next years are unknown, but in 1939 she was living with her unmarried sister, Alice and brother, William at No. 124 Felinfoel Road in Llanelli. She is recorded as not being then in paid employment. Presumably to attain a degree of anonymity she changed her surname to that of Johnson (the surname of her married sister Gertrude), whilst retaining her Christian names. In 1949, she was in west London helping her sister run a nursing home and she went with her solicitor and two of his clerks to attend the premiere of a play at Wimbledon Theatre. The play, *The Man they Acquitted*, was by Sir Edward Percy (1891-1968), M.P. for Ashford and was inspired by but not based on the Greenwood poisoning case. He had tried to contact any living relatives so as to avoid giving offence and said 'The only connection between this play and the Greenwood case is that it provided the all important inspiration'. In any case, the plot did have crucial differences, though the protagonist was a doctor, who was charged with murdering his wife by poison. The conclusion, though, was that the nurse had poisoned his invalid wife's wine. It does not seem that any legal action was taken.[54]

Mrs. Gwladys Greenwood (as Johnson) died in Llanelli on 14th January 1962 at Bryntirion Hospital, Swansea Road, having been living at No. 8 Parc Howard Avenue previously. She left £1,315 in her will, to five surviving siblings and her son. Unlike the press interest in the death of her late husband there was none here, over three decades later. It is probable that is how she would have wanted it. Gerald, whose surname was also Johnson, was resident in Johannesburg, South Africa in 1959. He is almost certainly deceased at time of writing (2024) and it is unknown whether he or his mother had any dealings with Greenwood's other children.[55]

Of Greenwood's first four children, their fates can be briefly recounted. Irene was employed as a governess in 1921, at the household of Mr. and Mrs. Hugh Duncan at Newfield Hall, Minshull Vernon in Cheshire, teaching the 8 year old Joan and the 6 year old Anne. She married Ernest Philip Martin Pearson in Kensington in 1928. They had at least one son, Brian Travers Pearson, born in 1930 and living in New Zealand by 1978. In 1939 Ernest Pearson was described as a bus lighting engineer, when the two of them were living in Woking (she was then not described as being in paid employment as per most married women at the time). She died in an old people's home in Wardle, Rochdale on 27th December 1980.

Mabel Eileen Greenwood was living in Whitefriars, Settle, with the family of Eustace Vant in 1921 and was then employed as a clerk. She passed her law exams in 1932 and became a solicitor like her father. She was clerk to the Giggleswick parish council, associated with the Settle branch of the National Farmers' Union and had been part of the Settle and District Light Opera company. She never married and was the first of the four siblings to die, which was in Settle, not far from her father's birthplace, on 26th May 1941 and was buried in Giggleswick. No reference was made to antecedents or her father in the small obituary and death articles.[56] Irene was allotted £100, John £50, Irene's son, Eileen and Norman Greenwood were given unspecified sums in the will of their uncle, Sydney Bowater in 1939.[57]

Norman Ivor Vansittart Bowater Greenwood lived in Croydon and worked in a bank, eventually becoming a bank manager. He married Irene May Brain (1908-1963) in Richmond, Surrey in 1931. He died in Barton-on-Sea, Hampshire on 12th February 1972 and his will left

£40,572. They had a daughter, Carolyn Bowater, in 1938, who married Geoffrey Waddell in 1964. Their daughter, Lindsay, grew up knowing next to nothing about her great grandfather. His younger brother, John Kenneth Greenwood, married Maisie Alloway in west London in 1938. By next year he was noted as being a motor engineer and dealer in Cheltenham. The two divorced. He then married one Pauline Ellen Wilson in 1945 and died in Aldershot on 19th June 1968. He and his first wife had one child; Diana Lucille Greenwood, born in about 1939 and who married one Donald Hewlett in 1956. She did not know of her antecedents until her 40s. Understandably their once well known ancestor was not a subject much discussed in the family.[58]

Dr. Griffiths survived Greenwood by a few years and died on 17th January 1934, a few months after his sister who was a possible contender for Greenwood's hand in 1919. The obituary noted his part in the Greenwood trial as a witness. His poor showing at the witness box does not seem to have affected his local popularity for he became deputy mayor of Kidwelly when in 1923 the town welcomed David Lloyd George as freeman of the borough and again served as an independent local councillor (topping the poll in 1928). He gave the land on which the town's war memorial was erected in 1924. The vicar of Kidwelly, the Reverend Jones, went on to write more books, became a Canon of St. David's Cathedral in 1930 and Rural Dean of Kidwelly in 1931 and retired in 1934, six years prior to his demise.[59]

Of the others involved in this case, Marshall Hall went onto defend others; unsuccessfully in the case of William Thomas Gray later in 1920 for the murder of Irene Munro at Eastbourne, and successfully with Madame Fahamy in 1923. Shearman was one of the appeal judges in the hearing of Major Armstrong, presided over the trial of Bywaters and Thompson in 1922 and was vehemently hostile to Mrs. Thompson, who subsequently was executed. In newspaper reporting of their deaths in 1927 and 1930 respectively, the Greenwood case was mentioned. Samson left the bar in 1923 and was appointed as stipendiary magistrate for Swansea. Hunter became Chancellor of the diocese of Swansea and Brecon in 1930. Lewis became a judge and his last murder trials were those of fellow Welshman Timothy Evans and then that of Donald Hume, both in the year of his death, 1950. Ludford was later county coroner and remained at his legal work until his death. Helby went onto become a detective chief inspector. Superintendent Jones was badly hurt in the strike riots of Ammanford in 1925, was awarded the King's Medal in 1926 and became deputy chief constable of the county. His obituary mentioned his part in the Greenwood case. Picton Phillips retired as chief constable in 1940 after 32 years in the job and 57 years in the police force.

In 1997 at the Manor Estates Auction Rooms the pocket watch and sketches made by Greenwood were on sale. They were being sold on behalf of Hugh Jones of Elgin Road, Pwll, and he was a nephew of Gwladys Jones. His knowledge of the case was limited but he gave his version; that it occurred in 1913, that Marshall Hall caused the body to be exhumed and when it was the pathologist found that it only contained that amount of arsenic that would normally be acceptable in a body and was not fatal, thus destroying the prosecution case.[60]

The play that concerned the second Mrs. Greenwood so much was the basis for an American television drama, broadcast in 1952 (it can be viewed on youtube.com). The story focuses on a Dr. Ralph Gordon, who lives with his wheelchair bound and almost universally detested wife, Elizabeth, and young daughter, Jennifer, together with a manservant, Barton, and a nurse, Miss Wayne. They live near London. Husband and wife row over him attending a conference to give a paper. A female visitor arrives and they take drinks. Dr. Gordon fetches a bottle of port from the cellar; the first bottle breaks so he takes another. He gives this to his wife, who almost immediately collapses. She is dead. Her husband diagnoses heart failure. It turns out that she has been poisoned with arsenic in the drink.

Dr. Gordon is put on trial for murder. His daughter tells the court that she drank from the same bottle (and is unscathed). The court acquits the doctor but on returning home finds an anonymous note pinned to the door telling him that he is no longer wanted locally. He talks to his daughter and she tells him she lied to save him, but considers him guilty.

The doctor then goes from his London home to Ireland and founds a successful new business. His manservant and nurse accompany him but not his daughter. He marries a younger woman and all seems well. Then his past is revealed by a journalist and his wife learns his secret. His practice collapses, though his staff remain loyal.

The doctor decides to take a ferry to Holyhead. Just as he is about to depart, Miss Wayne tells him that it was she who poisoned the port. She has been in love with the doctor and wanted to help him out of his predicament. So she poisoned the next but one bottle. Had he been found guilty at the trial, she would have confessed. Husband and wife are then reunited.

There are some similarities with reality; a professional man, with a name similar to Greenwood, and his wife argue; she dies of poison and he is put on trial for murder but acquitted. A key defence witness was his daughter who claimed to drink from the same bottle. Yet local opinion is still hostile and he leaves his home town. On the other hand, there is no reason to suspect nurse Jones of administering arsenic to Mrs. Greenwood; Mrs. Greenwood was not an unpleasant invalid but Greenwood was a womaniser and knew his second wife before his first died.

Although there was a two part television dramatisation of the Armstrong case, titled *Dandelion Dead* in 1994 (which makes no reference to the Greenwood case), the screen impact of the Greenwood case is far less. Also in 1994 was the television drama *Deadly Advice*, set in Hay-on-Wye and with explicit allusions to the Armstrong case; ironically the central family in the drama (a mother and two adult daughters) is named Greenwood. Two decades after the second Mrs. Greenwood's death there was a short television drama based on the case.[61] It was introduced and narrated by Sir Alwn Talfan Davies (1913-2000), Q.C. while Greenwood was played by William Vaughan; other actors played the judge, Marshall Hall, Dr. Griffiths and Hannah Williams. It was a half hour drama broadcast as part of a series titled *In this Case*, and was first shown on television on 22nd November 1985 on HTV between 10.30pm and 11.00pm.[62]

There was, in 1996, a half hour Radio 2 dramatisation of the story in a series about Marshall Hall's greatest cases, which starred Tom Baker as the barrister and was written by John Mortimer, former barrister and author. In this one, Greenwood is romantically linked to Gladys Griffiths, a piano teacher, who he is learning to play the piano with. Marshall Hall's clerk is named Mostyn and the discoveries made by Webster and Dr. Willcox post date Greenwood's incarceration in Carmarthen prison rather than the other way around. The story focuses on the trial, with Marshall Hall cross examining

Dr. Willcox, Dr. Griffiths and Hannah Williams – it is generally accurate though somewhat truncated by time constraints.

Finally there was an episode in the series *Crime Solver*, broadcast on ITV late on 15th June 2005 titled *The Murder Trial of Harold Greenwood*. This, as with the 1985 episode, seems to have vanished without trace.[63]

There are a number of books about Agatha Christie and true crime. Two refer to this case – curiously enough one which does not is one explicitly about poisonings and with arsenic in the title, possibly not surprising because Greenwood is not mentioned explicitly by name. Of the two that do, one considers only one of the stories discussed below and the other deals with them all.[64]

The story was cited, though not by name, in five Agatha Christie stories. The first was *The Cornish Mystery*, a short story published in 1923 and which later featured in *Poirot's Early Cases* in 1974. Here a middle aged woman living in a small Cornish town is concerned that her dentist husband is poisoning her and that he is rather attracted to his dental assistant, a young woman. The wife dies and the doctor ascribes her death to natural causes. There is suspicion, made all the more so because the bereaved husband then announces his engagement to his assistant. This leads to local gossip and suspicion. The corpse is then exhumed and it is found to contain arsenic. The dentist is arrested, the case is heard in the magistrates' court and he is assigned to the assizes for trial for the murder of his wife. Poirot reveals the true murderer and the motive; the dentist is innocent of murder. In the 1989 television adaptation, the actor playing the accused man looks startingly like Harold Greenwood.

Secondly, *The Tuesday Night Club*, published four years later as a short story and then in book form in 1932 as the first of *The Thirteen Problems*, which introduced the world to Miss Jane Marple. Mr. Jones is a middle aged and married travelling chemist. He is also a philanderer. He has been rather friendly with a doctor's daughter. One night after dinner with his wife and her companion, served by a young housemaid, Gladys Linch, the three diners become ill. The said doctor comes around that evening and gives Mrs. Jones opium pills. However, she dies, of food poisoning, says the doctor and is buried without further fuss. Mrs. Jones' will leaved Jones £8,000. Then a woman, comparing the case to another she has read about, finds a suspicious letter written by Mr. Jones. An exhumation takes place and arsenic is found in the body of Mrs. Jones. Jones is suspected but it seems impossible for him to have had the opportunity to commit the murder. Several features here have obvious parallels with the real case.

Then there is another short story, *The Lernaean Hydra* in *The Labours of Hercules*, which also makes reference to Major Armstrong. In fiction the invalid Mrs. Oldfield dies of gastric trouble; as Hercule Poirot remarks, 'the symptoms of gastric inflammation and of arsenical poisoning are closely alike – a fact which everybody knows nowadays. Within the last 10 years there have been at least four sensational murder cases in which the victim has been buried without suspicion with a certificate of gastric disorder'. In a discussion of murderers, a character in the story refers to 'Armstrong, for instance, and that other man – I can't remember his name'. This is an implicit reference to Greenwood, and as with the Miss Marple quote below, Agatha does not name him explicitly. Since he had died in 1929 and this had been widely reported, it is not certain why she could not have done so without fear of any legal consequences; possibly she had missed the brief obituary. In this case, it is the gossip of neighbours that lead the authorities to act. In the story it is the gossips that lead the widowed Dr. Charles Oldfield to summon Poirot following the death of his older wife. As the doctor tells him, 'I don't know how to fight this – this vile network of lies and suspicion'. In both cases there is the rumour that the widower poisoned his wife because he wanted to marry a younger woman.

In the story, however, the husband is entirely innocent of murder and at the end of it there is the prospect of a happy marriage with his beloved; unlike Greenwood he did not marry her earlier because of the cloud of suspicion that he lay under. Unlike Greenwood he is never charged with murder and never has to undergo the ordeal of a trial. One wonders if in making the two husbands innocent Agatha is suggesting that she believed Greenwood was not guilty of his first wife's murder.

Then there is the reference in *A Murder is Announced* (1950). Miss Marple tells Bunch Harman 'Family solidarity is a very strong thing. Very strong. Do you remember some famous case – I really can't remember who it was. They say the husband poisoned his wife.

In a glass of wine. Then, at the trial, the daughter said she'd drunk half her mother's glass – so that knocked the case against her father to pieces. They do say – but that may be rumour – that she never spoke to her father or lived with him again'.

Irene, his daughter, claimed to have drunk from the same bottle but without ill effect. However, following her father's remarriage she left the family home and lived with her mother's family, the wealthy Bowaters, in London. Her father had given her her mother's wedding ring but then demanded it back to give to Gwladys Jones – and he only told Irene about his forthcoming remarriage two days before the date. She was clearly able to support her father to the extent that she did not want him to suffer the ignoble fate of hanging and to have the notoriety of having a convicted murderer as her father, which would certainly not help her future prospects. On the other hand, after taking that crucial step, she did not want to have anything more to do with him and she and her sister did not attend their father's funeral, which suggests hostility. She may never have spoken to her father again, but this is unknown (but there is no evidence that she did).

However, the plot of the book has little or no connection with that of the Greenwood case. The killer goes on to kill twice again and is motivated by money. Their methods are dissimilar; shooting, poison and strangulation. Miss Marple is using the Greenwood case as an example about family solidarity in a murder case.

Finally, we might cite a comment made by Miss Marple at the end of another novel in which the spinster sleuth states, 'He wanted to marry the girl, you see. He is very respectable and so is she. And besides, he is devoted to his children and did not want to give them up. He wanted everything, his house, his children, his respectability and Elsie. And the price he would have to pay for that was murder'. Perhaps this provides a motive for Greenwood as well as the one in this story. Ironically in this story the poisoner is a solicitor and there is a Dr. Griffith and his sister, who is in love with the solicitor.

Another great 20th century British author alludes to the case in the same coy manner as Agatha Christie. In his essay of 1946, *The Decline of the English Murder*, George Orwell discusses the 'golden age' of classic English murderers (contrary to modern tawdry killers of the 1940s) as he cites Dr. Palmer, Jack the Ripper, Thomas Cream, Mrs. Maybrick, Dr. Crippen, Frederick Seddon, George Smith,

Major Armstrong, Bywaters and Thompson, and 'In addition, in 1919 or thereabouts, there was another very celebrated case which fits into the general pattern, but which I had better not mention by name, because the accused was acquitted'. This was clearly Greenwood. Orwell refers to these killers as being predominantly middle class, respectable people, who kill, often using poison, for often sexual rather than monetary motives (though Palmer, Smith and Seddon killed for money).[65] Clearly, as with Agatha Christie, Orwell did not know that Greenwood was long dead, though it was widely reported in January 1929 it was just a paragraph or two tucked away inside the newspaper and so easily missable by a casual reader. It may be coincidence that in 1945, the author's arguably most celebrated novel, *Animal Farm*, there is a minor character called Mr. Pilkington, an easy going gentleman farmer who enjoys fishing and hunting. If this is a reference to Greenwood then surely Orwell did know of his demise because it was only in the news of his death that his pseudonym was revealed.

We now turn to the locality of the crime. When John Rowland, a true crime author, visited south Wales in 1960 he found, on mentioning Greenwood, only four decades later, that he had been entirely forgotten there (though Major Armstrong had not).[66] Others had different experiences. Mr. G. H. Munford, a veteran journalist, writing later in the decade, thought that apart from the Crippen case, that of Greenwood was the most celebrated in the last half century or more. He wrote, 'In South Wales and in legal circles one can still hear echoes of the controversy the case provoked. Did he get away with a callous crime or was he the victim of cruel gossip?'[67] Furthermore, in 1997 it was stated, 'Mention the name Greenwood in Kidwelly and most people still remember the infamous case which put the town well and truly on the murder map'.[68] At the end of Bob Hinton's CD-ROM version of the story, he stated, 'So did Greenwood get away with murder or was he rightly acquitted? You will get an argument in Kidwelly to that question to this very day'.[69] In 2015 the local history society put on a re-enactment of the story at the town's carnival.[70] There was a lecture by Keith Evans to the Kidwelly Local History Society on the case in recent times. In conversation with the present (2024) vicar, the author learnt that he had been asked about the possibility for a gravestone for Mrs. Greenwood (the permission of her descendants would be needed for such) and about the chance of another exhumation of the remains to enable further scientific tests to be made (surely impossible at this late stage). He has also noted that flowers have been placed on the spot where her remains rest. He also told the author that a local archaeologist claimed that in later life Greenwood confessed to the murder of his wife, but on what basis this might have been is unknown. A descendant of the Bowaters alleged that the Bowater family looked down on Greenwood and that Marshall Hall thought that he was lucky to escape with a not guilty verdict.

As to the physical remains of the case, Greenwood's last home in Kidwelly, Rumsey House, remains, as does the former doctor's house opposite. Rumsey House had been converted as chapel and school room in the 1920s. In 1992 it was described as 'a mouldering white elephant', its grounds overgrown with weeds and brambles the monkey puzzle tree brown and dying.[71] It was sold in 2017 and is now known as Hillfields Villas, which is being transformed for educational and community use. It is a Grade II listed building, though at time of writing some of the exterior has certainly seen better days. Some of the outbuildings still stand, though some of the land once attached to the house has been sold. His first home there, Broomhill, was demolished in the 1980s and a new house with the same name stands on the site. Another of Greenwood's homes in Kidwelly, The Priory, in Lady Street, is still standing. Kidwelly town hall is now in a derelict state. Many of the streets and houses in central Kidwelly are much the same as they were in Greenwood's day. Elsewhere, his former offices in Llanelli had gone by 1961 as a department store was then established on the site. Although the guildhall in Carmarthen and the town hall in Llanelli are still there, the prison was demolished after closure in the 1920s though some of the castle ruins remain. At St. Mary's church in Ingleton, there are many memorials and gravestones to the Greenwood family, though the family house is long gone and holiday homes and a caravan park now stand on the ground, just to the south of the village

Chapter Ten

Conspectus

We now need to consider what actually happened at Rumsey House in June 1919 and whether a guilty man walked free or whether the guilty party could have been another. Most of those writing about the case have not felt able to provide a conclusion. Poison cases, unlike those involving stabbing, shooting, strangulation and bludgeoning have the potential to be ambiguous. They may be passed off as accidental or as suicide to a far greater degree than those four other methods of murder just mentioned. The same symptoms, too, can be argued to have been brought about by a variety of natural causes. So poisoning cases pose additional difficulties for the investigator.

There are several examples of such in the early twentieth century. In 1910-1911 three people died at Lancaster castle. It transpired that they had died of arsenic poisoning. There was a clear suspect. Circumstantial evidence pointed towards her. However, no one had seen her administer it and the motive seemed weak. The defendant was acquitted, yet someone had poisoned the three. It was an unsolved mystery.[1]

Before going into the specifics of this case, it may be worth examining the comments made in a study of poisoning by Dr. Thompson in 1937:

> The history of great poisoning cases shows that such crimes are usually planned in secrecy and the poisoner acts alone, for he rarely attempts the administration of his deadly weapon in the presence of another person. Criminal poisoning is not a matter of sudden impulse, but is generally thought out with considerable care some time before the plan is put into execution, for it is typical of the poisoner that he sets about his

> work with the utmost cunning, as to avoid suspicion or detection.

As to motive, 'such is the strange working of the human mind that what to some persons might seem a wholly inadequate motive … may seem sufficient to justify in their own mind a murder'. He adds:

> It has thus been found that should a peculiar combination of circumstances prevail in the environment of a person which renders it extremely difficult or impossible to satisfy some strong desire by any course of action permitted by convention, a state of mind is produced which prompts him to break that code. His mind becomes dominated by one fixed idea, and such is its power that it blinds him to facts and arguments, insomuch that at the moment there appears no risk in carrying out his design.

Dr. Thompson discusses various motives for poisoning, such as political assassination. As to others, money is the most common followed very closely by 'sex or lust' and this includes love, jealousy and hate:

> In such cases, it may be assumed that the mind of the individual becomes dominated by a fixed idea which becomes accentuated by constant dwelling on it. The mind becomes completely obsessed by it and the obstacle which stands in the way of the fixed idea has to be destroyed.[2]

Having dealt with generalities which seem worthy of note we must now pass to the details of this case by analysing the comments and conclusions of previous authors. The first substantial published work on the topic was by Winifred Duke, in her introduction to the volume of the *Notable British Trials* series, published in the year following Greenwood's death and thus able to conclude with whatever verdict she chose as she was unfettered by the law of libel.

Duke (1890-1962) was a historical novelist, who asked to edit the trial for publication. Apart from her introduction, which was very favourable towards Greenwood, casting serious doubts on any financial or romantic motive he might have had for murder, there was a transcript of the inquest, the magistrates' courts proceedings and the trial. Duke ends her introduction thus:

> It is possible that had the Greenwood case been tried in Scotland, the verdict would have been 'Not proven'. Despite the jury's finding, local believers in Harold Greenwood's guilt remained, like the unconvinced lady in the rhyme, 'of the same opinion still'. Guilty or innocent, the mind shrinks from contemplating the fate that followed him. He suffered outlawry, ostracism, exile from everything that he had hitherto known and enjoyed. The words of his counsel touching his social and professional ruin, whatever the outcome of the trial, became singularly true ... The chief actor in the brief drama vanished, following an abortive attempt to take up his old life ... Harold Greenwood. Whose fame once had been on everybody's lips, had made his last bow and exit from a world that had offered him little and deprived him of much. If innocent, his was a more than Greek fate.[3]

It was banned from Swansea public libraries because its content was seen as being objectionable (presumably because of the passages referring to adultery and the one explicit statement to 'sexual intercourse'), though it was a book that people wanted to read.[4] A contemporary journal noted that 'The introduction is very well done by the lady editor'. It was critical of her going easy on the prosecution when they suggested bringing Mrs. Greenwood as a witness as it suggested they were lacking in knowledge of the Criminal Evidence Act.[5]

According to Duke, 'The alleged motive was undoubtedly the weakest link in the chain of Crown evidence'. However, although she relates how family, friends, servants and the doctors all described the Greenwoods as being a happy couple, she then goes onto say that some who knew her, considered him to be a 'ladies' man' with

Gwladys Jones and Miss Griffiths in particular. The author fails to reconcile these contradictory points of view which she lays out.[6] Later she attacks the possible motive of remarriage as speedy marriages in and after the First World War such were commonplace, she alleges and the mourning habit was outdated, 'Death had lost its dignity and importance. Mourning was obsolete'.[7]

According to her, 'the verdict will be seen to be just and impartial'. She admits that Mrs. Greenwood was poisoned but does not give any explanation as to how or who was responsible. This she is unable to do because of the contradictory nature of the evidence.[8]

She concludes, with assumptions, a misleading reference to Gwladys Jones' age and a cautionary note 'Were the loss of over £600 a year, the companionship of a considerate and affectionate wife, the awful risk of the gallows, worth contemplating for the charms of a woman over 30, a lifelong acquaintance without money or expectations … yet murder may be committed without apparent motive, as instanced by Herbert Rowse Armstrong'.[9]

'There is much in the Greenwood case that can never be brought to light', due to witness discrepancies.[10] Duke's writing is full of unprovable assertions and exaggerations that are passed off as being fact. The relations between husband and wife are not known to have been demonstrably and undeniably good; contemporaries giving diverse views on the state of the marriage and the income she brought to the household is questionable. She also presumes that Greenwood acted by objective and rational criteria, which is not always the lot of humankind. Yet she is fair minded enough to leave the reader with a scintilla of doubt. Her introductory essay was republished with several other introductory essays to other trials in the series in 1954.[11] Her work has been the basis for all subsequent authors and for many this has been their sole source.

The story was published in various books since but never had a volume to itself. The results were not always happy. The first true crime book to deal with the case, though as a single chapter, was published shortly after Greenwood's death. Author Arthur Lambton endorsed the verdict of the court, writing, 'I believe the verdict to have been a just one and but for the hasty second marriage causing the contemptible tittle tattle that always has and always will poison English country life, there would have been no exhumation and no trial'.[12] In another compilation of poisoning mysteries, composed a few years later, Dr. Thompson was less certain and confessed that the mystery 'is never likely to be cleared up', whether it was murder or misadventure.[13] He was unable to conclude whether this was murder by arsenic or misadventure. Of the former he implied that the poison was not in the wine because Irene said she drank it and nor could it have been from the food as everyone ate it. He then suggests the medicine given to Mrs. Greenwood in the early evening (he neglects the brandy as a possibility). He does not give an opinion as to the poisoner.[14]

Decades later, another E. Spencer-Shew devoted four pages to the case in a compendium of true crime, took Greenwood's side. He was scornful of the gossips, adamant that Greenwood's dalliances with women were entirely innocent and that everyone thought the Greenwoods led a happy domestic life.[15]

Then there are books which deal with both the Armstrong and Greenwood poisonings. John Rowland, the author of the first of these, which is the only one to give a substantial amount of the book over to Greenwood, uses Duke's volume as his major source and seems to add nothing factual to that account, though he did visit South Wales during his research. He thought that if it was murder, that the motive was weak, 'Motive there seems none' for Mrs. Greenwood was pleasant and well liked and 'Harold Greenwood was not a man who might be likely to kill because of a sudden burst of passion', though the author had not known the man and the murder, if murder it was, was not necessarily the act of sudden passion.[16] Yet he produced no evidence for either assertation. As for money, Gwladys Jones 'had no financial expectations' and Greenwood by losing his first wife stood for the loss of 'some hundreds of pounds every year'. The former is true but the latter is exaggerated. He also noted the low level of arsenic found but thought that this might be deadly to a woman already in weak health.[17] He gives no suggestion as to how the arsenic was administered.

'It is indeed a mystery' he wrote. He stated that the dose of arsenic found in the corpse was insufficient to kill. He agreed, therefore, with the jury's decision because of the uncertainty of the evidence. 'And at this late date it seems very difficult indeed to answer them. There is, however, one point that must be briefly addressed before we take leave of the Greenwood case. How did Mrs. Greenwood die?' Could morphia or arsenic have been the cause? Rowland does not answer these questions. The author also paid a trip to Kidwelly and Llanelli as part of his research. He finishes with recounting a conversation he had in a hotel in Llanelli, where a man recalled the Armstrong case but not the Greenwood case.[18]

A contemporary newspaper found Rowland's book disappointing; 'slapdash and plagued with numerous irritating repetitions'. The commentator then added that Greenwood should never have been in court 'but for the incompetence of the police'.[19] Although written over six decades ago, Rowland's book is the lengthiest account of the case to date, though dealing with it in under 100 pages and using limited source material.

Then there are the three books which solely cover the Armstrong case; all with different conclusions. All deal with the Greenwood case as a prelude almost to the main event. None of the three authors, after their short summary of the Greenwood case, give an opinion on his guilt. This is probably sensible enough as they have not probed the matter very fully and there is no reason why they as biographers of Armstrong should have done so. However, for many readers of true crime, the Greenwood case is but an adjunct to that of Armstrong. That most recent of them, by Stephen Bates, refers in passing to Greenwood as 'the one who got away' suggesting that the author thought him guilty, though without expanding on this throw away line.[20] A book with a substantial chapter on Greenwood and Armstrong concludes that Mrs. Greenwood was murdered and that the chief suspects must be Greenwood and, the until then unique suggestion of Dr. Griffiths. He also made the novel suggestion that 'a disaffected maid' about to lose her job could have been responsible. Alas the author does not develop any of these three lines of argument.[21]

Although she never wrote a book on the topic, Mrs. Yseult Bridges (1888-1971), who did write some true crime books about the late Victorian poisoning cases of Charles Bravo and Adelaide Bartlett (neither officially solved), also studied the Greenwood case in great detail. She commented on Irene's part in her father's acquittal:

> If she had given evidence at the inquest as she did at the trial the course of the trial might have been quite different. At the time of the inquest the prosecution had not yet based their case on the theory that the poison had been administered in the wine drunk at lunch. The extraordinary blunder on the part of the authorities concerned in ignoring Irene's existence during the investigations and proceedings allowed the defence to produce her at the last moment, like a rabbit out of a hat, to demolish the prosecution's case … If this evidence had been given at the inquest the prosecution would have suggested another and more probable medium of administration of the poison, such as medicine or brandy.[22]

On the other hand, Tennyson-Jesse, editor of several editions of *Notable British Trials*, stated, 'Mr. Greenwood had quite rightly been acquitted, and much public money had been spent for nothing'.[23]

Since Rowland's publication of 1961 there has been no substantial work on the case. It has been written about as a chapter in numerous true crime compendiums. Often the case has been included in books about Major Armstrong, to whom Greenwood is often compared. The general consensus seems to be similar to that offered by Duke, that Greenwood may or may not have been guilty. Why so few authors have suggested that Greenwood was guilty is unclear since from 1929 it has been legally safe to do so, unlike the case of John Donald Merrett, given a verdict of 'not proven' in 1927 for the murder of his mother in Edinburgh in 1926 (he lived until 1954 and from then on no one has had any hesitation in stating that in 1927 he got away with murder).

The 21st century brought forward more part works. A local history publication in recent years by Kidwelly resident Eric Hughes, included a chapter on the case. This was based on the introduction to the *Notable British Trials* book and yet again the author does not suggest a definite conclusion.[24] Bob Hinton produced a narrative on CD-ROM which includes criticisms of the thesis that Greenwood was guilty but does not conclude either one way or the other.[25]

Some authors have stated that Greenwood was innocent, often citing the fact that gossip was the cause of Greenwood's being suspected. Hinton, in his book about South Wales murders, concludes 'Harold Greenwood was, quite rightly in my opinion, acquitted of the murder of his wife ... and the information I am discovering makes me more certain than ever that he was innocent'. He also had Diane Lazarus, a famous psychic, go to the house and her results backed up his opinion.[26] Kevin Turton, another author, wrote:

> But did Greenwood poison his wife? I would doubt it .... There was not, and is not, any viable evidence that would show the solicitor murdered his wife. Did the doctor, inadvertently, cause the death? That is obviously impossible to know ... In conclusion, whoever administered it could only have been the doctor, the nurse, Harold Greenwood and his daughter, Irene. They were the only people around her bedside throughout the whole of the time that mattered and surely one of them got away with murder'.[27]

However, there are two flaws in this argument. First, symptoms of poisoning occurred prior to the arrival of Dr. Griffiths and nurse Jones. Thus, having exonerated Greenwood already, the author is implicitly accusing Irene of the murder. Secondly, why should any of these people want to kill Mrs. Greenwood? Irene did much to persuade the jury of her father's not being guilty. The author's thesis is sadly under developed and unconvincing.

In a communication with the author, Hinton reveals his novel solution to the mystery. He is adamant that Greenwood was innocent. He argues that Greenwood was not a stupid man and would have known that, following the Seddon arsenic case in 1912, that there was general knowledge of the poison, making it the one not to use for poisoners. His theory is that Irene poisoned her mother because she was strict and did not allow her to take a job or to amuse herself. She may not have meant to kill, however. He claims that Greenwood knew his eldest daughter was guilty as she lied as to the drinking of burgundy during the lunch.

It is true that there can be detected a formality at least in Irene's relationship with her mother; she called her mother whereas she used the more affectionate term 'Daddy' for her father. Miss Phillips also detected a coolness in daughter-mother relations. Yet the limited evidence available does not show that Mrs. Greenwood restricted her eldest daughter's actions. Irene had spent time in London amusing herself in 1919, had 21st birthday celebrations that year at Rumsey House and worked in a bank in Carmarthen. It is also worth noting that other poisoners used arsenic after 1912; Major Armstrong for one, Beatrice Pace in 1928 and Annie Hearn for another.

As in the classic detective stories of this era there is a closed circle of suspects. Relatively few people had access to the victim. She was not killed by a stranger but by someone well known to her; a family member, a friend who was a frequent visitor to the house or someone she often had social intercourse with or possibly a servant. Yet she is not known to have been at odds with any friend or acquaintance.

Various accounts of the case have appeared in the press; usually short and often highly erroneous. A Yorkshire newspaper stated that Greenwood was a prosperous partner in a law firm, married to a woman called Joyce. He remarried his childhood sweetheart and was questioned at Rumsey House by Superintendent George Jones. Marshall Hall had recently triumphed in the Seddon case and was opposed to Dr. John Webster in court. Irene gave her testimony on the fourth day of the trial. Two decades later another newspaper repeated all these errors, adding more; Greenwood inviting a colleague and his wife for the fatal lunch. His wife in this version was 44 years old on death and a depressed invalid.[28]

Two youtube.com videos since 2020 have provided concise narratives of the story. They are generally accurate as to fact but neither gives the listener a definitive conclusion. Neither suggests lengthy research nor provides any new evidence. One suggests that someone other than Greenwood might have been guilty, though not who, why or how. The most popular youtube.com video on the case is *Death by Gooseberry Tart: The Murder of Mabel Greenwood, Kidwelly, 1919* by Mark John Maguire, which appeared in 2019 (and as a chapter in book form in 2023). The video is one of the first in his great (and, in 2024, ongoing) series which began in 2019 *They Got Away with Murder*. One of the advantages of youtube.com videos is that it allows comments (the other videos have little or none); and several hundred have appeared on this, most rightly congratulating the author on his work. One commentator has put that Greenwood was innocent and that Irene was the clue to the mystery. No further explanation is given and it would be intriguing to have known more. Another posits the theory that Greenwood and Dr. Griffiths were homosexual lovers and hence collusion in the case; no evidence supports this.

Maguire, unlike many previous authors, provides a clear solution and is the first to present the case for Greenwood as being guilty of murder, 'The evidence against Harold Greenwood was problematic from the start, and although he always looked likely to be the murderer ... Yet considering the circumstances in the case and weighing the probabilities, the evidence, although circumstantial, is compelling'.[29]

Firstly, Maguire is convinced that there are many good reasons for his thesis. On his wife's death, Greenwood 'clearly inherited property and money'. His second wife was 'from a wealthy family'. It is implied he needed money because of his gambling; apparently he 'liked a wager', and spent some of his time 'betting on sporting events' and there is a third reference to 'his betting habits' (quite apart from his philandering as referred to on pages 47-54). Secondly, he had purchased arsenic shortly before his wife's death by arsenic. Thirdly, his wife was older than him and in poor health and he wished to remarry. Finally, there is no viable alternative to him killing her as suicide and accident would seem even more unlikely.[30]

To conclude, 'No one else had the means and opportunity of administering the arsenic ... The weight of probability is heavily in favour of the husband administering the arsenic and it is surely reasonable that he did'. He discounts the alternative possibilities as suggested by Marshall Hall at the trial and states that Irene was 'heavily coached' in her answers in court to exculpate her father.[31]

In addition, he claims 'There was much to recommend the idea that there was some form of collusion between Dr. Griffiths and Harold Greenwood'. His reasoning is as follows. First, the two had been close friends for a long time. Second, there was a romance between Greenwood and Mary Griffiths. Third, Dr. Griffiths incorrectly diagnosed Mrs. Greenwood's illness and did not take samples when her condition worsened. Fourth he was very slow in responding to Mrs. Greenwood's condition on the night of her death. Fifth, he gave the cause of her death as heart failure. Sixth, if he had given morphia to Mrs. Greenwood on the fatal night this might have been to speed up the arsenic already administered to her by Greenwood. Finally, Greenwood took a great risk in poisoning his wife unless he knew he had the support of an ally – Dr. Griffiths.[32]

As with the previous consensus, this radical new hypothesis cannot go entirely unquestioned, though this is not to state that the main thrust of it is necessarily incorrect despite queries as to points of detail. There is little evidence that Greenwood benefitted materially from his first wife's death. True, he gained control of the £378 left by his wife in ready money and assets (for she left no will), but not her capital of £3,000 nor the income from it. He also gained Rumsey House, but this was mortgaged and in any case he needed a home for himself and his new wife and children, so was not a disposable asset but one which needed an income to maintain. His second wife had little or no money of her own (her father who died in 1917 only left £1,410 6s. 8d. but had a widow and ten children). There is also no contemporary evidence known to this author that Greenwood had an urgent need for money due to betting losses (had there been the prosecution would surely have used it).

We could also query the administration of arsenic. Here the thesis is that of the prosecution at the time; that Greenwood, as seen by Hannah, put arsenic in the wine for his wife to drink at lunch and that Irene falsely, but understandably, stated that she also drank it at that time. We are told that 'a sizeable quantity of arsenic' was found in the corpse. It was actually a little more than a quarter of a grain whilst Dr. Willcox stated that a killing dose was two. Of course, more than a quarter grain would have been ingested but much of it would have been expelled as it is known to have been done. The other point to consider is that if Hannah is accepted as a reliable witness, then this does not explain her claiming to have brought out two wine glasses at lunch nor in the evening, bringing out the same bottle which, if the prosecution thesis is accepted as it is here, had poison in it for the evening which was then drank again by Irene.

As to working with the doctor, it seems hard to believe that the wealthy and well established Dr. Griffiths would have risked so much for nothing. He would have known that to collude in murder was a capital offence and there was no reason for him to risk his neck, unless a financial pay off was in the offing, though there is no evidence he was in need of money. It is not unknown for doctors to misdiagnose murder; Dr. Hincks was to do in the Armstong case in 1921 and Dr. Galbraith likewise in the death of Minnie Everard in Cornwall in 1930, to name just two cases. It is not evidence of conspiracy. The doctor's known medical ineptitude, that has been already noted on page 33, was the more likely solution here.

All these caveats about details in the recent hypothesis by Maguire does not necessarily invalidate the overall thrust of the argument. However, before this is further discussed, it is perhaps worth considering another possibility that has hitherto only been mentioned once and that fleetingly. This suspect had motive, means and opportunity. This is Hannah Williams. Consider this. Because of her lateness in coming home one night, Mrs. Greenwood gave her notice to leave her current employment. There was the suggestion made that she drank the family's wine. This may have led her to harbour resentment against her mistress and thus supply a motive, weak as it may seem, unless there was more than that of which we know. Mrs. Greenwood may well have expected high standards from her servants; she was an upstanding churchwoman. Possibly Hannah did not meet the high standards expected. Secondly as she served the drinks on the fatal Sunday lunch, she had the opportunity to poison the wine and had access to the weedkiller in the garden sheds without being seen. She may not have wanted to kill but just wanted 'to teach her a lesson'. As a teenager at the time she may not have had that sense of control and maturity that an older person often possesses. Then she covered her tracks by pointing suspicion against Greenwood, whose behaviour was curious at the least, and was the major witness against him in court.

Little is known of Hannah Maggie Wiliams. She was the eldest daughter of at least five children born to David, a miner, and Letitia, his wife. She had been born in Ferndale in the Rhondda in 1901 and was resident there in 1911. After her brief employment at Rumsey House in 1918-1919, in 1921 she was again employed as a servant at the home of Thomas Morris, chief clerk to a brickworks company and resident at a house in Alstow Street, Kidwelly. She is not known to have married and apparently died in Pontypridd in 1964.[33] Because the focus of the investigation was always on Greenwood, little thought was given to any other person.

This theory covers the facts, but it is not a supposition that any contemporary thought of that we know of. In the golden age of detective fiction, servants were rarely guilty of murder, either. Is dismissal a reason for murder? Sometimes in real life it is, as in the case of servant, Kate Webster, who in Richmond in 1879 murdered her mistress, Mrs. Julia Thomas, after being given her notice. It was not that Hannah would have had any serious fear of being made destitute (servants were in high demand after 1918 and more so as many young working class women were employed in factories, shops and offices) and she found another job fairly quickly afterwards. It seems unlikely that she would have been a long term poisoner and this is what this crime most probably was as we shall soon see.

The most plausible solution to this problem is probably the one offered by Maguire, but not quite as he outlines it. Read on and see what you think. It is, by necessity, in the realm of speculation, because there is a scarcity of evidence from the lack of surviving personal papers and other sources but seems to meet the known facts.

In 1918, Greenwood has been married for over two decades. He was from a gentry background and had, he probably once thought, married well and had four children to which he is much attached. Yet he was now, in 1918, middle aged and his career in a slump. There is one bright spark in his life, but he cannot wholly seize it to the extent which he would if he was single. He has enjoyed the company of younger women, such as Miss Price, a governess once employed at The Priory, and has ceased sexual relations with his wife. One young woman in particular has now attracted his attention, a woman he has known for a long time but now sees as more than his late business associate's daughter. It is not an uncommon situation for a middle aged married man to find himself in. Just as importantly, she reciprocates his attentions. Possibly she has given up hope on her four year long engagement with a geographically distant fiancé which seems to be proceeding nowhere.

From the autumn of 1918 Greenwood and Gwladys Jones begin to spend time with one another **[1],** chiefly at Llanelli, conveniently out of the way of his wife and those who know him in Kidwelly, and when necessarily apart, on conversations on the telephone. Given that he asked a servant, and others, to lie for him this is probably more than a platonic friendship. There is no evidence that he ever introduced her to his wife and family, except Irene, and again this suggests an illicit relationship; if innocent why did he not do so? She could have been legitimately introduced as the daughter of a longstanding business friend, which indeed she was. Yet lovers are taking a risk in being together under the scrutiny of the spouse of one of them for they may inadvertently give themselves away by a gesture, a look or a word.

[1] Harold and Gwladys Greenwood.

At the same time it is noticed by those around Mrs. Greenwood that her health is in decline. She is losing weight and suffering from diarrhoea and fainting fits. She is less active than what she was. Greenwood had ordered weedkiller in both 1917 and early 1919. The first order may have been innocently done in order to combat weeds but it meant he had a supply to hand for more sinister uses. Given that his wife uses patent medicines it would be an easy task for him to insert small doses of arsenic into her bottles (and after her death he disposed of them all in the river at the bottom of the garden). Or it may have been in another medium and as a husband it would be easy to access such sources.

Poisoning by small doses over time is less dangerous than administering one substantial amount and so arising suspicion because it suggests that the victim is suffering from a long term illness and so death is not a great surprise to anyone. Many poisoners do so, such as Major Armstrong and later Annie Hearn. It is likely that this is what Greenwood did and it accounts for her gradual decline in health over time that was noted by many, but not with any suspicion. Mrs. Greenwood's reticent nature as noted (she did not even confide in her best friend about her drastic weight loss) would have led her to tell no one any suspicions she may have had. These she might have put down to natural ageing or even the will of God, and that was something she had to resign herself to suffering without complaint, as exemplified by the long suffering Job in the Old Testament, a story she would have known.

The final dose was given on the afternoon of Sunday 15th June and this led to Mrs. Greenwood's demise. It was given between about 1.00pm and 6.00pm. Whether Greenwood put a dose in her wine on Sunday lunch is another question. Hannah stated that she saw him in the dining room prior to lunch and that gave him the opportunity to do it. On the other hand, his daughter, whom Miss Phillips said had little love for her mother, but called her father 'Daddy', said that she also drank the wine and was unscathed. If we believe her, and the jury certainly did, then Hannah must have been mistaken and Greenwood did not poison the wine. Or Irene may have lied to save her father; possibly after a suggestion made by Marshall Hall. Yet as Hannah related that she brought out two wine glasses at lunch implying two wine drinkers and then brought out the same wine bottle in the evening and Irene drank from it suggests that there was never any arsenic in the wine.

It is possible that Greenwood poisoned his wife in another medium that afternoon. There were chocolates that she liked so much and may have had one or more after lunch, handed to her by her husband (poisoned chocolates featured in the Armstrong case; Oswald Martin being sent a box in which some had arsenic inside them). Or he may have given her a drink that afternoon, perhaps a cup of tea when their daughter was out with Foy. Or in the brandy that we know he gave her later that afternoon. Or it may have been more poison in the medicines, which he subsequently had disposed of.

Greenwood did not benefit much financially from the crime. Money is not the only motive for murder. But he did get to marry the woman of his desires. There may have been other motives; no one could know all that happens between man and wife behind closed doors and also in the mind of a murderer (it was never ascertained why John Christie killed his wife of 32 years but he was found guilty in 1953 of her murder all the same). We can never know what these were; perhaps resentments built up over years and for which the arrival on Greenwood's mindset of the attractiveness of Gwladys Jones was the catalyst for action. For this middle aged man, perhaps he saw this as his last chance for an opportunity of happiness, and lacking any moral scruples, took that chance, regardless of the possible consequences for him or for his current wife, thinking himself to be far too clever for the far from competent Dr. Griffiths.

Divorce as a legitimate way to have ended the marriage would have been ruled out. First of all, it was very rare and so socially it would have been a shocking scandal, especially in the small town society that Greenwood lived in. It would have meant the loss of Rumsey House and he would have lost his relationship with his children. His wife would have been unlikely to have granted a divorce on religious grounds. It was expensive and difficult. He wanted to maintain his current life in Kidwelly with Gwladys but without Mabel. Greenwood was emotionally greedy; he wanted it all, romantically and socially, but to do so meant murder.

We should not forget the first Mrs. Greenwood in all this. She was the innocent victim in her husband's mid-life crisis. That she was a fine upstanding member of the community committed to good works at the church and elsewhere may have been in part her undoing. She was aware of her husband's philandering, that we know, but there was little she could or would do about it. Divorce was ruled out on social and religious grounds. It was tragically a case of 'till death do us part'.

His plan went wrong, as has been stated. After the initial success based partly on the doctor's incompetence, and so no post mortem and a quick burial, Greenwood ran into trouble by his hasty remarriage. Clearly he thought that he had got away with murder and wished to enjoy the fruits of his actions without delay. In part this may have been on Gwladys' insistence (possibly because she believed she was pregnant) and clearly he did not want to lose her, because that would have meant the murder would have been for nothing. Yet he did not take into account the social constraints; possibly being at the apex of local society maybe he thought he was above all this, but he was not. The reverse was true as more would have been expected of him in moral and social terms. This led to gossip and then to an official investigation, incompetently caried out as it was (the failure to take statements from Irene and the failure to take hair and nail samples from Mrs. Greenwood's body being the 'highlights' here). And though he was found not guilty, the consequences of his crime remained with him forever. Although formally found 'not guilty' of murder, he did not get away with it because it led him to becoming a social leper, having to move from his pleasant home and to deal with professional ruin and relative penury. Perhaps life with his new wife and the birth of a son compensated for this outward collapse.

Justice, it would seem, did miscarry in Carmarthen in 1920. Marshall Hall exploited the weaknesses of the prosecution case, and as noted the investigation had been faulty. Irene played a crucial part in her father's acquittal. Greenwood should have been found guilty of the murder of his first wife but due to a weak investigation the evidence was lacking to convince a jury beyond all reasonable doubt. There seems little doubt that she died of slow poisoning and that he alone had both motive and opportunity to inflict it. No other solution seems to realistically work with the admittedly limited evidence to hand.

Notes

Chapter 1

1. Ancestry.co.uk, John Bentley, *History of Ingleton*, (2008), p.60.
2. Anthony Hewittson, *Visitors' Handbook and Guide to Ingleton*, (1886), pp.5-6, 9, 12.
3. Ancestry.co.uk; *Lancashire Gazette*, (7th January 1873 & 1st April 1876).
4. *Craven Herald*, (18th November 1876).
5. Will of William Norman Greenwood; *The National Archives*, IR26/3004, f.96.
6. *Yorkshire Post and Leeds Intelligencer*, (31st March 1883).
7. *Craven Herald*, (11th January 1879); Winifred Duke, *Six Trials*, (1934), P93.
8. *Lancashire Guardian and County Advertiser*, (7th April 1893).
9. *Illustrated Sunday Herald*, (14th November & 5th December 1920).
10. M. Mullins, *Giggleswick Grammar School Register, 1499-1913*, (1913); *Sydenham, Forest Hill and Penge Gazette*, (8th September 1888 & 22nd March 1890).
11. Ancestry.co.uk; *Lancashire Guardian*, (13th January 1894); *The Gentlewoman*, (24th November 1900); *Lancashire Standard and County Advertiser*, (17th April 1903).
12. *Lancashire Evening Post*, (11th August 1913).
13. *Illustrated Sunday Herald*, (4th December 1920).
14. Author's observations in church and churchyard, (2024).
15. Ancestry.co.uk.
16. Will of William Norman Greenwood.
17. *London Evening Standard*, (5th June 1896).
18. Ancestry.co.uk; *Craven Herald*, (23rd July 1897).
19. Ancestry.co.uk.
20. Ancestry.co.uk.
21. Information from Nicholas Gibbs, (2024).
22. *Sydenham, Forest Hill and Penge Gazette*, (19th November 1887, 22nd June 1889 & 10th January 1891).
23. *London Gazette*, (4th December 1903).
24. Ancestry.co.uk.
25. Mark John Maguire, *They Got Away With Murder*, I, (2023), p.185.
26. Winifred Duke, *The Trial of Harold Greenwood*, (1930), pp.22n & 177.
27. Will of William Bowater; *Tottenham and Edmonton Weekly Times*, (10th May 1907).
28. Will of Eliza Jane Bowater.
29. Winifred Duke, *Trial*, (1930), p.179.
30. *The Times*, (29th August 1907).
31. *Sydenham, Forest Hill and Penge Gazette*, (14th October 1882, 29th September 1882, 15th December 1888, 11th January 1890 & 27th September 1890).
32. *London Evening Post*, (7th April 1898).
33. Ancestry.co.uk; *Western Mail*, (11th January 1918).

34. Winifred Duke, *Trial*, (1930), p.341.
35. Ibid, Opp. p.347.
36. Ibid, p.341.
37. The National Archives, MEPO3/265b.
38. *Western Mail*, (26th, 28th, 30th March 1914, 7th July 1915, 18th January 1916, 20th, 22nd, 23rd, 25th January 1917, 22nd August 1916, 21st & 25th November 1918).
39. The National Archives, MEPO3/265b.
40. David Daven Jones, *History of Kidwelly*, (1908), pp.1, 98-107, 157; *Medical Officer of Kidwelly's Annual Report* (1925); *South Wales and Monmouthshire Directory*, (1920), pp.433-434.
41. Winifred Duke, *Trial*, (1930), pp.1-2.
42. David Daven Jones, *History*, (1908), pp.95-96
43. *Western Mail*, (18th January 1934).
44. *Daily Mirror*, (5th April 1921); The National Archives, DPP1/57; Ancestry.co.uk; *Nottingham Journal*, (5th April 1921).
45. The National Archives, MEPO3/265b.
46. Winifred Duke, *Trial*, (1930), p.102.
47. The National Archives, MEPO3/265b.
48. Census (1921).
49. The National Archives, ASSI72/46/7; MEPO3/265b.
50. Ancestry.co.uk; *Western Mail* (30th March 1917).
51. *Larne Times*, (24th April 1920).
52. Winifred Duke, *Trial*, (1930), p.215.
53. *Leeds Mercury*, (19th April 1920).
54. *Llanelli Mercury*, (8th February 1906).
55. *Herald of Wales*, (10th February 1906).
56. *Carmarthen Journal*, (20th January 1911).
57. Ibid, (15th December 1911).
58. Ibid, (14th April 1904 & 21st October 1910).
59. *Western Mail*, (6th May 1902).
60. Winifred Duke, *Trial*, (1930), p.83.
61. The National Archives, DPP1/57.
62. Winifred Duke, *Trial*, (1930), p.342.
63. *Larne Times*, (24th April 1920).
64. Ibid; *Evening Standard*, (4th November 1904).
65. *Western Mail*, (5th August 1899); *Llanelli Mercury* (22nd August 1901).
66. *South Wales Daily News*, (4th August 1898).
67. *Llanelli Mercury*, (21st November 1901).
68. *Carmarthenshire Journal*, (20th April 1906).
69. *Western Mail*, (24th October 1904).
70. *Llanelli Mercury*, (17th April 1902).
71. *South Wales Daily News*, (9th August 1898).
72. *Brecon County Times*, (29th January 1904).
73. *Llanelli Mercury*, (16th August 1906).
74. Ibid, (10th January 1907).
75. The National Archives, MEPO3/265b.
76. *Western Mail*, (2nd November 1915).
77. Ibid, (16th June 1920).
78. *Herald of Wales*, (4th November 1899).
79. *South Wales Daily News*, (26th October 1899); *Llanelli Mercury*, (4th January 1912).
80. *Carmarthen Weekly Reporter*, (10th April 1914).

Notes   259

81. *Llanelli Mercury*, (25th October 1900).
82. Ibid, (2nd May 1901).
83. *Carmarthenshire Weekly Reporter*, (30th October 1908).
84. *Carmarthenshire Journal*, (22nd September & 3rd November 1911).
85. Ibid, (10th April 1914).
86. *Carmarthen Weekly Reporter*, (16th August & 6th September 1901).
87. Winifred Duke, *Trial of Harold Greenwood* (1930), pp.2-3.
88. *Llanelli Mercury*, (28th June 1906, 13th August 1908 & 7th May 1908).
89. *Carmarthen Weekly Reporter*, (5th & 26th June 1908).
90. Ibid, (6th August 1909).
91. Ibid, (13th June 1913).
92. Ibid, (4th February 1910).
93. Ibid, (8th April 1913).
94. *Carmarthen Weekly Reporter*, (4th September 1903).
95. *Leeds Mercury*, (19th April 1920).
96. *The Daily Telegraph*, (18th June 1920).
97. *Yorkshire Post and Leeds Intelligencer*, (10th August 1912).
98. *Illustrated Sunday Herald*, (14th December 1920).
99. *South Wales Daily News*, (12th August 1898).
100. Ibid, (31st August 1898).
101. *Carmarthen Weekly Reporter*, (11th August 1899).
102. *Herald of Wales*, (26th August 1905).
103. *Western Mail*, (23rd November 1898).
104. *Llanelli Mercury*, (31st January 1907).
105. *Herald of Wales*, (6th May 1905).
106. *Western Mail*, (7th May 1915).
107. *Carmarthen Weekly Reporter*, (11th September 1914, 13th November 1914 & 27th July 1917).
108. Ibid, (22nd October 1915, 15th March 1918, 8th September 1916, 2nd October 1914 & 10th January 1919).
109. The National Archives, MEPO3/265b.
110. Winifred Duke, *Trial*, (1930), pp.315, 319, 321; The National Archives, MEP3/265b; Winifred Duke, *Six Trials*, (1937), p.97.
111. *South Wales and Monmouthshire Directory*, (1920), p.434.

Chapter 2

1. Duke, *Trial*, pp.3, 7.
2. Sally Smith, *Sir Edward Marshall Hall: A Law unto himself*, (2016), p.191.
3. Edward Spencer-Shew, *A Companion to Murder*, (1960), p.96.
4. C. J. S. Thompson, *Poison Mysteries Unsolved* (1937), pp.114, 117.
5. Mark John Maguire, *They Got Away With Murder*, I, (2023), pp.182, 190, 193, 185.
6. *Leeds Mercury* (19th April 1920).
7. Winifred Duke, *Trial*, (1930), pp.272, 294, 314, 319, 321.
8. Ibid, p.342.
9. Winfred Duke, *Trial*, (1930), pp.310-311.
10. The National Archives, ASSI72/46/7.
11. The National Archives, MEPO3/265b.
12. Ibid.
13. Ibid.
14. Ibid; Winifred Duke, *Trial*, (1930), p.215.

15. The National Archives, MEPO3/265b.
16. Ibid, DDP1/57.
17. Winifred Duke, *Trial*, (1930), p.216.
18. Ibid, pp.289-290, 116; The National Archives, DPP1/57.
19. The National Archives, MEPO3/265b.
20. Winifred Duke, *Trial*, (1930), p.286.
21. Ibid, p.230.
22. Ancestry.co.uk.
23. The National Archives, MEPO3/265b.
24. Winifred Duke, *Trial*, (1930), p.185.
25. *Illustrated Sunday Herald*, (28th November 1920).
26. The National Archives, DPP1/57.
27. *Illustrated Sunday Herald*, (14th November 1920).
28. Winifred Duke, *Trial*, (1930), pp.87-88, 211, 215.
29. The National Archives, DDP1/57.
30. *Illustrated Sunday Herald*, (21st December 1920).
31. Winifred Duke, *Trial*, (1930), p.270, 305.
32. The National Archives, DPP1/57.
33. Ibid, MEPO3/265b.
34. Ibid.
35. Winifred Duke, *Trial*, (1930), p.188.
36. Ibid, pp.220, 341-342.
37. *Illustrated Sunday Herald*, (28th November 1920).
38. Winifred Duke, *Trial*, (1930), p.288; The National Archives, ASSI72/46/7.
39. Ibid, pp.292, 294.
40. Ibid, p.83.
41. Ibid, p.293.
42. Ibid, pp.208, 342.
43. Ibid, pp.189, 216.
44. Ibid, pp.94-95.
45. Ibid, p.88.
46. Winifred Duke, *Trial*, (1930), p.284.
47. *Illustrated Sunday Herald*, (28th November 1920).
48. Winifred Duke, *Trial*, (1930), pp.289-290.
49. *Illustrated Sunday Herald*, (28th November 1920).
50. Ibid.
51. The National Archives, DPP1/57.
52. Winifred Duke, *Trial*, (1930), p.85.
53. Ibid.
54. The National Archives, DPP1/57.
55. Winifred Duke, *Trial*, (1930), pp.83, 273, 288; *Illustrated Sunday Herald*, (28th November 1920).
56. Winifred Duke, *Trial*, (1930), p.294.
57. Ibid, p.85.
58. The National Archives, MEPO3/265b.
59. *Illustrated Sunday Herald*, (28th November 1920).
60. The National Archives, MEPO3/265b.
61. *Illustrated Sunday Herald*, (28th November 1920).
62. Winifred Duke, *Trial*, (1930), pp.273, 210.

Notes 261

63. The National Archives, MEPO3/265b.
64. *Illustrated Sunday Herald*, (28th November 1920).
65. The National Archives, DPP1/57.
66. *Illustrated Sunday Herald*, (28th November 1920).
67. Winifred Duke, *Trial*, (1930), p.211; The National Archives, MEPO3/265b.
68. Winifred Duke, *Trial*, (1930), pp.76-77, 211.
69. Ibid, p.112; *Illustrated Sunday Herald*, (5th December 1920).
70. Winifred Duke, *Trial*, (1930), p.283.
71. Ibid, pp.77, 182, 211.
72. Ibid, pp.109-110, 112, 282, 316.
73. Ibid, p.112.
74. The National Archives, ASSI72/46/7.
75. Winifred Duke, *Trial*, (1930), p.282.
76. Ibid, pp.85-6, 344.
77. The National Archives, MEPO3/265b.
78. Winifred Duke, *Trial*, (1930), pp.86, 344.
79. *Illustrated Sunday Herald*, (5th December 1920).
80. Winifred Duke, *Trial*, (1930), p.85.
81. Ibid, pp.212-213.
82. Winifred Duke, *Trial*, (1930), p. 283.
83. Ibid, pp.94, 213.
84. Ibid, pp.78, 94.
85. Ibid, pp.86, 273; The National Archives, DPP1/56.
86. The National Archives, MEPO3/265b.
87. *Carmarthenshire Journal*, (2nd May 1919).
88. *Carmarthen Weekly Record*, (11th April 1919).
89. Winifred Duke, *Trial*, (1930), p.274.
90. The National Archives, DPP1/57.
91. Winifred Duke, *Trial*, (1930), pp.94-95, 270.
92. The National Archives, MEPO3/265b.
93. Winifred Duke, *Trial*, (1930), p.88.
94. Winifred Duke, *Trial*, (1930), pp.212-213.
95. Ibid, pp.86, 88, 103.
96. The National Archives, DDP1/57.
97. Winifred Duke, *Trial*, (1930), pp.284-285.
98. Ibid, p.88.
99. Ibid, p.86.
100. Ibid, p.103.
101. Winifred Duke, *Trial*, (1930), pp.270, 276.
102. The National Archives, MEPO3/265b.
103. Winifred Duke, *Trial*, (1930), p.270.
104. Ibid, pp.273-4.
105. Ibid, pp.86, 273.
106. Ibid, p.89.
107. The National Archives, DPP1/57.
108. Winifred Duke, *Trial*, (1930), p.274.
109. Ibid.
110. Ibid, p.215; The National Archives, DPP1/57.
111. Ibid, pp.96, 270, 276.
112. Ibid, p.271.
113. Ibid, p. 87; The National Archives, DDP1/57.

114. The National Archives, MEPO3/265b.

Chapter 3

1. Winifred Duke, *Trial*, (1930), p.277.
2. Ibid, p.288.
3. Ibid, p.290.
4. Ibid, p.277.
5. Ibid, & p.83.
6. Ibid, p.208.
7. Ibid, p.277.
8. Winifred Duke, *Trial*, (1930), p.283.
9. The National Archives, ASSI44/46/7.
10. Duke, *Trial*, (1930), p.280.
11. Ibid, p.211.
12. Ibid, p.286.
13. *Kensington News and West London Times*, (20th June 1919).
14. *Carmarthenshire Journal*, (20th June 1919).
15. *Llanelli Mercury*, (19th June 1919).
16. Winifred Duke, *Trial*, (1930), p.304.
17. The National Archives, MEPO3/265b.
18. *Illustrated Sunday Herald*, (5th December 1920).
19. Winifred Duke, *Trial*, (1930), pp.201-202.
20. The National Archives, DDP1/57.
21. Ibid, p.79.
22. Winfred Duke, *Trial*, (1930), p.58; The National Archives, MEPO3/265b.
23. Winifred Duke, *Trial*, (1930), p.318.
24. The National Archives, DPP1/57.
25. Winifred Duke, *Trial*, (1930), p.204.
26. Winifred Duke, *Trial*, (1930), p.22.
27. C. J. S. Thompson, *Poisoning Cases*, (1937), pp.135, 138.
28. Ibid, pp.337-338.
29. The National Archives, MEPO3/265b.
30. Duke, *Trial*, (1930), pp.181, 189.
31. Ibid, pp.189-190.
32. Ibid.
33. Ibid, p.74.
34. Winifred Duke, *Trial* (1930), p.190.
35. Ibid, p.191
36. Ibid, pp.105, 107.
37. Ibid, p.219.
38. Winifred Duke, *Trial*, (1930), p.278.
39. The National Archives, MEPO3/265b.
40. Ibid; Winifred Duke, *Trial*, (1930), p.336.
41. *Cambrian Daily Leader*, (3rd October 1919).
42. Winifred Duke, *Trial*, (1930), pp.23-24.
43. *Illustrated Sunday Herald*, (5th December 1920).
44. *Carmarthen Journal*, (24th October 1919).
45. The National Archives, MEPO3/265b.
46. Ibid, DPP1/57.

Chapter 4

1. *The People*, (30th June 1940).
2. *Welsh Gazette*, (15th April 1949).
3. Winifred Duke, *Trial*, (1930), pp.135, 276-278.
4. Ibid, p.92.
5. Ibid, p.312.
6. Winifred Duke, *Trial*, (1930), pp. 111, 317.
7. The National Archives, ASSI44/46/7.
8. Ibid, DPP1/57.
9. Winifred Duke, *Trial*, (1930), p.344.
10. Winifred Duke, *Trial*, (1930), pp.76-80.
11. Ibid, p.193.
12. Ibid, pp.80, 125.
13. The National Archives, MEPO2/265b.
14. Winifred Duke, *Trial*, (1930), pp.116, 272.
15. *Carmarthen Weekly Reporter*, (28th December 1919 & 14th November 1919).
16. Winifred Duke, *Trial*, (1930), pp.116, 272.
17. Ibid.
18. Winifred Duke, *Trial* (1930), pp.116, 272.
19. The National Archives, DPP1/57.
20. The National Archives, HO144/11780.
21. Ibid.
22. *Illustrated Police News*, (22nd April 1920); *Western Mail*, (16th June 1920).
23. The National Archives, MEPO3/265b.
24. Winifred Duke, *Trial*, (1930), p.92.
25. Ibid, p.201.
26. *Llanelli and County Guardian*, (22nd April 1920).
27. *Larne Times*, (24th April 1920).
28. Winifred Duke, *Trial*, (1930), pp.304-305.
29. Ibid, pp.304-305.
30. The National Archives, MEPO3/265b.
31. *Carmarthen Journal,* (19th April 1920).
32. *Evening News*, (17th April 1920).
33. *Weekly Despatch*, (17th April 1920).
34. *Illustrated Police News*, (22nd April 1920).
35. *The Times*, (17th April 1920).
36. Winifred Duke, *Trial*, (1930), p.217.
37. *Llanelli and County Guardian*, (22nd April 1920).
38. Ibid, (17th April 1920).
39. Winifred Duke, *Trial*, (1930), p.83; The National Archives, DPP1/57.
40. The National Archives, DPP1/57.
41. Winifred Duke, *Trial*, (1930), p.280.
42. Ibid, pp.326-327.
43. The National Archives, MEPO3/265b.
44. R. N. Ratnaike, *Acute and chronic arsenic toxicity* in *Postgraduate Medical Journal*, 79, (2003), pp.391-396; A. Duncan *et al*, *Homicidal arsenic poisoning* in *Annals of Clinical Biochemistry*, 52 (4), (2015), pp.510-515. (I am indebted to Dr Anna-Lena Berg for these references).
45. Philip A. Willcox, *The Detective Physician*, (1970), p.56.
46. The National Archives, DPP1/57.

47. Winifred Duke, *Trial*, (1930), p.343.
48. Ibid, p.344.
49. Ibid, p.343.
50. The National Archives, HO144/11780.
51. Ibid, MEPO3/270.
52. Ibid, MEPO4/346/85.
53. Ibid, HO144/11780.
54. The National Archives, MEPO3/265b.
55. Ibid.
56. Ibid.
57. The National Archives, HO144/11780.
58. Ibid.
59. Ibid.
60. Ibid.
61. Ibid.
62. The National Archives, MEPO3/265b.
63. Winifred Duke, *Trial*, (1930), p.337.
64. Ibid, p.292.
65. The National Archives, MEPO3/265b.
66. Ibid, DPP1/57.
67. Ibid.
68. Winifred Duke, *Trial*, (1930), p.112, 312.
69. The National Archives, DPP1/57.
70. Phillip Willcox, *Detective Physician*, (1970), p.10.
71. The National Archives, HO144/11780.
72. *The Times*, (3rd & 4th June 1920).
73. Winifred Duke, *Trial*, (1930), p.342.
74. Winifred Duke, *Trial*, (1930), pp.342-343.
75. Ibid, pp.340-341.

Chapter 5

1. The National Archives, DPP1/57.
2. Winifred Duke, *Trial*, (1930), p.269.
3. *Daily Mail*, (16th June 1920).
4. *South Wales and Monmouthshire Directory*, (1920).
5. Winifred Duke, *Trial*, (1930), pp.269-270.
6. Ibid, p.270-272.
7. Ibid, p.273.
8. Winifred Duke, *Trial*, (1930), p.274.
9. Ibid, pp.275-276.
10. Ibid, pp.277-8.
11. Ibid, p.279.
12. Ibid, p.280.
13. Winifred Duke, *Trial*, (1930), p.280.
14. Ibid, pp.280-281.
15. Ibid, p.281.
16. Ibid, pp.281-282.
17. Winifred Duke, *Trial*, (1930), p.282.
18. Ibid, pp.282-283.

19. Ibid, p.283.
20. Ibid, pp.283-284.
21. Winifred Duke, *Trial*, (1930), pp.284-286.
22. Winifred Duke, *Trial*, (1930), pp.286-287.
23. Ibid, pp.287-288.
24. Ibid, p.288.
25. Winifred Duke, *Trial*, (1930), pp.289-290.
26. Ibid, p.291.
27. Ibid, p.292.
28. Ibid, p.293.
29. Ibid, p.294.
30. Ibid.
31. Winifred Duke, *Trial*, (1930), p.295.
32. Ibid, pp.295-296.
33. Ibid, p.296.
34. Ibid, pp.296-297.
35. Ibid, p.297.
36. Ibid.
37. *Manchester Guardian*, (17th June 1920).
38. Winifred Duke, *Trial*, (1930), p.296.
39. *Western Mail*, (17th June 1920).
40. *Manchester Guardian*, (16th June 1920).
41. *Western Mail*, (17th June 1920); *Illustrated Sunday Herald*, (12th December 1920).
42. *Illustrated Sunday Herald*, (12th December 1920).
43. *Manchester Guardian*, (17th June 1920).
44. Winifred Duke, *Trial*, (1930), p.296.
45. *Western Mail*, (17th June 1920).
46. *Illustrated Sunday Herald*, (12th December 1920).
47. Ibid.
48. *Llanelli Guardian*, (24th June 1920).

Chapter 6

1. The National Archives, MEPO3/265b.
2. Ibid.
3. Ibid.
4. The National Archives, HO144/11780.
5. *Western Mail*, (3rd July 1920); *Llanelli and County Guardian*, (19th June 1919).
6. *Western Mail*, (18th June 1920).
7. *Evening Standard*, (17th June 1920).
8. *Western Mail*, (21st & 24th June 1920).
9. Winifred Duke, *Trial*, (1930), pp.299-300.
10. *Western Mail*, (2nd July 1920).
11. *Manchester Guardian*, (2nd July 1920).
12. Winifred Duke, *Trial*, (1930), pp.300-302.
13. Ibid, pp.303-304.
14. Ibid, pp.304-305.
15. Winifred Duke, *Trial*, (1930), pp.305-307.
16. Ibid, pp.308-309.
17. Ibid, p.309.
18. Ibid, pp.310-313.

19. Winifred Duke, *Trial*, (1930), pp.313-314.
20. Ibid, pp.314-315.
21. Ibid, p.316.
22. Winifred Duke, *Trial*, (1930), pp.317-318.
23. Ibid, pp.318-319.
24. *Western Mail*, (2nd July 1920).
25. *Manchester Guardian*, (2nd July 1920).
26. *Western Mail*, (3rd July 1920).
27. *Evening Standard*, (3rd July 1920).
28. *Western Mail*, (3rd July 1920).
29. Ibid.
30. Winifred Duke, *Trial*, (1930), pp.319-320.
31. Winifred Duke, *Trial*, (1930), p.321; *Western Mail*, (2nd July 1920).
32. Ibid, pp.321-322.
33. Ibid.
34. Ibid, p.324.
35. *The Times*, (3rd July 1920).
36. *Western Mail*, (3rd July 1920).
37. *News of the World*, (4th July 1920).
38. Winifred Duke, *Trial*, (1930), p.325.
39. Ibid, p.326.
40. Ibid, pp.326-327.
41. Ibid, pp.327-328.
42. Ibid, pp.329-330.
43. Winifred Duke, *Trial*, (1930), p.331.
44. Ibid, pp.332-333.
45. Ibid, p.333; *Western Mail*, (5th July 1920).
46. *Llanelli County Guardian*, (8th July 1920).
47. *Western Mail*, (3rd & 5th July 1920).
48. *The Globe*, (6th July 1920).
49. *Llanelli Guardian*, (8th July 1920).
50. The National Archives, MEPO3/265b.
51. Ibid.
52. Ibid.
53. *Daily Sketch*, (14th July 1920).
54. *Illustrated Sunday Herald*, (14th November 1920).
55. Ibid.
56. Ibid.
57. *Illustrated Sunday Herald*, (4th December 1920).
58. Ibid.
59. Ancestry.co.uk.
60. *John Bull*, (24th April 1922).
61. The National Archives, MEPO3/265b, DPP1/57.
62. Winifred Duke, *Trial*, (1930), p.135.
63. *Western Mail*, (9th July 1920).
64. The National Archives, MEP3/265b.
65. *Nottingham Evening Post*, (7th July 1920).
66. *Western Mail*, (2nd October 1920).
67. *Sheffield Daily Telegraph*, (4th October 1920).
68. *Birmingham Daily Gazette*, (6th July 1920).
69. *Law List*, (1920), p.245; *Who Was Who*, (1941-1950), p.1020.

Notes 267

70. *Law List*, (1920), p.167; *Oxford Dictionary of National Biography,* 33, pp.61-62.
71. The National Archives, DPP1/57.
72. Ibid.
73. The National Archives, MEPO3/265b.
74. Ibid, 24, pp.609-610.
75. Winifred Duke, *Trial*, (1930), p.347.
76. *Western Mail*, (22th September 1920).
77. Ibid, (13th October 1920).
78. *John Bull*, (22nd April 1922).
79. *The People*, (17th June 1934).
80. *John Bull*, (22nd April 1922).
81. Ibid, (29th October 1920).
82. The National Archives, DPP1/57.
83. Ibid.
84. *Western Mail*, (2nd October 1920).
85. Ibid, (20th October 1920).
86. Edward Marjoribanks, *The Life of Sir Edward Marshall Hall*,(1929), p.410.
87. Ibid, p.411.

Chapter 7

1. *Western Mail*, (3rd November 1920).
2. *Oxford Dictionary of National Biography*, 50, pp.140-141.
3. Winifred Duke, *Trial*, (1930), p.1.
4. *The Times*, (2nd November 1920).
5. *The Observer*, (7th November 1920).
6. *Western Mail*, (1st November 1920).
7. Ibid, (3rd November 1920).
8. *Evening Standard*, (2nd November 1920).
9. *The Daily Telegraph*, (4th November 1920).
10. *John Bull*, (22nd April 1920).
11. Winifred Duke, *Trial*, (1930), p.347.
12. *Evening Standard,* (6th November 1920).
13. *Western Mail*, (3rd November 1920).
14. *John Bull*, (24th April 1922).
15. Winifred Duke, *Trial*, (1930), p.63.
16. Ibid, pp.64-65.
17. Winifred Duke, *Trial*, (1930), pp.65-66.
18. Ibid, p.66.
19. Ibid, p.68.
20. Ibid, p.72.
21. Ibid, p.72-74.
22. Ibid p.75-76.
23. Winifred Duke, *Trial*, (1930), pp.80-81.
24. Ibid, p.82.
25. Ibid, p.83.
26. Ibid, pp.84-86.
27. Ibid, pp.86-88.
28. Winifred Duke, *Trial*, (1930), pp.89-91.
29. Ibid, pp.92-94.

30. Ibid, pp.94-95.
31. Winifred Duke, *Trial*, (1930), p.95.
32. Ibid, pp.96-97.
33. Ibid, pp.99-100.
34. Winifred Duke, *Trial*, (1930), pp.100-101.
35. Ibid, pp.101-102.
36. Winifred Duke, *Trial*, (1930), pp.103-105.
37. Ibid, pp.106-107.
38. Ibid, pp.108-109.
39. Ibid, p.109.
40. Winifred Duke, *Trial*, (1930), pp.110-112.
41. Ibid, p.113-114.
42. Ibid, p.114.
43. Winifred Duke, *Trial*, (1930), p.115.
44. Ibid, pp.115-116.
45. The National Archives, DPP1/57.
46. Winifred Duke, *Trial*, (1930), pp.117-118.
47. Ibid, pp.119-120.
48. Ibid, pp.120-122.
49. Ibid, pp.122-124.
50. Winifred Duke, *Trial*, (1930), pp.124-125.
51. *Western Mail*, (4th November 1920).
52. *The Daily Telegraph*, (6th November 1920).
53. *Evening Standard*, (2nd November 1920).
54. Winifred Duke, *Trial*, (1930), pp.126-130.
55. Ibid, pp.131-134.
56. Winifred Duke, *Trial*, (1930), pp.135-136.
57. Ibid, pp.137-138.
58. Ibid, pp.139-144.
59. Winifred Duke, *Trial*, (1930), pp.144-145.
60. Ibid, p.145.
61. Ibid, pp.145-146.
62. Ibid, pp.147-148.
63. Winifred Duke, *Trial*, (1930), pp.148-149.
64. Ibid, pp.150-151.
65. Ibid, p.152.
66. *Illustrated Sunday Herald*, (14th November 1920).
67. The National Archives, DPP1/57.
68. *John Bull*, (24th April 1922).
69. Winifred Duke, *Trial*, (1930), p.153-154.
70. Ibid, pp.156-157.
71. Ibid, pp.157-158.

Chapter 8

1. Winifred Duke, *Trial*, (1930), pp.158-159.
2. Ibid, pp.159-160.
3. Ibid, pp.160-161.
4. Ibid, pp.161-162.
5. Ibid, p.162.
6. Winifred Duke, *Trial*, (1930), pp.162-163.

7. Ibid, pp.163-164.
8. Ibid, p.164.
9. Ibid, pp.165-167.
10. Ibid, pp.168-169.
11. Winifred Duke, *Trial*, (1930), pp.172-174.
12. *The People*, (17th June 1934).
13. Winifred Duke, *Trial*, (1930), p.174.
14. Ibid, pp.174-175.
15. Ibid, pp.176-177.
16. *The Daily Telegraph*, (6th November 1920).
17. *John Bull*, (24th April 1922).
18. Winifred Duke, *Trial*, (1930), p.177.
19. Winifred Duke, *Trial*, (1930), p.178.
20. Ibid, p.179.
21. Ibid, p.180.
22. Ibid, pp.181-182.
23. Ibid, pp,183-184.
24. Winifred Duke, *Trial*, (1930), pp.184-185.
25. Ibid, pp.186-187.
26. Ibid, pp.188-190.
27. Ibid, pp.191-193.
28. *Evening Standard*, (6th November 1920).
29. Winifred Duke, *Trial*, (1930), pp.194-197.
30. Ibid, pp.198-200.
31. Ibid, pp.201-202.
32. Winifred Duke, *Trial*, (1930), pp.203-206.
33. *The Observer*, (7th November 1920).
34. Winifred Duke, *Trial*, (1930), pp.206-207.
35. Ibid, pp.208-210.
36. *Western Mail*, (8th November 1920).
37. *The Daily Telegraph*, (6th November 1920).
38. Winifred Duke, *Tria*l, (1930), pp.210-212.
39. Ibid, pp.213-215.
40. Ibid, pp.216-219.
41. *The Observer*, (7th November 1920).
42. *Sheffield Independent*, (11th November 1920).
43. *Weekly Record*, (13th November 1920).
44. Winifred Duke, *Trial*, (1930), p.220.
45. *Western Mail*, (8th November 1920).
46. *Illustrated Sunday Herald*, (14th November 1920).
47. *The Observer*, (7th November 1920).
48. *Illustrated Sunday Herald*, (14th November 1920).
49. *Evening Standard*, (8th November 1920).
50. *Western Mail*, (10th November 1920).
51. *Evening Standard*, (8th November 1920).
52. Winifred Duke, *Trial*, (1930), pp.221-222.
53. Ibid, pp.222-223.
54. Winifred Duke, *Trial*, (1930), pp.223-225.
55. Ibid, pp.225-228.

56. Ibid, pp.229-232.
57. Ibid, pp.233-234.
58. Winifred Duke, *Trial,* (1930), pp.235-239.
59. Sally Smith, *Marshall Hall*, (2016), p.189.
60. Archibald Bowker, *Behind the Bar* (Staple Press, 1948), p.85.
61. Winifred Duke, *Trial*, (1930), pp.239-242.
62. Ibid, pp.243-247.
63. Ibid, pp.247-248.
64. Winifred Duke, *Trial*, (1930), pp.249-252.
65. Ibid, pp.252-253.
66. Ibid, pp.253-254.
67. The National Archives, DPP1/57.
68. *Weekly Record*, (13th November 1920).
69. Winifred Duke, *Trial*, (1930), pp.255-256.
70. *Evening Standard*, (9th November 1920).
71. Winifred Duke, *Trial*, (1930), pp.257-258.
72. Ibid, pp,258-259.
73. Ibid, pp.259-260.
74. Ibid, pp.262-263.
75. Winifred Duke, *Trial,* (1930), pp.263-264.
76. The National Archives, DPP1/57.
77. *Illustrated Sunday Herald*, (14th November 1920).
78. Ibid.
79. Winifred Duke, *Trial*, (1930), pp.264-265.
80. *Western Mail*, (10th November 1920).
81. Ibid.
82. *Llanelli and County Guardian*, (11th November 1920).
83. *Illustrated Sunday Herald*, (14th November 1920).
84. Sally Smith, *Marshall Hall*, (2016), p.196; Stephen Bates, *Poisonous Solicitor*, (2022), p.29.
85. *Western Mail*, (10th November 1920).
86. Edward Marjoribanks, *The Life*, (1933), p.420.
87. *Western Mail*, (10th November 1920).
88. *Weekly Record*, (13th November 1920).
89. *Illustrated Sunday Herald*, (14th November 1920).
90. Ibid.
91. *Sheffield Independent*, (12th November 1920).
92. Winifred Duke, *Trial*, (1930), p.50.

Chapter 9

1. Winifred Duke, *Trial*, (1930), p.49n.
2. Philip Willcox, *Physician-Detective*, (1970), pp.160-161.
3. Ibid, pp.162-163.
4. Ibid, pp.163-164.
5. The National Archives, MEPO3/265b.
6. Ibid.
7. Durham University, *The Henson Journals, The Journals of Hensley Henson*, (1900-1939), Volume 29, p.36.
8. *Western Mail*, (15th November 1920).
9. Edward Marjoribanks, *The Life*, (1933), p.420.

10. Winifred Duke, *Trial*, (1930), p.52.
11. Ibid, pp.53, 52n.
12. The National Archives, HO144/11780.
13. The National Archives, DPP1/57.
14. *The Times*, (10th November 1920).
15. *Illustrated Sunday Herald*, (12th December 1920).
16. *The Nation*, (13th November 1920).
17. Ibid.
18. *The Times*, (18th November 1920).
19. Winifred Duke, *Six Trials*, (1934), p.136.
20. *Illustrated Sunday Herald*, (14th November 1920).
21. Ibid, (12th December 1920).
22. Harold Greenwood, *Greenwood's Thrilling Fight for his Life*, (1920).
23. *Daily Mirror*, (5th April 1921).
24. Winifred Duke, *Six Trials*, (1934), p.144.
25. *Weekly Record*, (13th November 1920).
26. Census (1921).
27. *Western Mail*, (8th March 1922).
28. Ibid, (23rd February 1921).
29. *Gloucester Citizen*, (7th March 1922); *Dundee Courier*, (8th March 1922); *Western Mail*, (8th March 1922).
30. Ibid, (23rd August 1921).
31. Martin Beales, *Dead Not Buried: Herbert Rowse Armstrong*, (1995), p.26.
32. John Rowland, *Murder Revisited*, (1961), p.186.
33. Douglas G. Browne & E. V. Tullett, *Bernard Spilsbury: His Life and Cases*, (1952), p.145n.
34. Robin Odell, *Exhumation of a Murder* (1975), pp.129-130.
35. Stephen Bates, *Poisonous Solicitor*, (2022), pp.242-243, quoting *John Bull*.
36. *Justice of the Peace Review*, (27th December 1930).
37. Stephen Bates, *Poisonous Solicitor*, (2022), p.98.
38. Ibid, pp.150-152.
39. Ibid, p.293.
40. *Western Mail*, (12th March 1923).
41. *The Scotsman*, (29th August 1923).
42. *Western Mail*, (29th November 1923).
43. Philip Willcox, *Physician-Detective*, (1970), p.163.
44. *Nottinghamshire Journal*, (7th February 1923).
45. *Herefordshire Directory* (1926), pp.194-195.
46. *News of the World*, (20th January 1929); *Daily Mail*, (20th December 1930).
47. *South Wales Daily Post*, (13th January 1934).
48. *Hartlepool Daily Mail*, (18th January 1929); *Daily Herald*, (18th January 1929).
49. *Yorkshire Post and Leeds Intelligencer*, (21st January 1929).
50. *Western Mail*, (22nd January 1929).
51. Winifred Duke, *Six Trials*, (1934), p.145.
52. *Weekly Despatch*, (20th January 1929).
53. *Western Mail*, (20th May 1929).
54. *Western Mail*, (14th & 18th October 1949); *The Daily Herald*, (18th October 1949); *The Welshman*, (21st October 1949).
55. Will of Mrs. Gwladys Johnson.
56. *Yorkshire Post and Leeds Intelligencer*, (27th May 1941); Ancestry.co.uk;

Lancashire Guardian, (30th May 1941).
57. Western Morning News, (29th June 1939).
58. Ancestry.co.uk.
59. Ibid.
60. Llanelli Star, (10th April 1997).
61. Carmarthen Journal, (15th November 1985).
62. Liverpool Daily Post, (22nd November 1985).
63. Bray People, (15th June 2005).
64. Kathryn Harkup, *A is for Arsenic: The poisons of Agatha Christie*, (2015); Anne Powers, *True Crime Parallels in the Mysteries of Agatha Christie*, (2019).
65. Tribune, (15th February 1946).
66. John Rowland, *Murder Revisited*, (1961), pp.109, 185.
67. Tewkesbury Register, (21st April 1967).
68. South Wales Post, (27th January 1997).
69. Bob Hinton, *Death Came to Dinner* (2009), p.16.
70. Keith Morgan, *Kidwelly Through Time*, (2015), p.22.
71. Frank Jones, *Beyond Suspicion: True stories of Unexpected Killers*, (1992), p.82.

Chapter 10
1. Philip Willcox, *Physician-Detective*, (1970), pp.38-41.
2. C. J. S. Thompson, *Poison Mysteries*, (1937), pp.15-18.
3. Winifred Duke, *Trial*, (1930), pp.56-57.
4. Western Mail, (12th February 1931).
5. Justice of the Peace, (27th December 1930).
6. Winifred Duke, *Trial*, (1930), pp.7-8.
7. Ibid, p.23
8. Ibid, pp.50-51.
9. Ibid, p.56.
10. Ibid, p.56-57.
11. James Hodge, *Famous Trials: 4*, (1954).
12. Arthur Lambton, *Thou Shalt Do No Murder*, (1931), pp.67-68.
13. C. J. S. Thompson, *Poison Mysteries Unsolved*, (1937), pp.147-161.
14. Ibid, (1937), p.161.
15. E. Spencer Shaw, *A Companion to Murder*, (1960), pp.96-100.
16. John Rowland, *Murder Revisited*, (1961), p.193.
17. Rowland, *Murder Revisited*, (1961), pp.183-184.
18. Ibid, pp.193-195.
19. Bristol Evening Post, (17th November 1961).
20. Stephen Bates, *The Poisonous Solicitor*, (2022), unnumbered page, plate caption.
21. Frank Jones, *Beyond Suspicion*, (1992), p.69.
22. Philip Willcox, *Physician-Detective*, (1970), p.164.
23. Bob Hinton, *Death Came to Dinner: The Greenwood Murder*, (2009), p.16.
24. Eric Hughes, *Kidwelly: Memories of Yesteryear*, (2003), pp.48-78.
25. Bob Hinton, *Death Came to Dinner: The Greenwood Murder*, (2009).
26. Ibid; Bob Hinton, *South Wales Murders*, (2008), p.144.
27. Kevin Turton, *Britain's Unsolved Murders*, (2017), p.90.
28. Huddersfield and Holmfirth Examiner, (24th August 1978); Grimsby Daily Telegraph, (8th November 1995).
29. Mark John Maguire, *They Got Away with Murder*, I, (2023), p.190.

30. Ibid, pp.190-191.
31. Ibid, p.191.
32. Ibid, pp.191-192.
33. Ancestry.co.uk.

Further Reading

Bates, Stephen, *The Poisonous Solicitor: The true story of a 1920s murder mystery*, Icon Books, (2022), ISBN 978-1-785788-17-8, 324 pages. The most up to date and fair minded of the books about Greenwood's fellow solicitor who was also tried for poisoning his wife.

Christie, Agatha, *The Thirteen Problems,* (1932); *The Moving Finger,* (1943); *The Labours of Hercules,* (1947); *A Murder is Announced,* (1950); *Poirot's Early Cases,* (1974). All these give thinly disguised versions of the true story.

Duke, Winifred, *The Trial of Harold Greenwood*, W. Hodge & Co., (1930), 347 pages. This is a crucial text which gives the transcript of the trial, but the editor's introduction is weighted towards Greenwood's innocence.

Maguire, Mark John, *They Got Away With Murder*: Volume One, Lightfast Publishing, (2023), ISBN 978-1-838485-82-5, 212 pages. The first book to include a chapter advocating Greenwood's guilt.

Oates, Jonathan and Berg, Anna-Lena, *The Crimes that Inspired Agatha Christie: The facts behind the fiction*. Pen and Sword, (2025). One chapter summarises the case and discusses all the Agatha Christie stories which are linked to it.

Powers, Anne, *True Crime Parallels to the Mysteries of Agatha Christie*, McFarland, (2019), ISBN 978-1-476679-46-4, 172 pages. Includes a chapter about the case and one Agatha Christie story linked to it.

Rowland, John, *Murder Revisited: A Study of Two Poisoning Cases,* John Long, (1961), 200 pages. Until now the lengthiest narrative of the Greenwood case; also includes that of Herbert Armstrong. Both show signs of age.

Smith, Sally, *Marshall Hall: A Law unto Himself,* Wildy, Simmonds and Hill Publishing, (2016), ISBN 978-0-854901-87-6, 302 pages. The most recent biography of Greenwood's defence barrister.

Willcox, Philip, *Physician Detective: The Life and Work of Sir William Willcox,* Heineman Medical (1970), ISBN 978-0-433362-01-2, 332 pages. Important work for its chapter about the forensics of the case.

Index

A

Armstrong, Major Herbert 7, 51, 112, 222-224, 231, 233, 235, 237, 242-245, 247, 253.

Arsenic 7, 33, 56-57, 73, 89, 101, 104-106, 110, 114-117, 119-123, 128-132, 134, 136-138, 144-146, 162-164, 166, 168, 172, 177-181, 183-186, 188, 195-198, 200-202, 209, 211-213, 216, 219, 223-224, 226, 232-235, 239, 243-244, 246-249, 253-254.

B

Bodkin, Sir Archibald 99, 224.

Bowater, Edith 21-22, 24, 26, 44, 57, 72, 76, 78, 82, 86, 95, 119-121, 142, 188, 193.

Bowater, Eliza 21, 23-24, 44, 62.

Bowater, Sir Thomas 21, 23-24, 36, 77-78, 106, 119.

Bowater, William 21-23.

Bowker, Archibald 198.

C

Cardiff 152, 207, 211, 217, 221.

Carmarthen 29, 38, 44, 59-60, 72, 87, 99, 111-112, 114, 135-136, 141, 145-146, 150, 154-155, 157-158, 160-161, 180, 188, 195, 209, 215, 220, 238, 247, 255.

Carmarthen Castle 132, 148, 160-161, 174, 175, 238.

Carmarthen Guildhall 157, 159-160, 174, 238.

Christie, Agatha 7, 9, 234-237.

Crippen, Dr. 114, 157, 236-237.

D

David, Gwyneth 56, 90, 128, 140, 173, 190.

Dick, Dr. Alexander 101, 103, 137, 173.

Duke, Winifred 8, 23, 47, 79, 84-85, 143, 158, 214, 219-220, 228, 240-243, 245.

E

Edinburgh 31, 113, 133-134, 143, 173, 245.

Edmonton 20-21, 23, 26-27.

Enfield 26-27.

F

Ferryside 60, 95.

Forest Hill 18-23, 25, 185.

Foy, Thomas 62-63, 65-66, 90-91, 164, 197, 254.

G

Greenwood, Eileen 28, 37, 43-44, 132, 146, 194, 209, 221, 230.

Greenwood, Gerald 227-228, 230.

Greenwood, Harold
 Childhood 11-12, 14-17, 147.
 Education 16-21.
 Marriage 20-21, 25-26.
 Career 26, 37-39, 41, 44.
 Hobbies & Interests 35, 40-43.
 Relations with Wife 47-49, 62, 78, 107, 116-117, 136-137, 142, 187-188, 227, 241-242, 254-255.
 Relations with Gwladys Jones 49-54, 58, 76, 79-82, 84-86, 89, 96, 110, 125-127, 129, 142-143, 152, 163-164, 169, 172-173, 177, 184, 188-192, 199, 201, 242, 251-252.
 Relations with Miss Griffiths 52-54, 70-71, 82-83, 125, 168-169, 181-182, 189-190, 231, 242.
 Relations with Other Women 31, 47-49, 53-54, 83-84, 97, 125-126, 138.
 On Day of Wife's Death 63-67, 69-74, 124-125, 129, 134, 136-140, 142, 145, 150, 162-164, 169-170, 175-176, 197, 199.
 Questioned by Police 91-98, 112, 137, 163, 174-175, 190.
 Buys Arsenic 113-115, 129, 133-134, 143, 164, 173.
 Arrest 130-131, 150, 163.
 At Magistrates' Court 132-146.
 In Prison 132-133, 135, 147-150, 154, 175, 196.
 On Trial 158-162, 174-175, 177, 179-181, 183, 187-192, 195-196, 201-205.

Index 279

Release 205-211, 224.
Writes Newspaper Articles 85, 214, 216-220, 224.
Later Life 221-222, 224-228.
Death 228-229, 240, 242.
Mentioned 7-8, 29, 34, 44-45, 54-62, 75, 77, 100, 103-104, 112, 119, 127-128, 150-151, 155, 185, 192-193, 197-198, 209, 211, 213, 223, 232-233, 237-238.
Fictional Depictions 229, 232-236.
Verdicts 240-255.

Greenwood, Irene 27-28, 36, 44, 49-50, 54, 56-57, 60-67, 69, 71-74, 76, 78-80, 83, 86, 90, 92-96, 103, 111, 119, 126, 132, 136, 140, 142, 152, 155, 164-165, 169-170, 176, 179, 183, 192-195, 197, 199-200, 202, 209, 216, 221, 224, 230, 236, 243, 245-249, 252-255.

Greenwood, Isabella 14-17, 19.

Greenwood, John Kenneth 28, 33, 44, 56, 63-65, 69, 71, 90-91, 193, 221, 227, 230-231.

Greenwood Legh 13, 16, 19, 20.

Greenwood, Mabel
  Childhood 21-24.

Marriage 20-22, 25-26.
Finances 23-24, 78, 113, 121, 152, 184, 187.
Interests 35-36, 40, 43, 79.
Health 54-57, 97, 104-105, 107-108, 110, 115-117, 127-128, 137-138, 140, 142, 144-146, 165, 167, 172, 178, 185, 189, 193, 198, 223, 252-253.
Days Leading up to Death 57-63.
Sunday Lunch 63-65, 123, 128-129, 139-140, 142, 162, 169-170, 175-176, 193-194, 196-197, 201.
Final Afternoon and Evening 65-73, 91-94, 137-138, 144-145, 164-165, 171, death of, 73-77, 90, 94-96, 98, 110, 120-125, 128, 130-131, 136-137, 154, 162, 167, 183, 197-198, 209, 212, 242, 244.
Rumours of Foul Play 87, 90, 98, 106-107, 190.
Theories of Death 78, 97-98, 100, 103-104, 106, 117, 126, 140, 154, 164, 179, 185-186, 190-191, 199, 213.
Funeral and Burial 75-78, 91, 96, 173, 200.
Exhumation 96, 98-100, 103-104, 173.

Other References 7-8, 21, 30, 34, 44, 49-50, 54, 78-79, 133, 164, 182, 193-194, 197, 212, 227, 238, 243-244, 246-250, 252-255.

Greenwood, Norman Ivor 28, 33, 36, 43-44, 146, 221, 230.

Greenwood, Oscar 14, 19.

Greenwood, Percy 14, 17-19, 42, 208-209.

Greenwood, William 14, 17-19, 157.

Greenwood, William Norman 12, 14-15, 19-20.

Griffiths, Mary 30-32, 34, 36, 43, 48, 50-53, 57, 66, 70-71, 76, 82-83, 87, 98, 124-125, 139-141, 146, 163, 168-169, 181-182, 189-190, 231, 242, 248.

Griffiths, Dr. Thomas 8, 31-33, 36, 41-42, 44-45, 48, 52, 55, 57, 66-67, 69-74, 78, 90, 92-101, 103, 107, 110, 114, 120-121, 125, 129, 134, 136-138, 146, 162-163, 165-169, 171-172, 177-178, 181-182, 184, 189, 192, 198, 200-202, 212, 216, 220, 231, 233-234, 244, 246, 248-249, 254.

Groves, Annie 50-51, 58, 75, 126-127, 129, 142, 172, 177, 201.

H

Haigh, Chief Inspector Ernest 30, 108-115, 130-136, 146, 151, 164, 175, 213.

Hearn, Annie 219, 247, 253.

Helby, Sergeant Henry 109, 136, 150, 212, 232.

Hunter, Trevor 153, 192-193, 199, 231.

I

Ingleborough 17, 19, 42.

Ingleton 11-12, 14, 16-17, 21, 26-27, 194, 238.

J

Jones, Reverend David Ambrose 8, 33-34, 36, 56, 60, 75-76, 78-79, 87, 90-91, 94-95, 103-104, 121, 126, 140, 164, 191, 231.

Jones, Nurse Elizabeth…48, 53, 57, 66-69, 71-73, 75-76, 78-79, 81, 83-84, 90, 93-94, 97, 99-100, 110, 120-122, 126, 129, 137-138, 146, 165-167, 181, 184, 190-192, 194, 197, 200, 233, 246.

Jones, Gwladys Amelia 35, 49-54, 56, 58, 62, 76-84, 86-87, 91, 96-97, 115-117, 125-129, 132, 134-135, 142-144, 149-150, 152, 163-164, 169,

172-173, 184, 187-192, 194, 197, 199, 201, 207, 215, 220, 226-230, 232, 241-243, 251-252, 254-255.

Jones, Superintendent Samuel 89-91, 96-98, 100, 103, 112, 114, 131, 135-137, 143, 145, 147, 164, 174-175, 181, 189-191, 212, 232, 247.

K

Kidwelly 11, 24, 27-28, 31-33, 35-36, 39-44, 52-53, 56, 58-60, 62, 76-77, 80, 84-85, 87, 89-91, 103-104, 106-107, 111-113, 115, 121, 127-128, 131, 133, 140, 143-144, 146, 154, 161, 164, 166, 173, 176, 181, 188, 200, 207, 212, 221, 224, 226, 231, 237-238, 244-245, 250-251, 254.

Kidwelly Castle 31, 43, 57-58.

Kidwelly Town Hall 40, 43, 59, 100, 102-103, 119, 130, 238.

Kirk, Gerald 15, 17, 43, 227.

L

Lewis, Sergeant Hodge 87, 90-91, 100-101, 103, 110, 112, 119, 128, 130-131, 136-137, 150, 152, 175-176, 212.

Lewis, Wilfrid 151-152, 154, 164, 169-170, 231.

Llanelli 28, 34, 38-39, 41-42, 49-50, 53, 56, 58, 60, 75-79, 81, 84, 87, 89-90, 101, 104, 107, 112, 115-117, 119, 127-128, 131, 133-134, 136, 141, 145, 148, 161, 172-173, 209, 213, 220, 229-230, 238, 244, 251.

London 12, 18-19, 21, 23-27, 31, 33, 36-37, 41, 57, 77, 79, 86, 89, 91, 96, 101, 104, 106, 111, 119, 133-134, 147, 151-152, 155, 157-158, 166, 173, 176, 183, 200, 207, 221, 229, 231-232, 235-236, 247.

Lloyd-George, David 221, 231.

Ludford, Thomas 39, 103, 112, 119-121, 123, 125-126, 128, 130, 132, 136-143, 145-147, 151, 153-154, 167-168, 208, 214, 230-231.

M

Manchester 21, 181.

Marshall-Hall, Sir Edward 85, 151, 153-155, 164-179, 181-186, 192, 196-198, 201-203, 207-208, 213-214, 216, 223, 231-233, 238, 247-248, 253, 255.

Meredith, Mrs. Sarah 44, 68, 75, 83, 121.

Morris, Margaret 44, 48, 65, 123-124, 142, 169.

Morris, Martha 48, 56-57, 60, 76, 128, 192-193.

Munro, Irene 89, 231.

N

Newspapers 15, 20-21, 27, 28, 30, 35-36, 38-39, 42-44, 48, 50, 52, 54, 75-77, 87, 76-77, 84-85, 100, 103, 106-108, 112, 115-117, 125, 130, 134, 141, 143, 145, 147, 154, 157-158, 160, 173-174, 191-195, 205, 211, 214-216, 218, 220, 222, 228-229, 231, 237, 244, 247.

Nicholas, Inspector David 91, 96, 175.

Nicholas, John William 99-100, 103, 119, 121-123, 128-130.

O

Old Bailey 151, 217.

Orwell, George 8, 236-237.

P

Pearce, Seward 119-121, 133, 136-138, 145, 155.

Phillips, Florence 33-34, 43, 48. 54. 56-57, 60-62, 65-67, 69-73, 78, 81-83, 87, 90, 93, 97, 114-115, 120, 138, 164-165, 194, 197, 199, 246, 253.

Phillips, Picton William 72, 87, 89, 91, 96-99, 108, 112, 115, 131, 136, 155, 232.

Powell, Lily 44, 48, 64, 128, 142. 169-170, 221.

Price, Lilian 28, 31, 251.

Priory, The, Kidwelly 27-28, 31, 238, 251.

R

Rumsey House 28-31, 34, 42, 44, 50, 53, 60-61, 66-67, 69, 71-72, 75-78, 80, 84, 86, 90, 96, 100, 103, 112, 119-120, 128, 130, 133, 143, 150, 154, 164, 167, 169, 173, 178, 194, 207-208, 211, 220-222, 224-225, 238-239, 247, 249-250, 254.

S

St. Mary's church, Kidwelly 31, 33-34, 36, 61, 78, 83.

Samson, Sir Edward 151-152, 154-155, 161-167, 169-170, 172-173, 175-178, 185-186, 188-191, 194, 198-200, 211, 219, 231.

Seddon, Frederick 101, 114, 144, 153, 179, 187, 236-237, 246-247.

Settle 12, 16, 194, 221, 230.

Shearman, Justice 157-158, 160, 162, 165, 167, 169, 171-172, 175, 180-181, 191, 195-196, 198, 200-202, 204, 206-207, 209, 211-213, 231.

Smart, Mrs. Annie 36, 43, 68, 76, 83, 87, 90, 104, 121.

Smith, George Joseph 114, 153, 236-237.

Spilsbury, Dr. Bernard 102, 114, 144-145.

Stephens, Alfred 28, 39-40.

Swansea 184, 186, 231, 241.

T

Toogood, Dr. 49, 151, 154, 184-186, 199, 223.

V

Vant, Edmund 205, 209, 230.

W

Walford 226, 228.

Webster, John 101, 104, 108, 119, 144, 146, 155, 162, 177-178, 180, 184, 186, 199, 201, 219, 223-224, 226, 233, 247.

Williams, Benjamin 143, 151, 221.

Williams, Hannah 44, 57, 62-66, 69, 71, 73, 76, 78-79, 90, 98, 114, 123-124, 126, 129, 133, 137, 139-140, 142, 162, 170-171, 175-176, 182-184, 197, 199, 201, 233-234, 249-251, 253.

Willcox, Dr. William Henry 114, 121-124, 128-130, 132, 137, 144-146, 154-155, 162, 166, 177-180, 185, 196, 199, 201, 211-212, 219, 223, 226, 233-234, 249.

World War One 25, 30, 43, 49, 53-54, 59, 84, 96, 114, 152, 154, 158, 227, 242.

www.ingramcontent.com/pod-product-compliance
Lightning Source LLC
Chambersburg PA
CBHW071146160426
43196CB00011B/2021